OUR DADDY WHO ART IN HEAVEN

David Grant Gallagher

Our Daddy Who Art in Heaven

Copyright ©2016 Moondream Publishing, LLC

All rights reserved. No portion of this book may be reproduced, stored in a retrieval system, or transmitted in any form or by any means–electronic, mechanical, photocopy, recording, scanning, or other–except for brief quotations in critical reviews or articles, or as specifically allowed by the U. S. Copyright Act of 1976, as amended, without the prior written permission of the publisher.

Published by Moondream Publishing Company

Unless otherwise noted, Scripture quotations are from the Holy Bible, New International Version (NIV). Copyright © 1973, 1978, 1984. International Bible Society. Used by permission of Zondervan Bible Publishers.

Quotations designated ESV are from THE ENGLISH STANDARD VERSION. © 2001 by The American Bible Society. Used by permission. All rights reserved.

Quotations designed KJV are from the King James Version.

Quotations designated NASB are from the NEW AMERICAN STANDARD BIBLE, © 1960, 1962, 1963, 1968, 1971, 1972, 1973, 1975, 1977, 1995 by The Lockman Foundation. Used by permission.

Quotations designated NKJV are from the New King James Version, copyright 1979, 1980, 1982, Thomas Nelson, Inc., Publishers.

Quotations designated NLT are from the Holy Bible, New Living Translation, copyright © 1996, 2004. Used by permission of Tyndale House Publishers, Inc., Carol Stream, Illinois 60188. All rights reserved.

Library of Congress Cataloging-in-Publication Data

978-0-692-64706-6

Cover Design: Joseph Bobzien & Caroline Shirota
Cover Image: Gennady, Shutterstock

Printed in the United States of America

16 17 18 19 20 21 [   ] 6 5 4 3 2 1

DEDICATION

This book is dedicated to....

My two daughters, Diana & Belle, whose presence in my life has given me the greatest gift of all—getting to be a daddy.

My Daddy in heaven, who in His foresight, wisdom, and calling, has entrusted me with the privilege of learning how, and from whom, an earthly dad can acquire and implement the attributes of heaven for his children right here on earth.

CONTENTS

Introduction   7

Chapter 1   Daddy, Are You There?   11
Chapter 2   Daddy, Do You Care?   27
Chapter 3   Daddy, I'm Hungry   45
Chapter 4   Daddy, Can You Help Me With My Mess?   61
Chapter 5   Daddy, Can We Spend Time Together?   75
Chapter 6   Daddy, I'm Tired   91
Chapter 7   Daddy, Can We Talk?   107
Chapter 8   Daddy, Are You Always There For Me?   123
Chapter 9   Daddy, Will You Hold Onto Me?   137
Chapter 10   Daddy, Can You Get Me Where I Need To Go?   151
Chapter 11   Daddy, Will You Help Me To Feel Better?   167
Chapter 12   Daddy, I'm Growing and Changing; Will You Help Me Through The Changes?   185
Chapter 13   Daddy, Will You Teach Me What Is Right?   201
Chapter 14   Daddy, Will You Protect Me?   217
Chapter 15   Daddy, Can You Teach Me To Give?   231
Chapter 16   Daddy, Can I Count On You?   247

Epilogue   261

About the Author   265

INTRODUCTION

Although it happened more than twenty-five years ago, I still remember it as though it took place this morning. As my friend Rosi Hinton walked up to me, I noticed she held something in her hand.

It was a tiny sock. A pink one.

"David," she said, "I've been praying for you, and God showed me that someday you will have a baby girl." She pressed the sock into my hand. "I want you to have this baby sock as a reminder that what He has spoken to me–and now to you–will one day come to pass."

The moment caught me completely flat-footed. I didn't know what to say or how to respond. I trusted Rosi as a spiritual woman and a friend, but I was a single young man in my late twenties at the time. What in the world could this mean? It made no sense to me.

But I kept the sock.

As the years passed and I moved from one house to another, I always took care to take that little pink sock with me. I packed it away as a reminder of what my friend believed God had showed her. When I finally got married at age thirty-nine, I thought the sock might at last find an owner. But for a decade, Rachel and I tried unsuccessfully to get pregnant, and I began to seriously wonder whether that sock would ever warm a daughter's tiny foot.

In 2002, Rachel and I visited Eldoret, Kenya, on a medical mission trip. We fell in love with the place and with the people, but especially with the orphaned and homeless boys and girls who, despite worlds of potential, had almost no hope of seeing any of their dreams come true. Almost two years later, we founded Open Arms International, an organization designed and dedicated to raising up a new generation of African leaders equipped to confront the difficult issues facing their people and bring about lasting change within their countries. The organization grew, and Rachel and I began spending most of our time in Kenya at the Open Arms Village that we helped to build.

More years passed. Good years. Blessed years. But still the little pink sock remained footless.

And then at 4 p.m., August 17, 2009, something different happened. Very different. On that day, I instantaneously and unexpectedly became a dad. It was my birth-day as a dad.

Phillip, the district children's officer in Eldoret, called to ask Rachel a question: could we take a one-month-old baby into our care? This baby had just been rescued from the rough-and-tumble streets of the city. Her nineteen-year-old mother, a street girl herself, had willingly given up her infant after Phillip had convinced her that the streets were no place for a newborn. It took courage and selflessness for this young girl to give up her baby daughter. She herself had lived on the streets since age eleven, along with her mother, father, brothers, and sisters.

Phillip's call deeply touched us. But what were we supposed to do? From the outset—from the beginning of all our plans—we had made a firm, intentional decision not to take babies in the Open Arms Village, and not because we didn't love babies or care very deeply for them. Our very limited resources simply couldn't begin to stretch to cover the extra work, attention, and cost of caring for these little ones.

It simply wasn't part of the plan.

Which is to say, it wasn't part of our plan. As Rachel and I looked at each other, it began to dawn on us that there might be another plan beyond our own—one that would forever change the course of our lives and ministry.

Introduction

About two hours later, Belinda Caroline arrived at our rented house. I'll never forget the day we received her into our family. Her skin had grown very dark from being exposed to the hot sun while living on the streets, and she reeked of glue and grime from life in the garbage dump. Bathing her, putting her in clean clothing, and wrapping her in a clean blanket was our first great joy–a joy that would continue through the days, weeks, and years. From the moment she joined us, we shortened her name to Belle, which means "beautiful" in French. She certainly was that to us.

And that pink sock? It became Belle's to fill.

I now laughingly say most couples have nine months to prepare for parenthood. Rachel and I had ninety minutes, although Rachel still insists it was closer to forty-five. In any event, it happened really fast. I suppose God knew we had little time to spare, since I was only a few months shy of my fiftieth birthday.

As I crawled into bed at the end of that hectic, unexpected, and most eventful day, I no longer saw only Rachel lying next to me. There, atop a recessed chiropractic pillow, lay a little dark bundle named Belle, with Rachel to her other side. Belle's presence marked the beginning of a surprising journey of discovery into fatherhood that will last the rest of my life.

Only Part of the Story

While the story of our peculiar family adventure provides the catalyst for this book, that's really only part of the story. As we have taken care of our little surprise and miracle girls–first Belle, and then Diana–I have been immersed, not always willingly, in many of the mysteries of fatherhood, along with its surprises. It seems that every day as I live with my daughters, care for them, and grow with them, I gain additional insights into what a dad is, does, and should be.

Because we became Mommy and Daddy to Belle when she was just twenty-nine days old and we didn't become Mommy and Daddy to Diana until she was three years old, many of the stories in this book focus on experiences with Belle when she was an infant. I am not playing favorites with my two lovely daughters. It's only that the seeds of what has become this book were germinating in me as I was Daddy to Belle during her infancy and toddler stages.

I might have had a late start as a father, but I don't think it put me behind. Not when I have a heavenly Father who has been so willing to open the book of fathering to me.

That's the idea behind the book you hold in your hands. I want to tell a very important story about dads, and one that starts and ends with our heavenly Daddy.

I didn't have a great experience with my earthly father, and Rachel had a much worse time with her own dad. For both of us, "dad" was closer to a four-letter word than it was a three-letter one. My learning curve about being a father, then, didn't start in my childhood. It really began on that incomparable day when Belle suddenly dropped out of heaven into our arms. Almost immediately, as if I had tuned into a new radio station I'd never heard before, I began seeing God as Father—God as Daddy—in a whole new and wonderful light. My experience as a dad is also helping me to learn what it means, under the care of my heavenly Daddy, to be a son.

Because of what I've learned (and continue to learn), I pray that our daughters will have a healthy, joy-filled experience in our home, quite unlike what either Rachel or I had growing up and what so many millions of others have had to endure. I pray that as you read, you may see that the only four-letter word ever meant to be associated with "dad" and "God" is love.

Long after I'm gone, I want my girls to know that they had a dad who loved them. And from that deep knowledge, I want them to know even more that they have a Daddy in heaven who will never leave them nor forsake them, one who loves them far more intimately and passionately than I ever could.

If I can help you to start seeing the same thing, I will be glad that I wrote this book.

Chapter 1

DADDY, ARE YOU THERE?

My father died when I was sixteen years old. Two years later, my mom remarried. She and her new husband, Vince, felt thrilled to have the companionship.

More than twenty years into their marriage, Vince asked me to help him set up a new scanner for his computer. After everything got plugged in and connected, my eighty-one-year-old stepdad reached into his wallet and pulled out a small black-and-white photograph, a picture I'd never seen. He had carried it with him for decades, ever since he was a young man.

I marveled at the worn photo–an ancient image of his father, who had abandoned the family when Vince was only six years old. In the years since the desertion, Vince had seen his dad only once–as he lay in his coffin at his funeral. And now, more than half a century later, the first thing Vince wanted to do with his new scanner was to enlarge the image of his father from an old, wrinkled photo.

As Vince took the new, bigger picture from the printer tray, a very odd thing happened. This tough, old, weathered building contractor began to weep. I didn't know what to do. How should you respond when you see your rugged old stepdad weeping over an enlarged photograph of his long-deceased father? So I said nothing. I just accepted the privilege of seeing a human being–eighty-one years old in body but still six years old in his soul–express his deep, heartfelt longing for his father.

I learned that day that, even after eight decades of life, a man needs to know his dad is near.

He longs to be assured that if he calls out, "Daddy!" he'll receive an answer. He needs to know his dad is close by.

A Desire for Reassurance
"Daddy!"

That shout from our daughter, Diana, when she was a toddler, always brought a smile to my face, no matter where I was in our house and no matter what I was doing. I couldn't resist stopping whatever I was doing to follow the sound of her cry. I just wanted to be with my precious little girl. Whenever I heard her shout for me, I knew she wanted some reassurance that I was close by, somewhere within earshot.

The same thing was true of her sister. Just four months after Belle joined our family, we returned to the U.S. for Christmas. We took our five-month-old daughter to a Christmas gathering, and of course, everyone wanted to hold her, hug her, kiss her, squeeze her, and just cuddle with her.

At one point I was doing a presentation, holding Belle on my forearm as she faced out toward the audience. Every few minutes, she would look up and around at me, just to make sure that the larger-than-life protective presence called Daddy was still right there with her. Even at the tender age of five months, she already needed that deep sense of reassurance and security.

Daddy, are you there?

I can be working away on my computer–the machine that Rachel sometimes calls my "second wife"–and Belle will come up to me and make it clear that she wants some focused, uninterrupted time with me. If I've been on the computer too long, she will crawl up into my lap and insert herself between me and the noxious trespasser.

At those times, as much as possible, I will lay aside my computer and focus completely on her. I want her to know that I am there for her–all of me–and not just part of me.

When Daddy Isn't There

The impact of knowing that your daddy isn't there can bring a tremendous amount of anxiety, stress, and insecurity. I recently read how divorce had significantly wounded the lives of several celebrities. Nicole Richie said, "When my dad divorced my mom, it was kind of like him leaving me also." Justin Timberlake confessed, "My parents divorced when I was three. I'm humbly and honestly finding out that I have a lot of issues with that."

When your daddy goes absent through death, the loss takes a huge toll; but that's almost easier to take than knowing he's still "out there" somewhere, alive and well, but you lack full access to him.

In the years following my own father's death, I rationalized that his passing was probably for the best; otherwise, I thought, he might have had a very negative impact on me. I know I'm not alone in such thoughts. Putting positive spins on otherwise very hurtful and unhappy situations allows us to cope. Often, however, these positive spins simply mask a deeper pain. Unless we deal with the core issue, head on, we'll struggle to engage as we need to in healthy, vital, and authentic relationships.

The need for reassuring glances from our dads is not only about security and protection, but also about the joy of knowing that one of the people we care most about is right there, just in case something goes right. When things go right, we want to know that someone we love–and who loves us–is there to share in our joy.

I know a medical doctor who suffered through a terrible upbringing at the hands of a perfectionistic father. In school, even as a very young boy, anything short of all A's on his report card got him a violent physical beating. Years later, when he was accepted into medical school, he told me, "When I opened the letter and saw that I had been accepted into medical school, it was, in the same moment, the happiest day of my life but also the saddest. It was the happiest day because I had worked so hard for so long and had achieved my goal. It was the saddest day because I had great news, but no one to share it with."

He admitted that he waited a long time to tell his parents, "because I knew that they wouldn't share my joy. In fact, when I finally got around to telling my father, all he could say was, 'Are you sure they got the right guy?'"

For far too many people, the reassuring sideward glance looking for their fathers gains them nothing but emptiness. Looking around a crowded room for the dad they desperately need to know is there for them, and who can give that reassuring glance back, evades them. And so they feel lost, alone, confused, and scared. That's why a lot of adults put on a tough façade that screams, "I've got it all together and don't need anyone or anything." That façade often masks the truly scared little boy or girl inside who looks around for Dad's reassuring presence and loving gaze.

How incredibly important a daddy's presence is!

The biggest problem with a father leaving the picture, whether mostly or entirely, is the deafening silence in the vacuum that is left where his presence was meant to reside and where his voice was meant to be heard. And so, whether we are three years old or eighty, we run through our houses, calling out, "Daddy?!" with an earnest hope that he is somewhere close by.

Right Where We Live

We all need to know that our Daddy God is in the "house" of our souls and within earshot if we need anything. We desperately need to know that we aren't alone in the world and that He has pitched His tent in our camp.

When the Bible says that Jesus, the Word, *"became flesh and made His dwelling among us"* (John 1:14), it literally means that Jesus pitched His tent in our camp and set up His living quarters with us, right where we live. He wants us to know that we are never alone in the world, but that He is right here with us.

May I suggest three key times in life when your Daddy God wants to bring reassurance to you? He wants you to know that you can always count on His presence. He wants to give you a growing confidence that brings a profound sense of security to your heart, the core of who you are inside.

God is with You at the Start of New Adventures

Did you know your Daddy God was with you at the start of the biggest adventure of all–your life? He was with you when you were born, even when you were conceived. How cool is that?

Today, many dads have the privilege of being with their children on the day of their birth. It's officially encouraged in western culture. Beautiful birthing suites are the norm and at many hospitals, Dad can even have a bed in the room. In 1960, when I was born, dads were actively discouraged from getting too close to the maternity ward. I've heard dads of that era say that nurses actually chased them away (truth be told, many of those dads responded with smiles of relief). They either paced around outside or went to the local watering hole, where they could drown their sorrows and their apprehensions about becoming a new father. Maybe they pulled out cigars and smoked nervously as they fretted about their new life sentence: I'm committed to this baby for the rest of my life!

I didn't have the privilege of being present when Diana and Belle came into the world, and neither of their biological fathers were present at their births. It's even possible that their fathers didn't know they'd become fathers. Both of my girls entered this world in stressful and dangerous circumstances. Belle was born on the streets, and Diana was born into immediate rejection, as neither her sixteen-year-old mother nor her extended family wanted her.

Even though I wasn't with my girls when they were born, their Daddy in heaven was. Their Daddy God was right there when they arrived, filled with excitement and joy–and He made sure they found their way to safety and acceptance.

Do you know someone who was born into rejection? Was that person you? If so, do you know that your Daddy God was right there and bursting with joy and excitement upon your arrival? David wrote about this when he said in a prayer to God, *For you created my inmost being; you knit me together in my mother's womb. I praise you because I am fearfully and wonderfully made; your works are wonderful. I know that full well. My frame was not hidden from you when I was made in the secret place* (Psalm 139:13-15).

David means that God, your Daddy, was not only present at your conception, but He made something someone wonderful. And He takes great pride in everything He makes!

In Mrs. Ginther's eighth grade art class, I once made a pottery pitcher. I took strips of clay, molded and shaped them into my pitcher, glazed my work, and fired it with some fancy colors. I remember how proud I felt of that pitcher. Was it perfect? No. Did I care that it wasn't perfect? No. Was it beautiful? Maybe not to others, but it was to me. In fact, I didn't see how it could have been more beautiful. Did I love it? Absolutely. Why? Because I created it. I didn't much care what anybody else thought. I loved it because I created it. And to this day I still have it.

Your Daddy God loves you because He created you. Are you perfect? Of course not. Are you beautiful? Maybe on a good day. Does He love you even though you aren't perfect and even though you have more bad hair days than good ones? Absolutely. He loves you utterly and thoroughly.

Why? Because He made you to take after Himself. You are His creation and He's very proud of you. You weren't an accident. He created you intentionally, tenderly, carefully. Your loving Daddy God wanted you to be born. He knew you needed to be in the world, and He's deeply pleased with what He made in you. He created a place in this world with your name on it.

Is it too much to believe that you weren't a cosmic accident?

Is it too much to believe that even though you may have been rejected by the very people who gave you birth, that you have a Daddy in heaven who did cartwheels of excitement at your arrival?

Is it too much to believe that the One who created you has a plan for your life and that His plan was in place long before anyone on earth had even the remotest thought of your existence?

Is it all just too much? Well, don't let it be. All these things are true–every one of them. Your task is simply to believe.

I will never forget how God instructed me to go to Bible college after I graduated from university with a degree in business. And while I had no doubt that my heavenly Daddy was guiding me, I didn't necessarily agree with where He was sending me.

To Bible school? In Texas?

I remember vividly how I battled oceans of fear as I drove away from my home state of Oregon. *Am I doing the right thing? What on earth is happening here?* I had chosen to leave everything comfortable and familiar in order to plunge into the unknown.

But I went through with it. Why? Because I knew my Daddy was with me, even in this new and unknown adventure.

When Rachel and I started Open Arms International from a room in our Oregon home, we could never have guessed that God was preparing another home for us halfway around the world. It was one thing, setting off from Oregon to Texas; but now, from Oregon to Kenya?

I will always remember stepping off the plane and onto the soil of Africa for the first time. *David, I thought, what have you done?* And then another thought hit me: *Oh, my God, what have you done to me?*

But despite those fears, I knew He was with me in this new adventure, just as He was with me on my drive to Texas all those years before.

What new adventures beckon you forward? What fears keep you from moving ahead?

Remember that your Daddy God promises to be with you at the start of any new adventure He asks you to undertake.

A couple of years ago, I learned that the second annual worldwide Gallagher family reunion was to take place in Ireland's county Donegal. I began reading about it on the Internet and started sending queries to its Irish organizers. Although I don't like making long trips by myself, eventually I decided to go solo. Rachel didn't feel she could go at the time, and I had invited my siblings, even offering to help them offset their costs, but none could make it. So I went alone.

I felt a bit scared as I started on my journey, and my fear and anxiety only intensified the closer I got to the reunion site. I kept saying to myself, "David, what have you done? Why did you do this?" I questioned myself, even though I've spent a good portion of the last twelve years traveling internationally. Do you know what my problem was? I needed to know that, despite being alone, I wasn't really alone.

And so I reminded myself that my Daddy God is with me wherever I go.

In fact, I had a fantastic time at the reunion. I met a number of amazing Gallaghers from around the world. The group I got to know the best hailed from Canada—two Gallagher ladies and two non-Gallagher friends. We had a blast, sightseeing and eating meals together. One day, the four of them invited me to spend the night in the extra bedroom they had at their beautiful rented house. They prepared a wonderful meal, and we sat and spun yarns and laughed throughout the evening. And there, in faraway Ireland, I made some lifelong friends. I'd left home feeling scared and anxious and returned far richer in friends...and more courageous for the future.

Do you have any intriguing opportunities that have presented themselves to you, but you've chosen instead to put your life on hold, unwilling to venture out because you feel a little scared about launching out on your own? Are you playing it safe, but in the process keeping yourself isolated and alone?

Remember this: You are not alone—ever. Even from the moment you were born, your heavenly Daddy has been with you. He delights in being with you at the start of new adventures. So take a deep breath, say a prayer, and book your tickets.

God is with You at the End of Old Adventures

Sometimes the hardest life transitions don't involve starting something new but rather coming to the end of a long journey. It's then that we sometimes most need the reassurance of our Daddy God's presence.

For seven years of my life, I got to live my dream of working in the world of broadcast television. I served as host and executive producer of a nationally syndicated television program called Night Light, beamed into small-to-medium U.S. markets on a Christian-based network. To that point, those were both the best and the worst years of my life. They were great because I was living my dream. They were awful because I never struggled more.

As virtually all Christian-based television is funded by donations rather than by generating revenue through commercial advertising, we had a constant struggle to raise funds—especially since we didn't ask for donations on-air. Even though we worked hard to create a show financed through the sale of advertising, we never could turn that corner.

Finally, after seven long years of plowing very tough soil, we had to pull the plug. The money just wasn't coming in, and you can't live forever on life support.

If ever there was a time when I needed to feel confident of my Daddy God's presence, it was then. My dream had died, devastating me. I had to consciously recite aloud the scripture, *the Lord gives and the Lord takes away; blessed be the name of the Lord* (Job 1:21). I had invested seven very taxing and difficult years launching and successfully producing a television program. When it all came to a screeching halt into a dead end, I felt lost and abandoned.

Daddy, are you there?

It didn't feel like He was. I found it very difficult to hear His voice calling back to me.

Despite the silence, however, I knew He was there. I knew it because that is the kind of Dad He is. I knew it because that is His character and His nature. He doesn't abandon us when we hit tough times. Regardless of what we may feel, He's always there when we need Him. I knew His words to Joshua were also His words to me: *The Lord himself goes before you and will be with you; he will never leave you nor forsake you. Do not be afraid; do not be discouraged* (Deuteronomy 31:8).

Unfulfilled hopes and dreams, especially at the end of long and tiring journeys, are often the most difficult to handle. I understand only too well that sometimes it's nearly impossible to see the positives when it looks as though the big picture vision has gone unfulfilled.

Recently we held an international Open Arms board retreat in Kenya where board members from the U.K., the U.S., and Kenya all met together. One of the items on our agenda was succession planning, pointing to the fact that Rachel and I will not be around forever.

Indeed, the springs from the fountain of youth are beginning to wane. We must face the reality that someday we won't be able to be actively involved in the day-to-day running of Open Arms. As the organization grows and changes, new people will come in to take up leadership roles. Letting go and empowering others to make decisions and to lead can be a scary and intimidating process. But in order for Open Arms to expand and mature and thrive, we know that we must let go.

So what is our comfort in planning for succession? It's this: our Daddy God is present at the end of old adventures. And not only present, but eager to tell us, *Well done, good and faithful servant! You have been faithful with a few things; I will put you in charge of many things. Come and share your master's happiness!* (Matthew 25:21).

God is with Us in the Middle of This Adventure We Call Life
Have you ever lost the plot? Strayed off course? Gotten lost? Of course you have. All of us occasionally lose the plot and end up lost. And nowhere do we tend to get lost with such frequency as in the area of dependency on God.

Our Daddy God created us in such a way that at the beginning of our lives, as babies, and at the end of our lives, in our old age, we depend a great deal on others to help us. The bookends of our lives, childhood and old age, consist largely of dependency.

In the middle of our lives, however–when we seem to be strongest, most self-sufficient and self-reliant–we tend to forget about dependency, especially our dependency on God. We seldom remember how much we actually do depend on Him. We think we just don't need our Daddy.

Living in Kenya has given me a perspective radically different from the one I'd surely have if I'd never made my home in Africa. The difference in my perspective comes from the fact that in Kenya, the vast majority of men and women live day-to-day. They have to believe that, somehow, they will have enough sustenance to survive each day.

We know so little of this kind of dependency in the West. When we need food, we run to the supermarket. When we need clothes, we run to the department store. When we need entertainment, we run to the computer or the theater. When we need healing, we run to the doctor. Far too often in our self-sufficiency, we leave little room for needing anyone or anything beyond ourselves. We don't even leave room for God. Who needs God if you can provide everything for yourself? Why pray when you have money in the bank?

People in developing countries, however, can't just run to a store or an ATM to get what they need. They tend to depend on other people and they depend on God. They tend to think about God more than we do. They tend to think about others more than we do. They tend to pray more than we do. They live a life of much greater dependency—and as a result, they run far less risk than most of us westerners of getting lost in a maze of material possessions. Their spiritual eyes aren't quite so blinded by the glare of economic success as ours tend to be.

No matter where we live in the world, though, we face the temptation of loving and depending on money and things more than we love and depend on God. We all need to be reminded about what the Bible means when it says, *Keep your lives free from the love of money and be content with what you have, because God has said, 'Never will I leave you; never will I forsake you.' So we say with confidence, 'The Lord is my helper; I will not be afraid. What can mere mortals do to me?'* (Hebrews 13:5-6).

We in the West so easily put our trust and our hope in money. I know that is very easy for an mzungu ("white person" in Kiswahili) to say, since most of us have access to a great number of resources. But when I go to Kenya and see men and women with far fewer resources than we commonly have in the West—and yet I see them with genuine and infectious smiles on their faces, the corners of their mouths pointing toward heaven—I often wonder, who is actually richer?

They ask all the time, "Daddy God, are You there?" Not is the food there or is the doctor there or is the money there, but Daddy God, are You there? That's the cry of many of my Kenyan friends. They not only depend on God; they also know they're dependent on Him.

But what about me? In reality, I need to be just as dependent as they are; but am I? Do I remember how dependent I truly need to be? Do I live it? Do my actions reveal it? The truth is, whatever happens (or doesn't happen) in this adventure we call life, I need to know and remember that my Daddy God is there.

I have a friend whose mother used to beat her terribly. One of the most difficult things she had to deal with was the knowledge that her father would retreat into his room during the beatings and do nothing to stop the abuse.

Some people have suffered terrible blows in life at the hands of others, some by the very hands that should have loved, nurtured, and embraced them. In circumstances like that, no matter our age and regardless of our gender, we need to know the whereabouts of our Daddy God. We want to know where the One is who will protect us.

It's possible that you, like my friend, have grown up with a dad who wasn't there for you. Sadly, many in your situation have transposed what they experienced at the hands of their earthly dads to what they can expect from their heavenly Dad. They therefore see Him as a distant, uncaring, and perhaps even as a terrifying figure.

But that's not your Daddy God! He is neither distant, nor detached, nor uncaring. Jesus, the personification of God in this world, said to His disciples, *And surely I am with you always, to the very end of the age* (Matthew 28:20). They needed to know that He would never, ever abandon them. We need to know the very same thing.

Is He Still Watching?

We all have that need for a reassuring glance, just a quick look to see if Daddy is still here, right now, ready to sweep in and hold us. We long for the security of knowing that someone far bigger than us, someone who loves us, is right there to watch over everything. We also want to know that the One we care most about, and who cares most about us, is right there, just in case something goes very right. Our Daddy God doesn't abuse you, neglect you, or abandon you. Quite the opposite! He builds you up and encourages you. He's attentive to you and to your needs. And He doesn't run off anywhere. He sticks with you through thick and thin, no matter what.

If you've ever asked the question, "God are you there?" then you're in great company. Every human being who has ever walked the planet, even atheists and agnostics, have, at one time or another, asked that question either out loud, silently, or somewhere in between.

Can I encourage you to bring God closer to home by asking, "Daddy, are You there?" I know I've asked that question many

times, when I've faced all kinds of circumstances. I've asked the question when…
- I'm scared
- I'm performing
- I'm needy
- I'm hurting
- I've failed
- I've been rejected
- I'm succeeding
- I'm boasting
- I'm being greedy

The answer always comes back the same: "Of course, I am. And no matter what, I'm not going anywhere."

It doesn't matter how large our bodies grow. Deep down inside we are all like little children with a multitude of emotional and spiritual needs. And we all ask,

Daddy, Are You There?

I need to know the answer. I need to know that He is there and that I have His complete attention. When I know He's there and that His presence in my life is for my good, then I stand a fighting chance of being a healthy presence in the lives of those around me.

In the same way that Belle used to wheel her head around to see if I was still there–to see my face and to look into my eyes–so too, we need to actively turn our faces toward our Daddy God. God never intended for us to stare outward at life while He holds us, without us occasionally turning toward Him. If we will but take the time and energy to turn toward Him in prayer, we will see His lovely, reassuring gaze.

Diana's shout for me, ringing throughout our house, is not unlike the shout in the house of my own soul. I need to see if my Dad is "in the house." We all have a very basic need to know that our Dad is around.

We were not created to be alone or even to feel alone in the universe. Our Daddy God created us to be in relationship with Himself and in relationships with others like ourselves.

I've never needed to know that my Daddy God was present in my life more than I have while working with Open Arms. Every day, it seems, I face one major challenge after another. It can all grow very tiring! But along the way, my Daddy God gives both Rachel and me some wonderful blessings that encourage us deeply and keep us going. In a thousand different ways, we confess our dependency on Him:

And even when I am old and gray, O God, do not forsake me, until I declare Your strength to this generation, Your power to all who are to come (Psalm 71:18 NASB).

And we hear Him promise in reply,

Even to your old age and gray hairs I am he, I am he who will sustain you. I have made you and I will carry you; I will sustain you and I will rescue you (Isaiah 46:4).

And so we move forward, secure in the knowledge that whether our life adventure is new, old, or somewhere in between, our Daddy God will always be right there. Just turn around and see for yourself. He's the One who is holding you.

Chapter 2

DADDY, DO YOU CARE?

From the time she was an infant, Belle has shown a great fear of animals. We have no idea where the fear started, but regardless of the size of the animal, they terrify her. Cats in particular seem to produce a loud shriek, sometimes so unexpected as to send us (and anyone within earshot) into cardiac arrest.

Whenever Belle gets scared, I get "The Look." Her little mouth goes vertical and forms a long oval. Her eyes squint. And very quickly, if I don't respond swiftly enough, the tap gets turned on, the tears flow, and she gets very vocal. Her desperate, wide-eyed, frantic stare cries out, "Daddy, I'm scared! And I'm in trouble. Can you please come to me…now?! I need to know that you care for me."

I've learned that her summons for help means several things:
1. Pick me up!
2. Remove me far from this danger!
3. Hold me close so that I can feel truly safe and secure in the arms of someone whom I know won't allow any harm to come to me!

The Look reminds me that it's one thing to recognize your daddy is "in the house." It's quite another thing to know that he actually cares enough to respond to you when you need him.

Whether it's a hangnail or a skinned knee or a gushing wound that requires stitches, we all need to know that our daddy is present when we really need him. Every child, whether five years old and forty pounds or forty-five years old and 210 pounds, has a need for safety and security. All of us need to know we have a daddy who gives us both.

Jill's World

Unfortunately, countless individuals on our planet have no idea that anyone cares about them. Solitude like this drives many people to an early grave. Broken hearts brought on by loneliness do kill.

Jill is in her early sixties and I got to know her when she came to visit us at the Open Arms Village. I noticed during her early days at the Village that she was somewhat withdrawn and wasn't engaging as fully as she could have with our other visitors.

What I found interesting was the fact that she had traveled with a small group and she knew many of the people she had come with. But she was still distant.

Toward the end of her time in the Village, I spent some time with Jill. As I got to know her and talk about her life, I discovered that when she was three years old her dad had left her and her mom. She told me that as long as she could remember, her mom was distant, cold, and uncaring. And she hadn't been able to reconcile with her dad's departure when she was so young. Understandably, the idea of a loving, caring daddy has eluded her.

Jill believed in God, but found it terribly difficult, if not almost impossible, to believe in God as a Daddy who would care about her and care for her when her own father had abandoned her at such a young age. I would suppose that is the point: her Dad was a "'father" but never a "Daddy."

After Jill and I talked for a while, we prayed together. She prayed "Lord" this and "Lord" that. Finally, I put my hand on hers and asked her to pray to "Daddy."

She said she couldn't. I encouraged her to try. A big step of faith. I also encouraged her that scripturally, since she has been adopted into God's family, that the Bible says we cry out *Abba* (Daddy) *Father*

(Romans 8:15). I told her that I wasn't asking her to do anything that wasn't scriptural or truthful.

She then prayed to Daddy. Was it awkward? Yes, terribly awkward. Was it uncomfortable? Yes, very uncomfortable. Was it foreign? Yes, the language of "Daddy" was completely foreign to her.

At the end of the day, Jill needs to know God as her Daddy. Even though Jill is a grown, adult woman, she still carries the weight that came as a three-year-old girl when she felt abandoned, alone, and desperate to know the love and care of a daddy she never had the chance to get to know. With a cold, uncaring mother and an absent father, she found herself disconnected and detached. But her Daddy God has other plans for her. Psalm 68 says God sets the lonely in families and that He is a Father to the fatherless. He no longer wants her alone and feeling isolated. And even at sixty-something years old, it isn't too late.

Making a Quantum Leap
My own father left our family when I was fourteen. All my siblings had already exited the house, so Mom and I had to fend for ourselves. Dad left it up to me to see that he and I got together occasionally. I could either walk the two miles to his apartment, ride my bike, or take a bus. It never dawned on him that, as my father, he should take the initiative to reach out to his teenage son.

Dad made me feel guilty for not reaching out to him, or for not making a more determined effort to see him. But our relationship had never been great, even when he lived with us, so I thought, Why should I make special attempts now, when he's made very few attempts to see me?

Within six months of his leaving Mom and me, doctors diagnosed my dad with an acute form of leukemia. In 1975, that was pretty much a death sentence. He died eighteen months later, in August 1976.

After all these years, and with the advantage of maturity and of knowing something of the heart of my heavenly Daddy, I now have the perspective to see my Dad as broken and ignorant, as someone who simply had things backwards. Unfortunately, he had so focused on himself that he couldn't begin to see the effect his words and behaviors had on my siblings and me.

As Belle's dad, I pay attention when I see her get that long face, her eyes begin to squint, and her breathing gets fast and shallow. That means she's scared. She needs me. Unfortunately, my dad just couldn't see the signs that his two little girls and two little boys were hurting and that we all needed to know he cared.

More painful to swallow for me is the possibility that Dad did see the signs of our need for his care, but it just didn't matter to him, or he simply didn't know how to respond. I honestly don't think my dad had a clue. Up to the day he died, I don't think he ever really had a clue.

Many of us have had similar experiences with our dads. So when our hearts get broken by them, our "creator" (with a small c); when our needs don't get met by our small c creator - can we possibly make the quantum leap to believe that our Daddy in heaven, our Creator with a big C, could actually care for us?

It may be a quantum leap, but it's one that God wants us to make. The great news is that He doesn't expect us to make that leap alone. If we ask Him to, He will, by His Spirit, pick us up and jump with us over that canyon called "unbelief" or "distrust" or whatever we want to call it. He knows it's too large a chasm for us to cross on our own.

I have to do that with my two girls quite often. On our walks, maybe we come upon some muddy patch or a stream of water or a ditch. I'll have to pick them up and make the leap with them in my arms, since it's just too big a leap for them by themselves.

That's exactly what God does with us, if we'll let Him. The biggest chasms to cross in life are distrust, unbelief, and rejection. God has never expected us to cross them by ourselves. He's our Daddy and

He wants to make those jumps with us and for us. While the gaps are simply too big for our little mortal legs, they aren't big at all for His massive, immortal legs.

God is a great Daddy. We never make the first move toward relationship. He does that, every time. In fact, He's done it since the beginning of time.

God Cares About the Small Stuff—Especially You

We have a saying in the West about keeping our eyes on the big picture and refusing to let little, niggling issues get to us. We say, "Don't sweat the small stuff."

When you consider our tiny place in this gargantuan cosmos, it quickly becomes clear that you and I are the small stuff. But amazingly, to God we're also the big stuff. That's why David marveled:

> *When I consider your heavens,*
> *the work of your fingers,*
> *the moon and the stars,*
> *which you have set in place,*
> *what is man that you are mindful of him,*
> *the son of man that you care for him?"*
> (Psalm 8:3-4).

When David gazed up at the vastness of God's universe and then around him at the majesty of this amazing world, he couldn't help but wonder, How is it, Lord, that you would even notice me?

He does, though. He notices, and He cares. Even in the whole panorama of the universe and in the immensity of our galaxy, in the vastness of our solar system and our world, and in the nation, Kenya, and our county, Wareng, and our area, Mlango, and the Open Arms Village…I know that God does sweat the small stuff. And so He cares about me. He cares about each one of our Kenyan houseparents. He cares about our babies who live in our baby home. And likewise, in the whole panorama of the universe, and in the immensity of our galaxy, and in the vastness of our solar system and our world, and in whatever continent you live on and whatever country and county you live in and whatever city and street you call home, God cares about you.

You might be small stuff in your eyes, but not in His.

The Scripture says that God sees and records when even one sparrow falls to the ground. If He cares enough to see and record that, then He sees and cares about what happens to each of us individually (Matthew 10:29, 30). He is a great Daddy. And He makes me want to be like Him.

Recently, Belle rediscovered a battery-operated Bible-story songbook she had last seen at age two. She pushed the buttons, trying to make it play, but nothing happened. After more than two years, it obviously needed some new batteries. Several times over many days she asked me to fix it, and finally I said to her, "Okay, honey. Daddy will have it fixed for you by this evening."

By this evening.

I went about my business on that day, fully intending to stop somewhere and get some batteries. On my way home after a long day, and within just blocks of our house, I remembered that I hadn't followed through on my promise. Oh, she can wait another day or two, no problem, I thought. But then I checked myself: You told her in no uncertain terms that you would have it fixed by this evening. You want your little girl to be able to trust your word. You need to go and get those batteries and have it fixed by this evening, as you promised.

So I passed my regular turnoff and headed for a store that stocks the required batteries. I installed them as soon as I got home and instantly the songbook came back to life. I felt so happy to give it to Belle when she came home a little later with her mommy. Not only had I kept my word, but Belle knew that I cared about her.

I had felt tempted to think that getting the songbook working again was a small thing. I felt tempted to not sweat the small thing, and just put off its repair until a more convenient time. But that songbook was not a small thing to Belle. And neither was my word to her. I needed her to know that I care about whatever she considers important.

In a much greater way, Daddy God cares about you, and that is why He made a deliberate decision to give you some space on this planet. He gave you some turf to occupy, even though that space now comes at a premium. But He knew you–you and not someone else–and that you needed to fill it. Your Daddy God cares about you because He made you and created you for a purpose uniquely tailored to you and for you.

Do you know your Daddy's love and care for you? Do you know that He sweats the stuff that might be small to Him but that is gigantic to you? He cares that much for you.

God Wants to Carry the Heavy Loads That Weigh You Down
My eighty-eight-year-old mother, Gerry, is a breast cancer survivor. Two mornings per week she volunteers at the local hospital to assist with patients. She wears hard-to-miss bright-pink sequined tennis shoes, which serve her intended purpose of bringing equally bright grins and smiles from the faces of the patients she is serving.

On one of those two days per week, she serves in the cancer clinic taking tea and coffee around to the folks who have been diagnosed with cancer and who are receiving their chemotherapy treatments. More than just serving coffee and tea, she serves up smiles and encouraging conversations with people about her own journey with cancer and the victory that she gained over it. She plays a small but extremely important part in lifting people's very heavy loads with the testimony of her own survival and the hope that comes from the knowledge that cancer can be defeated. My mother is a bright-pink sequined-tennis shoe angel in disguise who firmly believes that her Daddy God is working through her to help carry others' frighteningly heavy loads.

What scares you? What makes you feel like something is pulling your legs out from under you? What leaves you petrified, certain that you're going down if someone doesn't intervene?

What terrifies you to the point that you need to know your Daddy is present and will respond to you? Think of that thing or of those things—and then allow these words from David, the king of Israel, to sink into your soul:

> *The cords of death entangled me*
> *the torrents of destruction overwhelmed me.*
> *The cords of the grave coiled around me;*
> *the snares of death confronted me.*
> *In my distress I called to the Lord;*
> *I cried to my God for help. From his temple he heard my voice;*
> *my cry came before him, into his ears.*
> *He parted the heavens and came down;*
> *he reached down from on high and took hold of me;*
> *he drew me out of deep waters.*
> *He rescued me from my powerful enemy,*
> *from my foes, who were too strong for me.*
> *He brought me out into a spacious place;*
> *he rescued me because he delighted in me*
> (Psalm 18:4-6, 9, 16, 17, 19).

Pay special attention to these words: "*He heard my voice; He parted the heavens and came down; He took hold of me; He gave me room to breathe* [my paraphrase] *and did all these things because He delighted in me.*"

Do you really know your Daddy's delight in you? So many people don't. Can you imagine how different this world would be if people really knew their heavenly Daddy's delight in them? Oh, the security, the comfort, the settledness, the peace that would change so many people and families, if this truth were able to soak into their souls!

Regardless of our age, we all need to know that someone

cares about us. We need to know that when we need something, something we can't provide for ourselves, that Someone stands close enough to be in touch with our situation, caring enough about us to do something about it.

What heavy loads weigh you down? What weighty problems keep you low to the ground? God knows and understands how terrifying it can feel when our feet slide out from under us. He knows the weight of fear we carry when we feel ourselves going down, with no one to save us.

On one of our family vacations, we spent four glorious days at the Disneyland and California Adventure theme parks. We had an awesome time, but also a sobering one. We walked every day, all day long, with then five-year-old Diana and four-year-old Belle. The experience sometimes took many steps of faith–especially because Rachel and I didn't bring any means of transportation for the girls. No stroller, pram, horse, donkey, camel, or wagon.

All around us we saw parents who seemed entirely prepared to take the load off their kids' feet (in part, I'm sure, so they could take the load off their own ears by eliminating the wails, "I'm tired! My feet hurt!"). In our family, Daddy became the pack mule. Is there such a thing as a pack ass? If so, I was it. I became the beast of burden for my girls.

I must say, they didn't utilize me as much as I expected. They walked a lot and didn't need Daddy as often as I thought they would. But whenever I needed to lend a helping back or shoulder, I felt happy to do so.

Our Daddy God is far more prepared to carry our loads and our burdens than I was.

The Bible tells us, *Cast all your cares on the Lord, for He cares for you* (1 Peter 5:7). Whether He's helping us to carry the weight of careers or relationships or financial debts, or He's carrying us because we just can't walk another step, our Daddy God loves to carry our loads and burdens.

Don't be afraid to admit that you yourself might be the biggest care or concern that you need God to carry. I know that sometimes I am the biggest weight that I have to ask my Daddy to carry. God knows your disabilities, weaknesses, and limits. He knows your constraints. He knows how desperately you want to fly, to soar. He knows when you can't get off the ground—or even get out of bed.

When you allow your heavenly Daddy to put you on His shoulders, whatever your limitations, those limitations fall away because He carries both you and the weights you bear. He wants you to let Him carry you, to show you how much He cares for you. He is all for your freedom and He wants you to soar as high as you can... which means, as high as He can.

God Stoops Down to Make Us Great

I've told you already that cats terrify Belle. In fact, she fears anything that crawls at her level, and when confronted by some such animal, as I've already said, she lets out bloodcurdling screams. A few months ago in Ushindi House in the Open Arms Village, she let out one such horrible scream when a cat walked into the house and wandered under the table where she was sitting. Her howls sent the whole house into a panic and nearly sent houseparent Daddy Tom and me to an early grave.

When Belle gets scared like this, I swoop in to pick her up and lift her above the things that terrify her. Even though I know the cat won't hurt her, she doesn't. She isn't old enough or mature enough to have an adult perspective. She just senses her danger, and she needs her Daddy's help to escape the fearsome thing.

Really, none of us are so very different from Belle. We all live our lives at ground level, where we get embroiled in the scraps and scrapes and battles we call daily life. Often we can't see above the fray to know how we're going to survive our difficult situations. We honestly think we won't make it. That's why Psalm 18:35 gives me such deep encouragement: *You give me y your right hand sustains me; you stoop down to*

In just one sentence of twenty words, this tremendous hope out of deep desperation. It of Someone much bigger than I, my Daddy in Himself toward me. He gives me His heavenly ... pective that offers me sight beyond my lowly fighting plane, and so I receive the hope that comes by seeing above the battle, by taking in the fuller picture available to God.

When you know your Daddy in heaven, you come to understand that His plans and purposes completely transcend our day-to-day living. He gives us perspective that allows us to grasp that what seems completely hopeless to us is actually just a blip on the radar screen of life. We will get through it, and rise above it, with His help.

Our heavenly Daddy knows full well our human condition. He knows where we have given up and when we are dying (or have died) inside. He loves to bring things back to life, especially His kids. And so He stoops down, pulls us up above ground level, and gives us His perspective. He breathes His life back into us and promises that He has a destiny for us to make us great. Isn't that awesome? Our heavenly Daddy, the One who gives us life, Himself stoops down to make us great.

As the author of life, God doesn't like His children dead. He wants you and me fully alive, and He wants to lift us up to places of greatness. Greatness doesn't necessarily (or even often) mean fame, wealth, and honor, although it could. Greatness is health, life, purpose, and a sense of belonging in the world.

The Bible does not picture God as way up there, demanding that we struggle, strain, and labor to climb up to Him. Just the opposite! God left His comfortable home in heaven, in the person of Jesus, and came down to our level in order to have relationship with us. Jesus lived at our level so that He could raise us up to His. Because He bowed low, we can rise up.

felt the gravity of earth and got down in the mud with us so that He could take our filth upon Himself, away from us. He broke the power of sin in our lives, enabling us to achieve greatness.

A String of Caring Mentors

I have seen the tender care of God displayed toward me through the presence of many loving, caring men who became, as it were, surrogate fathers for me after the death of my biological father.

When Mom remarried and her new husband, Vince, came into our lives, he became a father to me. At the time, he wasn't a Christian, so we couldn't share any spiritual depth or understanding. But he was loving, kind, thoughtful, and generous.

Vince worked as a contractor and cared for me and provided for me as he hired me to work on a couple of his house projects. I have great memories of being on the job site. After starting work by 6:30 or 7 a.m., around 10 a.m. he would say, "Hey! It's doughnut and coffee time!" and we would get in his construction van and go sit and have coffee and a doughnut at the little shop in the area.

Vince also helped me buy my first house. In fact, the house belonged to him and my mom.

He worked with me to assume his veteran's mortgage at a low interest rate. He also agreed to take a bit less for the house so I could afford it. From Vince, I learned firsthand that healthy fathers care for their children. I got to see what God is like through Vince's love and care for me.

In my last year of Bible school, at the age of twenty-five, I moved in with a family who attended my church. Bill and Sandi Davis became my dad and mom away from home. Because Bill was a strong Christian, I could share spiritual matters with him. Interestingly, he, too, was a contractor, and he hired me to assist him on job sites. In doing so he helped to provide financially for me as I finished school. Once again, I learned firsthand that a father cares. I saw a glimpse of what God is like through Bill's love and care for his family and for me.

Even now, in middle age, God has blessed me with a wonderful friendship with Brian Bittke. Brian is in his early seventies; I have known him for about ten years. He is a wonderful example to me of a loving husband and father, and he has been an inspiration to me as a mentor. Brian has had a fatherly influence and role in my life, and not just for me, but for countless others as well.

In the decade I've known him, Brian stayed very close to me when all hell started breaking loose. He would invite me to coffee or breakfast (we're both early morning guys) so we could check in with each other so he could make sure I was doing all right. I can't begin to tell you how many times Brian has reached across the breakfast table, grabbed my hand, leaned over with his steel-blue eyes peering over his glasses, and said, "David, you're like a son to me. Everything is going to be okay. I'm with you. If you need anything—and I mean anything—will you tell me? I mean it."

Brian has been a rock to me. Again, I have learned through Brian that a father cares. I see a glimpse of what God is like through Brian's love and care. I see my Daddy God when I look into Brian's eyes.

Because of God's gracious blessing on my life, many wonderful men like these have come into my life as role models. As fathers, they've guided me and mentored me and instructed me. Their influence makes me want to do the same for others. I want to pass along what has been so freely shared and invested in me.

I never want my daughters to wonder, even for a moment, whether I care about them. When Belle was an infant and I would be sitting and working on my laptop, she would sometimes crawl over and stand up beside me, wanting to come up and see me. I would make every effort to stop what I was doing, put my work to one side, and pick her up so I could hold her and play with her. To this day, when my girls come to me—no matter what I'm in the middle of doing at the moment—I make every effort to be with them and focus on what they want or need. I don't ever want them to think that anything is more important than they are.

Daddy, do you care?

I pray that I will be a daddy who cares and who loves to show my care to his daughters.

Even when events at the happiest place on earth don't go so well.

Beware the Loud and Dark

I knew we were in trouble on our very first day in Disneyland. I knew it by the very first attraction we visited, the Enchanted Tiki Room.

It all seemed benign enough. You sit in a tropical-looking room in which a bunch of robotic birds come to life and sing to you. But when the room grew dark and an artificial thunderstorm began, Belle lost it and began screaming hysterically.

We hastily left there and headed over to the Tarzan treehouse, where a loud, unexpected growl from a leopard perched on a branch frightened Belle. She was so scared I almost had to jump out of the treehouse with her in order to get her to safety.

We then made a beeline for Winnie the Pooh, *where we thought, surely, we will be safe on this ride*—but once again, she screamed and cried hysterically.

Finally, we boarded a carousel and held our breath. We thanked God because she loved it. And then on to Dumbo the Flying Elephant, which she also adored. We were two-for-two and seemed to be moving in a good direction.

As a little boy, my favorite ride was Mr. Toad's Wild Ride, so we decided to try that. Belle rode with Mommy in Mr. Toad's car... and from the moment she entered in to the time she emerged from his crazy house, hysterical screams once again bellowed out of her little mouth.

We finally realized that the rides and attractions that really scared Belle were the ones that go through the dark, accompanied by loud noises. I assured her, as her Daddy, that I would do my best to protect her from such rides. I told her I would keep her out of the dark and away from loud noises.

The next day, we visited California Adventure, where the big ride attraction in Car Land is called Radiator Racers. It appeared to be an outdoor ride, in the light, and we heard no loud noises. So we got Fast Passes for the late afternoon.

Unfortunately, while most of the ride took place in the daylight, one section did not–and that section had some very loud noises. This was the one part of the ride where the cars actually went slower–prolonging Belle's agony away from the light of day. If that wasn't bad enough, to make matters worse, the car then took off at lightning speed, racing against another car. Belle was beside herself.

Just when I didn't think it could get any worse, it did. Throughout the most offensive part of the ride, whipping around hairpin curves, I kept hearing her scream behind me as she rode with Mommy, "Daddy lied! Daddy lied!"

The ride came to an abrupt end with a braking halt and Belle cried hysterically as I pulled her from the car. As I carried her to safety, she clung to me for dear life, sobbing uncontrollably. After her screams and tears finally subsided, I took her to a quiet, shady spot, looked her in the eye, and apologized. "Honey," I said, "Daddy needs to ask for your forgiveness, because I didn't check out that ride carefully enough to make sure you wouldn't be scared. I am so sorry. I would never intentionally put you in a place where I thought you would be terrified like that. I didn't lie to you on purpose. Will you please forgive daddy?"

Her horrific cries of, "Daddy lied! Daddy lied!" had seared me to the core. I had failed my daughter in a big way, as earthly dads are prone to do. At a very deep level, my daughter had come to conclude, at least for a while, that I really must not care enough about her to protect her from the things that terrify her.

Later that evening, we got tickets for the World of Color water show. I didn't know how quickly I would once again be put to the test.

It never occurred to me that anything in a water show might scare Belle. But from almost the beginning, she came unglued.

Rachel and I couldn't believe it. This time we had no question as to the problem: the loud PA system. She stood there, shaking, covering her ears and sobbing.

I picked up my daughter and held her close, and even though she calmed down a bit, she was still agitated, afraid, and full of anxiety. I knew I had an opportunity to show my little girl that I did cherish her. I told Rachel that I needed to take her out. I had some repair work to do in order to rebuild Belle's trust that her daddy really did care about her.

We left Mommy and Diana to enjoy the show while I took Belle away to find a much quieter place where we could sit. Belle laid her head in my lap, and soon I felt confident I had begun to make the transition from "Daddy lied!" to "Daddy cares."

Whoever I'm "daddy" to—my own girls, children in the Open Arms Village, or others—I hope and pray that they know, without any doubt, that I care. I care because I have learned something about God's concern and care for me, displayed through those who learned to be great dads long before I began my lessons. I'm far from perfect. But I want my actions to remind them all of their heavenly Daddy.

A Great Transformation

When they were toddlers, Rachel and I would often bring our girls to our bed first thing in the morning for some playtime. On one occasion, Belle had a long-lasting cold and sinus infection. It didn't matter how much we wiped her nose, we just couldn't keep up. One morning, after our playtime, seeing the residue that was left on our bed, Rachel said, "It looks like a slug has been crawling around on our sheets."

I really didn't need that visual.

In Belle's sickness, I had to take saline solution and a small rubber "snot sucker" to her nose.

She didn't like the snot sucker, at all. She would get a panicked look in her eyes as soon as she'd see me pick it up. She'd begin wailing uncontrollably and flailing her little limbs, while I would try to restrain her.

After days of this routine–snot sucker comes into view, eyes grow large, the evil device approaches, screams and crying commence, restraints get imposed, suckage takes place, accompanied by flying snot–suddenly a change occurred. When I grabbed the snot sucker, her eyes didn't grow large. As I approached, no hysterical screams or crying commenced. I didn't need to use restraints. As suckage began and snot went flying, quiet reigned. We accomplished the intended aim and purpose, without all the dramatic side effects.

What had happened?

Belle finally understood that after snot suckage, no matter how strange, uncomfortable, or weird it might feel, came relief. Somehow, I think Belle figured out that I used the dreaded instrument because I cared about her. I believe she finally began to understand that I had her best interests at heart. I wanted her well-being. I desired her health and wellness and I was willing to forge ahead, despite her wailing and hysterics, to make sure she felt better.

Daddy, do you care?

Yes, indeed. *No discipline* [read, "snot sucker"] *seems pleasant at the time, but painful,"* God tells us. *"Later on, however, it produces a harvest of righteousness and peace for those who have been trained by it* (Hebrews 12:11).

I'm still learning. But at least I've learned, beyond a shadow of a doubt, that whatever my Daddy God does in my life–even if it seems weird or uncomfortable and I don't understand it–He does because He cares for me.

Like my wonderful friend Brian speaking to me, hear your Daddy God saying to you, "Everything is going to be okay. I'm with you. If you need anything–and I mean anything–will you tell me? I mean it." Now that's a Daddy who cares.

Chapter 3

DADDY, I'M HUNGRY

It's quite a shock when you go overnight from sharing a quiet home with your wife to caring for a twenty-nine-day-old infant who does all the things babies tend to do. That little girl turned our lives upside down and sideways in every way conceivable. Constant feedings and preparing bottles suddenly became part of my daily routine.

So did the crying. (Belle's, I mean.)

Babies cry when their diapers get dirty. They cry when they don't feel well. They cry when something startles them. They cry when someone doesn't let them have their way. And, of course, they cry when they're hungry.

Belle, like most babies, had an internal clock whose alarm went off about every four hours. Her body let her know when she needed food and, being a baby, the only way she had to communicate her need was to cry. We could be playing or cuddling one moment and the next moment she would get fussy and upset. I'd look at my watch and see that, sure enough, it had been about four hours since her previous feeding.

Time to eat!

The last thing I liked to hear, I admit, was my daughter's hunger cry. It's not that hearing my little girl cry aggravated or upset me. Nor did I just want peace in my home. Hearing Belle cry bothered me because I couldn't stand the thought that she felt upset or uncomfortable or hungry. I always got the message:

Daddy, I'm hungry!

Those became moments of total agreement between my daughter and me. We both knew I needed to get that bottle ready *and as quickly as possible.*

Precious Teaching Moments

I thoroughly enjoyed feeding Belle. I know a lot of guys—really good friends of mine—who, although they truly loved their children, never fed their kids a bottle. The idea of actually sitting with a child in their arms as that child ate just never appealed to them.

Too bad for those guys, I say!

As I cradled Belle in one arm, I felt amazingly privileged and blessed as I gazed down and saw in her eyes a look of total satisfaction and comfort. I felt a deep joy in seeing her at rest and in such peace that soon her eyes grew heavy, her breathing slowed, and in no time at all she drifted off to sleep.

In those blissful moments, Belle had no thought of paying off a mortgage or studying for a final exam or finding a counselor to help her work through some difficult personal problem. She felt content . . . and that was all.

God used those precious moments to teach me something wonderful about Him, His nature, and how He relates to His own children. Just as my daughter felt at rest as I held her in my arms, so God wants our souls at rest in Him as He holds us and nourishes us. And just as earthly parents provide food and nourishment for their children to enable them to grow and develop, so our Daddy God provides us with everything we need to grow and develop spiritually and emotionally.

The Need for Well-Balanced Meals

I know very well a child's need for nutritious and well-balanced meals. One of our regular programs at Open Arms International is a feeding program for 300 children, five days per week in Kambi Teso - a slum outside of Eldoret, Kenya. When we started our feeding program there, only 20 percent of the children attended school regularly. With a higher than 70 percent alcoholism rate in this slum, more parents spent their money on alcohol rather than on better food for their children. The malnourished kids couldn't function in school. Their brains starved for lack of protein.

Two years after we started our feeding program, more than 60 percent of these children were enrolled in school. Every day we see the difference that proper nutrition makes.

When my two girls get hungry and want something to eat, I am often reaching for things on shelves in the kitchen cabinets that are well outside their grasp. Try as hard as they might, because of their small size, there are things in our cupboards that they would never be able to reach for themselves.

In a similar way, God does not want His kids to struggle through life, wounded and weak, as they await eternity in heaven. Rather, He wants us to be well-nourished, growing, strong children of God–shining reflections of Himself. For that reason, our Daddy God reaches to the Top Shelves, those lofty places that remain out of our grasp, and gives us everything we need to nourish us and to keep our souls and spirits growing and healthy.

Just as I respond quickly when Belle's hungry, so our Daddy in heaven responds quickly whenever our hungry souls cry out. He makes sure we receive the emotional and spiritual nourishment we need.

I've watched our Daddy God nourish us and revitalize us in several crucial ways. Let's focus on just four Top Shelf items that only our Daddy in heaven can reach and bring down to us.

Nourished Through a Love That Brings Life

Multitudes of children grow up around the world never knowing the love of a daddy and mommy. It's heartbreaking. These precious young souls have no idea what it feels like to be loved and cared for, no idea what it's like to feel safe and secure, no idea what it feels like to have their daily needs met. For far too many of these children, life is nothing more than a daily struggle for survival.

About a year before Belle came to live with us, I observed the saddest real-life example of a lack of love and security that I've ever seen. When Belle's older biological half-sister, two-and-a-half-year-old Beatrice, came to live in the Open Arms Village, she knew nothing of family love and provision. Her parents had left her alone on the streets at the age of two, where she quickly found life to be nothing more than "survival of the fittest." Even the youngest street children learn to beg, steal, and scrape together every scrap of food they can find, just to make it through another day.

It broke our hearts to watch Beatrice at mealtime in her new family's home. Instead of sitting at the table to eat with the rest of the family, she would "duck and cover" with her bowl, moving far away from the others and hovering over her food to guard it and keep it out of the sight of any potential thief. She'd keep one eye peeled on her surroundings, constantly monitoring for anyone who came too close.

As our daughters have grown up, they have learned that in this home "survival of the fittest" does not reign. They live instead in a house of love. They know they don't have to fend for themselves and fight for every scrap of food. They know that there will always be enough. They take it for granted that when they say, "Daddy, I'm hungry," they will be fed. They live in a house of safety and provision. They know their Daddy will always work to meet their needs.

Children who grow up in homes where they know they are loved, even if they can't put into words what they know, are usually the healthiest, happiest, and best-adjusted children in their communities. That's because they grow with parents and other family members who do everything possible to supply them with a great environment. That kind of love makes kids feel protected, covered, completed, affirmed, and encouraged—in other words, safe and secure.

Children who don't feel safe and secure at home can go in a very different direction. Instead of living confidently that Mom and Dad are looking out for them, they develop some highly honed, self-protective (but ultimately very destructive) survival skills, skills that keep that child from giving and receiving love.

Our home offers a picture, admittedly an imperfect one, of the perfect home of safety and provision God wants to give all of His kids. In that home we can cry out to God, "Daddy, I'm hungry," and know that He will answer, "Of course I will feed you, sweetheart. I love you, and I want your hunger satisfied. You live in My house, and I will make sure you are well-fed."

My wife and I don't meet our daughters' needs merely out of a sense of duty or legal obligation. We do it willingly and joyfully because we love our two beautiful girls. We do it because, more than anything in the world, we want them to become all that their Daddy in heaven has created them to be.

Daddy God's love for His children is perfect. He doesn't love us and provide for us merely out of a sense of duty, as if He has to do it. No. He wants to feed us, wants to give to us, and wants to provide for us so that we can become what He has always intended for us to be.

How many countless millions of human beings don't know the safety and security of life in our Daddy God's house of love? They can't comprehend the truth that Someone created them to live in the safety and security of His love. But our heavenly Daddy never wants us to forget that.

When we understand that we have a Daddy who loves us and has devoted Himself to taking care of us, we no longer believe that we must somehow care for and fend for ourselves. We are no longer like Beatrice–always ducking and covering, escaping and hoarding, and constantly protecting ourselves. We are more like Belle and Diana, believing with everything in us that our Daddy God provides us everything so that we never need to live in hunger. Even more, we're free to give to others from what God has given us.

I never want my sweet daughters to question my love for them or my commitment to meeting all their needs. Likewise, your Daddy in heaven never intended for you to spend one second of your life outside of His house of love. He wants you to stay at home and allow Him to take care of you and to provide for you throughout your life.

King David understood the beauty of God's house of love, a place he never wanted to leave:

> *I have seen you in the sanctuary and beheld your power and your glory.*
> *Because your love is better than life, my lips will glorify you.*
> *I will praise you as long as I live, and in your name I will lift up my hands.*
> *I will be fully satisfied as with the richest of foods;*
> *with singing lips my mouth will praise you*
> (Psalm 63:2-5).

With singing lips my mouth will praise you. Linger over that description. If you've ever spent time in a home where the children feel safe and secure, where they are loved and fed and cared for, you'll hear the unmistakable sounds of joy. You'll hear children laughing and singing and enjoying life.

In the same way, when you're in the awesome presence of your heavenly Daddy, when you live in a home of love that is better than life, you too will be driven to song (even if you can't really sing) because you're happy, content, and at peace in His presence. As the psalmist wrote, your soul "will be fully satisfied as with the richest of foods."

A friend of mine has an insightful phrase taped to his desk, handwritten by a godly and beloved uncle who passed away a couple of years ago at the ripe old age of ninety-nine. I can see why he keeps it prominently displayed: "Joy is the most infallible sign of the presence of God."

Nourished Through Fulfilled Desires

As an eight-year-old boy, I got my first taste of having my desires fulfilled by my heavenly Daddy. My mother and I were shopping at Lynch's Market when I saw a giant banner advertising canned vegetables. A model train cleverly used those canned vegetables as its cars. For the whole store to hear, I shouted, "Mom! Do you see the train? Do you see it? Isn't that neat?" To make sure she heard me, I kept repeating myself.

An elderly gentleman soon approached my mom and said, "Excuse me, ma'am, but I couldn't help but overhear your son's enthusiasm for the train. I just wanted to introduce myself to you because I am an engineer with the Banks Railroad, and I want to invite you to bring your son out sometime. It would be my privilege to have him ride up in the locomotive with me."

A few weeks later, there I was, living the dream and riding in the locomotive of a full-scale steam engine.

Coincidence? Hardly. What are the odds that in the span of about fifteen minutes, we just "happened" to be at Lynch's Market at the same time someone who worked with the only railroad in 2,000 miles that gave short, public train rides was also there? Not only that, but he was an engineer who had the authority to invite an eight-year-old boy to join him for a ride in the engine of a steam locomotive? A long time ago I decided to "salt" my experience in Lynch's Market with a dose of faith. I chose to believe that Someone far greater than me, Someone who knew my innermost desires, had worked to make my dreams come true. From the time I was able to recall that experience as a young adult, I made a decision to give my Daddy God all the credit for making my dreams come true. I believe in God as my heavenly Daddy. I believe that He nourishes my heart by satisfying my innermost desires–just as He does for all His children.

David wrote in Psalm 103:2-5:
Praise the Lord, my soul, and forget not all his benefits—
who forgives all your sins and heals all your diseases,
who redeems your life from the pit and crowns you with love and
 compassion,
who satisfies your desires with good things so that your youth is
 renewed like the eagle's.

David knew his Creator satisfied his deepest desires.

Daddy God knows our desires can feel like a gnawing hunger craving to be satisfied. God also knows whether what we hunger for will feed our souls and spirits or kill them. He knows what will cause our spirits to rise and what will cause them to fall.

If we want truly satisfied souls, then we have to lean on our Daddy's estimation of the things we desire. It only makes sense that we should go to the One who made us and allow Him to speak into our desires. We need God to tell us what will give us ultimate satisfaction.

What do you believe about your Daddy in heaven? Do you believe that He wants to fulfill your desires? As you answer that question in your own mind, don't be afraid to wrestle with where you land on what you believe about God.

Do you believe that you have been left alone in the universe to feed yourself, make your own way, and satisfy your own desires?

Are you willing to salt your experiences with a dose of faith to believe that the One who gave you life is looking after you and satisfies your healthy desires so that you are well-nourished from the inside out?

I hope so.

Nourished Through Our Daddy's Presence

Even before I became a father, I understood that it is every dad's responsibility to provide his children with the things they need to grow healthy and strong and to live comfortably. I have gladly and joyfully worked to fulfill that duty.

I never want my daughters to wonder, even for a moment, if I will fail to provide the things they need. But I also want them to live in the assurance that I will share with them what any loving father most desires to share with his kids: himself.

Call it "bonding time," but the delightful moments I spent giving Belle her bottle felt to me like far more than a father caring for his child's need. It was a daddy who, on a very personal level, shared himself with his daughter. Over time, she learned that I was more than just a provider. She understood that I wanted to share myself with her and allow her to share herself with me. My presence brought nourishment to my daughter and satisfied a hunger that a bottle never could.

The very best thing I can give my daughters is the gift of myself, the gift of my presence. My daughters need time with their daddy, minutes and hours and days with the one who can give them the things money can never buy: love, protection, healing, validation, security, and a sense of belonging.

My own Daddy in heaven provides the perfect example of what every dad should be. He created us and provides for us physically, but He gives us so much more! He has shared Himself, including the most personal way possible, by giving us Himself in the form of His Son, Jesus Christ.

Jesus once declared, *"I am the bread of life. Whoever comes to me will never go hungry, and whoever believes in me will never be thirsty"* (John 6:35). Jesus didn't choose His words randomly. By calling Himself "the bread of life," He reminded us that God has placed within us a hunger for knowing Him–and that He is the only way to satisfy that hunger.

We all have an empty place in our souls that we long to have filled, and our Daddy God wants to fill it to overflowing. Sadly, we often turn to many other things in a vain attempt to dull our inner hunger for meaning, for security...for God. We turn to food, to alcohol, to sex, to shopping, to sports, to hobbies—make your own list.

I saw an example of this one night in Eldoret. That evening, the phone in my hotel rang, and a voice on the other end told me I had visitors. When I came downstairs, I found two young women, whom I had met earlier in the day at the grocery store, both dressed to the nines and obviously "looking for love in all the wrong places," as the old song goes. These single ladies, desperate for love and attention, had bought into the myth then current that married people couldn't give or contract HIV. I knew of husbands and wives all over town who indulged their libidos with other married people because of that myth. But single people, like these two young women, had been left out in the cold.

God did not create us to remain alone or to fend for ourselves. Survival is not for the "fittest," but for those who decide to live in their Daddy's love. That night, it occurred to me that these young women were just two among millions trying to fill the Dad-shaped God Space inside themselves with anything that might quench the thirst and satisfy their hunger.

We run into an insurmountable problem when we try to find answers to our spiritual and emotional hunger by depending on anything or anyone outside of God. None of these "answers" can deliver anything but temporary results.

The numbing effects of alcohol and drugs wear off.

Great food loses its taste shortly after the last swallow.

The buzz of sex dissipates once the orgasm ends.

Your team loses in the playoffs. Even if they win it all, the euphoria is short-lived.

The stuff you get on your shopping spree goes on a shelf or in a drawer (or in your garage), and once you own the thing, the excitement ends (and reality hits when the credit card statement arrives or the first loan installment comes due).

The pleasures of this world—many of them good and right—offer nothing but temporary relief. But our Daddy God and His love last forever. More than anything else, He wants you to allow Him to share Himself with you and spend time with you. He has a passion to satisfy your soul with His own Son, the bread of life.

Nourished Through His "Good Gifts"

At seven years of age, I felt desperate to get my own, brand-new Schwinn bicycle. I didn't go for subtlety when I let my parents know what I wanted. I made it unmistakably clear that I just had to have a new bike, one with all the options: a headlight, a horn, and a book carrier.

I had a big problem, however. I had been born on April 16, just one day after tax day, when many families have to use all their resources to pay Uncle Sam. My family was not well-to-do, and mid-April never was a good time for unnecessary expenditures. On many years, as my birthday approached, my Dad would tell me, "It's tax time again. Money is tight, so there won't be any birthday presents this year."

But somehow, some way, my parents made it happen that year. The big kahuna. On the morning of April 16, 1968, they took me into their bedroom to reveal my birthday gift. I stood there, wide-eyed and nearly breathless, as I fixed my gaze on the magnificent, gleaming object before me. It had everything I had hungered for: gold color, headlight, horn, and a book carrier. While I don't remember every detail from that morning, it must have been quite a scene—me, over-the-top excited, and my Daddy and Mommy, giddy with joy because they had found a way to give me my heart's desire.

Loving parents get a special "rush" from giving their children the extra things they hunger for, things that aren't so much needs as desires. Love always motivates us to give, and good parents take great pleasure in giving good, even extravagant, gifts to their children.

Like any loving parent, your heavenly Daddy loves to pour out good gifts on you.

And He's not bound by a lack of resources, due to tax day or any other occasion.

God promises to meet our physical and material needs, but He doesn't stop there. Your heavenly Daddy, who lives and moves in the spiritual realm, promises to pull things down from His Top Shelf in heaven to give you the things you could never reach on your own–or buy at your local Walmart or Saks Fifth Avenue store, things you can't touch, feel, hear, or see with your five senses. Things like:

- Peace
- Patience
- Understanding
- Wisdom
- Joy
- Kindness
- Perspective (seeing things the way He does)
- Unconditional love

Do you hunger for any of these things? If so, never doubt that your loving, caring, generous Daddy God wants to give them to you and in spades. Listen to a remarkable promise that lies at the heart of your Daddy's desires, straight from the mouth of His Son, Jesus Christ:

> *Which of you, if your son asks for bread, will give him a stone? Of if he asks for a fish, will give him a snake? If you, then, though you are evil, know how to give good gifts to your children, how much more will your Father in heaven give good gifts to those who ask him!* (Matthew 7:9-11).

Good gifts to those who ask Him. Don't let that phrase escape your notice. In many ways, I see few differences between Belle's crying out to her earthly daddy and her fifty-something-year-old earthly daddy crying out to his Daddy in heaven. In both cases, small people cry out to someone much bigger to satisfy needs and desires they can't satisfy on their own.

When I cry out to God–when I pray–I don't use the words, "Daddy, I'm hungry! Can you give me something to eat?" But I know I can cry out to God, even when I can't put into words what I'm hungry for, and know that He can and will meet the longings and needs of my heart.

Best of all, He's not merely willing to satisfy my hunger, He's happy to give it! He told His people long ago–and He tells them still today–*"I am the Lord your God, who brought you up out of Egypt. Open wide your mouth and I will fill it"* (Psalm 81:10).

What Makes You Hungry?
God knows about our gnawing hungers even before we mention them to Him. He knows the desires lurking in our hearts, and He knows that we don't feel satisfied until the cravings stop. But more importantly, God knows which of our desires are good for us and which feed our souls.

Our Daddy in heaven is just like any good parent, except that He's perfect in every way. He knows what is truly good for us. He knows whether what we hunger for will feed our souls and spirits or kill them. He knows what will cause our spirits to rise and what will cause them to fall.

While we hunger for many things that can nourish our souls and spirits, not all of our desires are good for us. In fact, they leave us malnourished, hungrier and thirstier than before and emotionally and spiritually stunted.

My wife and I know what foods are best for our daughters. We know that sugary, high-fat foods do not nourish their bodies. At times, therefore, we don't feed them what they want but rather what they need. We want them to develop in a healthy way.

Our Daddy in heaven is far wiser than even the best earthly mommy and daddy. And when He answers our hunger cries, He does so in ways far beyond anything we can ask or imagine.

What makes you hungry? Do you crave power? Money? Position? Respect? At some level, we all desire these things, and in and of themselves they aren't necessarily bad for us. They can be among the "good things" that God may choose to give us.

But God wants us to hunger even more for the gifts He knows are the very best for us, things like personal integrity, honesty, humility, a heart for service, and meekness. When we cry out to God for these things, hungering and thirsting for them–even though the world often sees them as weakness–He will never let us down. In fact, He makes an incredible guarantee to those who bank on His ability and willingness to bring them the very best: *Then you will know that I am the Lord; those who hope in me will not be disappointed* (Isaiah 49:23).

Depending on Daddy

I've often thought about where my daughters might be today if Rachel and I hadn't taken them into our home. Belle, born to a nineteen-year-old street girl whose own parents had lived on the streets and raised her on the streets (I am told that, as of this writing, Belle's biological father is in prison somewhere in Kenya), almost certainly would have had a life going in a drastically different direction than it is. Diana, born to a sixteen-year-old girl and rejected by her family and tribe, would have been killed, abandoned or thrown down a pit latrine and left to die if her grandmother hadn't whisked her away to safety.

Our girls depend completely on Rachel and me to meet all their needs. As small children, they cannot do much of anything to feed themselves, so they must depend on their Mommy and Daddy. And I wouldn't have it any other way–not because I want to maintain control over them, but because I'm their daddy. I want them to understand that I have gladly chosen to love them and provide for them. I want my girls to know that I meet all their needs because I want to.

That sounds a lot like our Daddy God, doesn't it?

God knows what kind of nourishment we need each day in order to please Him by our lives. But the greatest news of all is that He *loves* to feed us whatever we need. He loves us so much that He wants us to completely depend on Him for everything–*everything!*– we need.

Every time we receive good things from God, things we know we could never provide for ourselves, we have the opportunity to remember how much He wants to provide for us. His great desire that we depend on Him for everything flies in the face of a current way of thinking that screams, "Don't depend on anyone or anything, because you might get hurt! You'll certainly get let down, and you'll appear weak and vulnerable."

The best answer to this popular line of thinking is a long, sustained gaze at Jesus Christ. If you take a good look at the life of this ultimate man of strength, the one who came to earth to bear the sins of the whole world, you will see the foolishness of such a position. Jesus never forgot that He was the Son and not the Father. He purposely and joyfully lived in His Daddy's shadow and never once thought about leaving it. He never wanted to separate from His Dad, even for one moment, because He knew that every bit of His power, sustenance and provision depended on continually staying close to His Dad and listening to His voice.

All of us have an inner hunger for love, for validation, for security, and for a sense of belonging. God Himself put those hungers within each of us. But our Daddy in heaven never intended for us to try to find satisfaction for any of these hungers apart from Him.

We recently took a little girl named Ann into our Open Arms Village. Ann had lived her first three years on the streets, where malnourishment had severely stunted her growth. She wasn't merely underweight; she looked about the size of an eighteen-month-old.

Ann needs proper nourishment to grow and thrive physically. She must regularly eat healthy food, or her body will fail to develop. Stunted growth is just one sign of malnourishment; starved young brains can fail to develop and so consign an innocent child to a life of hardship.

We intend to give Ann a fresh chance at life and take her in. We wanted the privilege of caring for her, providing for her, and preparing her for a life of joy and satisfaction. But for her to move in that direction, she had to trust us. She had to depend on our willingness and ability to care for her and provide for her. She had to come to believe that we are there to help her thrive.

In a similar but far greater way, God wants us to trust Him, to depend on Him. He wants to meet our needs and satisfy our hunger. Perhaps most of all, however, He wants us to know that He's a Daddy who will never turn a deaf ear to His kids when we cry out, "Daddy, I'm hungry!"

Chapter 4

DADDY, CAN YOU HELP ME WITH MY MESS?

Belle was about eighteen months old when she secretly grabbed a bottle of her mommy's lotion. Do you have any idea how much fun a little girl can have in just five minutes? She smeared liberal amounts of the stuff all over her face, arms, legs, hair…and all over the carpets in our house.

How could such a sweet little girl create such a huge mess in such a short time?

If you're a parent, it probably didn't take you long to realize that babies and messes—of every shape, size, form, and color—just go together. There are the food messes…all over their faces, hands, torsos, and clothing, as well as on the floor and walls. (By the way, you should take a few pictures of these mini-disasters. They may very well provide some smiles in later years, when your little ones have grown up and moved far away.) Then there are the daily messes that come in the form of dirty diapers. And, of course, there are the messes that come when your baby gets sick—the mucus from colds and sinus infections, the messes from gastrointestinal problems like diarrhea, and messes that come as a result of nausea and upset stomachs.

Belle is no exception. Her five minutes alone with that bottle of lotion was far from the only time she's created a muddle. She regularly makes messes of all kinds, usually all over herself. As her daddy, I've had plenty of experience cleaning up Belle's messes. By now, I've gotten pretty good at it. And her messes remind me that we live in a messy, messy world.

Life is Full of Messiness

As much as we'd like to think otherwise, life's moments of chaos and confusion don't stop when we grow from infanthood into childhood, then from childhood into adolescence, and then on to adulthood. Life is messy, and while the fumbles and jumbles I make usually look different from the ones my daughters make, I still find myself in various kinds of messes of my own making... and probably more regularly than I'd like to admit.

And then–just when you have emerged from the chaos of several minor disasters and imagine that you're in for a season of open pathways and smooth sailing–life ushers in a brand-new set of messes that you had never remotely anticipated.

The wreckage in each of our lives comes in all shapes and sizes. Relational troubles, spiritual difficulties, emotional pain, financial hardship...it's a never-ending list. These messes also come from a variety of sources. We inflict some of them on ourselves as a result of our own poor choices. Others grow out of the actions of others, or simply because we live in a fallen world. But wherever they come from, someone has to clean them up.

I made a small mess for myself one Christmas Eve in Eldoret, Kenya, when I was driving around with some friends. The thought suddenly occurred to me that my friends really needed to see for themselves my phenomenal driving skills. After all, driving in Africa requires a stunt driver's license. I put on quite a show for them! And just as I thought I had privileged my friends to experience the greatest driver this side of Jeff Gordon, I rear-ended someone.

I probably should have read Proverbs to begin my day: *Pride goes before destruction, a haughty spirit before a fall* (Proverbs 16:18).

Fortunately, God delivered a mostly gentle correction. Yes, I felt embarrassed–and humbled.

The crash injured no one, and the police handled the situation very well. In the bigger scheme of things, I hadn't created a huge disaster, but the situation could easily have turned out much, much worse. Had I caused a more serious accident, I could have brought a tangle of pain, confusion, and inconvenience into the lives of a number of innocent people.

Sometimes, our poor choices and botched decisions result in only minor messes. But some of our missteps can produce huge messes, for others as well as for ourselves. My mind immediately leaps to some of the headline-grabbing fiascoes of the past few years, whether presidential misdeeds or celebrity debacles or the well-publicized failures of various religious and ministerial figures. Your mind no doubt creates a similar list.

The fact is, smart, talented, gifted, inspiring, and highly productive people can also make major, tabloid-worthy messes. All of us are prone, at times, to making irresponsible and reckless decisions. We take our eyes off the ball and act selfishly, greedily, or lustfully. And when we make bad decisions, those flawed decisions have the power to create mayhem in our lives and the lives of others.

Some years back, my brother, Bill, found himself in a mess that even his worst enemy wouldn't have wished on him. He didn't cause the situation, but it landed on his head courtesy of the person closest to him, the individual who should have had his trust above anyone else.

Bill and Deborah had been married for several years. While they didn't exactly live in marital bliss, Bill believed he had a fairly solid marriage.

That all changed one morning when he got up to get ready for work. After showering and dressing, Bill walked out the door to jump into his car, only to discover that there was no car to jump into. Deborah's car had vanished too. It didn't take long for Bill to learn that the repo man had come in the dead of the night to tow away the cars. Why? Deborah had failed for some time to make the required monthly payments. And then it got worse. A short time later, Bill learned that the bank was about to foreclose on his house. Same reason.

How could such a huge mess sneak up on Bill? My brother had entrusted his wife with paying all the household bills, and for some time, she did a good job keeping the checkbook balanced. Eventually, however, a concealed drug habit began to get the best of her. The money earmarked for car payments and the mortgage went to support her habit instead.

Deborah's addiction–and the illicit actions she took to feed that addiction–took a terrible toll on my brother and on his whole family. Before Bill had a chance to do anything to head off this terrible mess, he found himself up to his eyebrows in a frightening financial catastrophe.

The fact is, we live in a world filled with fallen, imperfect, and sometimes dysfunctional people. And for many (if not most) of us, it's only a matter of time before someone does or says something that makes a mess in our lives, whether a small muddle or a huge one. Has someone ever made a mess in your life by doing any of the following?

- A coworker lied about you, and the lie kept you from getting the promotion at work you had hoped for.
- A family member or so-called "family friend" physically and emotionally abused you as a child, leading to a string of serious issues later in life.
- Your reputation got trashed when someone spread false rumors about you.
- You got unjustly accused of something you didn't do.
- An identity thief blew up your finances.

The messes that others create don't always come out of malice, of course. I once decided to clean up the kitchen in the children's ministry building at our church. Because I didn't know any better (this will tell you how kitchen-savvy I am), I put liquid dish soap into the dishwasher and then left the premises. Not long afterwards, a literal wall of suds came cascading out of the kitchen, creating a white lava flow that snaked its way down the hall of the building. Afterwards, someone told me that screams pierced the air, some of them bordering on profanity–and that my name figured prominently in the outbursts. I ended up creating a mess of rather amazing proportions.

But I didn't have to clean up that mess myself. I wasn't around to do it. That fell to my friend, Caroline.

Messes, as they say, don't clean up themselves.

Who's Cleaning Up This Mess?
When Belle was a baby, she'd often be sitting in my lap when I'd notice the unmistakable evidence of a big mess in her diaper.

What kind of father would I have been had I just refused to clean up her messes? What if I had just looked at my messy little girl and declared, "Hey, you made the mess, so you get to clean it up. Now go away and don't come back until you've cleaned yourself up"?

Of course, I would never say such a thing. I love Belle far too much to do anything other than what any loving daddy would do. I cleaned her up, talking to her and encouraging her all the while. And while I might not have relished that task, I still did it gladly. Why? Because I love my daughter, and knew that she needed someone bigger than herself to help her out of her predicament.

Did I just use the word "gladly"? Let me reiterate that I *hated* the mess, hated the smell, and was thoroughly grossed out to the point of gagging. But at the same time, I *wanted* to jump in and help my little girl. I didn't want to change my daughter's diapers so I would feel more comfortable. I didn't brave the stench because I wanted to improve my quality of life.

No, I jumped in to help Belle because I love her.

I don't want her to be uncomfortable–or sad or hungry or fearful or lonely. I hate to hear her cry, because I want the best for her.

I knew that *someone* needed to change Belle's diapers, and I felt glad that "someone" could be me.

Some dads, I know, would do almost anything to get out of diaper duty. If they had a choice between changing a dirty diaper and fighting a fire-breathing dragon armed with nothing but a toothpick and a ham sandwich, they'd pick the latter (at least they'd get a meal out of it). Not me. To help my little girl I'd choose to face the noxious fumes, which at times were as deadly and terrifying as a fire-breathing dragon. That's not to say that there weren't times that I waited just a bit longer to get around to changing the diaper in the hopes that Belle's mommy would walk through the door and do the duty. Come on—I'm still a *guy*.

I love Belle, and I knew that, like any small child, she wasn't old enough, physically mature enough, or emotionally or intellectually developed enough to clean up her own messes. So if she was going to remain clean and smelling good—and that's what I wanted for her, more than my own comfort—then her daddy and mommy would have to deal with her messes by cleaning her up and bathing her.

It's very much like that with God, our heavenly Daddy.

God is certainly present and able to step in and help us when we find ourselves in nasty situations. As the psalmist says, He is an ever-present help in trouble (Psalm 46:1). But more than that, He wants to do it. He wants to help. He longs to step into our lives and do for us what we could never, ever do for ourselves.

Now, I understand that the wanting part of this equation is difficult for many people to wrap their heads around, including many believers. In fact, it's so difficult for them that it keeps them from turning to the one place they should always turn first when life gets messy: to our Daddy in heaven.

Why Not Your Daddy?
Imagine for a moment that you're in one of life's big messes, up to your eyeballs in trouble. It really doesn't matter what kind of chaos you're in—or whether you created it yourself or it fell on you out of

the clear blue sky. Maybe you were just in the wrong place at the wrong time making the wrong decisions.

Whatever the situation, you're in a mess too big to handle yourself, and you need help to get it cleaned up.

Where do you turn first? Whose number do you dial?

The real question is this: Do you deep-down and truly believe that God wants to hear from you in such a time? And how do you think He'd answer if you were to reach way down inside yourself and muster up the courage to ask Him, "Lord, please, will You help me to get out of this mess I'm in?"

How you answer these questions, especially as you read this book in relative comfort, should tell you a lot about what you really believe about God. It may be that, even at this moment, one or more of the following thoughts is rambling through your mind:

I'm not sure there is a God, but even if there is, He's nowhere to be found. He's left me alone, to fend for myself.

I know God must be out there somewhere, but I'm not sure He wants to help me, especially in this particular mess. Maybe He will, maybe He won't.

God has no interest in helping me out of this mess, because I've created it for myself. This is my problem, and I must solve it myself.

The whole thing is just way too complicated. Maybe even for God. I wouldn't even know how to explain it to Him or where to begin.

I have found each of these perceptions of Daddy God to be extremely common, as well as deeply flawed. Where do you think they come from?

If your earthly father abused you, abandoned you–or maybe just ignored you–you may find yourself wondering if your heavenly Father will follow the same pattern. Your own dad didn't seem to care what happened to you, so why should God? Your very own father didn't trouble himself to help you, talk to you, or develop a relationship with you, so why should you expect some distant "heavenly Father" to do any better?

As I've mentioned, my father died when I was sixteen. While for years I rationalized that his early death "might have been for the best," that point of view became more and more difficult to hold onto as I grew into adulthood. No matter how I tried to spin that loss, no matter how I attempted to shrug it off, I really couldn't pretend that it didn't matter to me.

It did matter.

It does matter.

It has always mattered.

One of the effects of fatherlessness here on earth tends to be a lack of trust in our Father in heaven. Some men and women who grew up without fathers deny that there is a God at all. Others might shrug their shoulders and say, "Well, even if there is a God, He/She/It doesn't have anything to do with me. I can't see God helping me or caring about me when life gets messy."

Men and women with such a dim view of God often make "going it alone" into a lifestyle—and a noble and courageous lifestyle at that. Since their earthly daddy wasn't there for them, and since there is no one "up there" to come to their aid, they believe that anyone looking for such divine assistance is weak and addicted to crutches. And because they themselves aren't weak, they see it as entirely up to them to sort out their own messes.

Without question, we do need to take responsibility for the messes we make. I'm certainly not advocating irresponsibility here. But many of the messes we must deal with in the course of life are simply bigger than us. What then?

Let me offer you another perspective on who God really is, a biblical perspective that I've seen played out over and over in my own life. I believe that someone who knows God as a loving heavenly Daddy also knows that He is committed both to them and to dealing with the complexities and difficulties and disasters in their lives. There will be times when the challenges we face are simply too high to climb over, too deep to tunnel under, or too wide to get around.

Our Compassionate Daddy
One time I was playing with Belle in our house—throwing her around, giving her pretend airplane rides, roller coaster rides, and sky diving lessons. She was laughing, I was laughing. We were having a ball!

Then suddenly, as little girls and boys sometimes do when their Daddies are airplaning them around, she burped up a tiny amount of milk onto the front of my sweatshirt.

No big deal! I thought, and quickly and happily wiped it off. Belle and I went back to playing, but this time on a much lower-key level. (No point in tempting fate!)

I went to bed that night, having forgotten about the small mess on my sweatshirt. The next morning, I got up and, before I showered and dressed for the day, I put on that same sweatshirt. As I walked down the hallway toward our family room, I caught a whiff of a terrible odor, one I couldn't identify. I just happened to be by the door of Belle's bedroom when I smelled it, and so I naturally thought, *Goodness! Belle really needs a diaper change.*

I didn't think anything more of the odor until I seated myself to work on my laptop in the family room. And then I caught another whiff.

"What is that?" I asked myself. At that moment, I remembered the little decoration Belle had left on my sweatshirt the night before. I leaned down to sniff the sweatshirt at the approximate spot where Belle had made her evening donation.

I nearly passed out.

As I later thought about the incident, it seemed like a small example of how the messes children make always affect their parents. Belle hadn't done anything wrong, but the mess from the day before continued to affect me into the next day.

The truth is that when our babies make messes, they affect loving mommies and daddies. That doesn't stop when they become toddlers, then grow into children, and then proceed to adolescence.

It really doesn't stop even when they grow into adults. The only difference is the *types* of messes they make. Those messes, however, will always have an effect on us as loving parents. Now, it's one thing to clean up your baby when it's diaper change time, or to clean up your children at the dinner table after mealtime.

I've done those things willingly and joyfully, just because I love Diana and Belle and know they can't yet do those things for themselves.

But it's something else altogether when your child gets to an age when he or she can make choices that result in real messes. The child's age doesn't matter at that point. When he or she is in a mess due to poor choices—whether due to inexperience, ignorance, or sin—it hurts a loving parent to the very core.

That's just part of the price of love, isn't it?

Love can be messy. Life can be messy. And you simply cannot experience true love without experiencing difficulty, challenges, disappointments, and heartaches.

Our Daddy in heaven knows this well. In the Bible, we read all kinds of accounts of Him looking down on the messes His children made and feeling grief, anger, and heartache for them—and sometimes all of those emotions at once.

By definition, sin is an offense to God. He doesn't take sin lightly, because it hurts His relationship with His most treasured creation, His kids. But even so, in the midst of all that, our Daddy God continues to feel compassion for His kids:

As a father has compassion on his children, so the Lord has compassion on those who fear him; for he knows how we are formed, he remembers that we are dust (Psalm 103:13-14).

Like a dad with his kids, my Daddy in heaven has compassion on His kids. His kids are those who fear Him—not a cowering, shaking, quivering, terrified kind of fear, but a fear declared and broadcasted by the honor and reverence they gladly show to Him, seasoned with healthy doses of love and awe.

How awesome that this Daddy God, who is rightly reverenced and honored, would also show me His compassion when I mess up and make poor choices! Rather than curse me, scold me, punish me, belittle me, mock me, or harass me, the Bible says He remembers that I am "dust." He shows me grace and mercy because He knows how fragile, vulnerable, and weak I am. When I bring disaster on myself and I'm honest about it (and even when I'm not honest about it), He shows me His love and compassion. His grace and favor in the midst of my failure and disobedience drives me to want to change and improve. It also drives me to want to extend that kind of love and compassion to others when they create disasters of their own.

I love a lot of things about my Daddy in heaven, but at the top of the list is this: He knows I make messes in my life, He knows about my bad decisions, and yet He still loves me. He knows about my stubbornness and rebellion against His desires and ways, yet He still willingly and compassionately forgives me. And then He comes in, cleans me up, and scours away the messes I make.

I can't begin to tell you how much solace I take in knowing that my Daddy in heaven remembers that I am "but dust." This doesn't mean that He devalues me or looks down His nose at me, as if I'm nothing more than dirt to Him. On the contrary, it means that He shows me grace and mercy when I fail because He knows my weakness and vulnerability. He remembers that, at the very beginning, He made human beings from the dust of the earth and then breathed into them the breath of life.

So how can someone made "in the image of God" also be made of dust? How do those two vastly different realities go together?

It's an amazing mystery, but it's almost as though the Lord were saying, "I love you and delight to spend time with you, walk with you, and speak with you. And just to show you that I'm not afraid to get My hands dirty in My relationship with you, I'm going to craft you from the earth itself."

This verse reminds me to always, *always* make a beeline straight to my Daddy God whenever I've made a mess, especially when it's so big that I can't handle it on my own.

Running to Your Daddy God

I'll never forget the blood-curdling scream that rattled our house one day from the direction of a kitchen window. Belle was playing there and had found what looked like a dead doo-doo ("bug" in Swahili) on the windowsill. As a curious little girl, she reached over and touched the bug, probably even tried to pick it up. But it wasn't dead, and it certainly wasn't harmless. An angry bee rewarded my daughter's curiosity with a nasty sting to her hand.

Now, what's the first thing a child does when he or she gets hurt? You don't have to be a parent to know that the child cries out and runs to mommy or daddy. Maybe it's a natural reaction to pain and discomfort, or maybe it's just something the child learns. Either way, children somehow just know that Mom and Dad are a source of comfort when something hurts them.

I think that's part of what Jesus was getting at when He told His disciples, *"Truly I tell you, unless you change and become like little children, you will never enter the kingdom of heaven"* (Matthew 18:3). On one level, that sounds like a stern warning. And perhaps it is. But if you look more deeply at Jesus' words, you begin to understand that God wants His relationship with us to beautifully reflect the way a helpless child completely depends on his or her mommy and daddy.

As Diana's and Belle's Daddy, I know my daughters completely depend on Mommy and me to clean up their messes and to offer comfort when they get hurt. And what's even more beautiful is that they know it too.

Unless you become like little children…

When we find ourselves in a mess, when we have painted ourselves into an impossible corner, our heavenly Daddy wants us to do one thing: run straight to Him, just as a small girl runs to her mommy and daddy for help and comfort after a bee sting.

When we run to our Daddy God with some mess we've made ourselves, He cleanses and restores us in the same way that Jesus forgave and restored Peter after the apostle had denied Him not once, not twice, but three times (John 21:15-25). He cleanses us and restores us, just as the father in the parable of the Prodigal Son welcomed home his wayward son with great fanfare, even after the boy had made a complete hash of his young life (Luke 15:11-20). When we run to God after we have made a mess, He offers us healing and uses the hurtful situation for our (and His) very best.

Your Daddy in heaven will never leave you alone to fend for yourself or insist that you clean up your own failures and disasters. You are His kid and He is your loving Daddy God, and He wants you to know that you can bring even your worst messes to Him.

So when life becomes messy, don't hesitate. *Run* to Him!

He's Not Going Anywhere

Your Daddy in heaven isn't going anywhere. He's always there for you, just a prayer away when you need Him. He loves you so deeply and broadly that He'll always welcome you into His loving arms whenever you need to be held.

Your heavenly Daddy's concern and care for you doesn't depend on whether He's too busy for you (He never will be) or whether He's tired of hearing about your problems.

That simply won't happen. Ever.

When it comes to responding to your needs, God will never be too tired, too distracted, too burned-out, too frustrated, or too disgusted with the mess in which you have thoroughly immersed yourself. He knows you and understands that you are going to make messes–and lots of them. As the apostle James reminds us, *We all stumble in many ways* (James 3:2). He will always be ready to forgive you, clean up your messes, and offer you healing and restoration.

"Daddy, can you help me with my mess?" Hear his answer: *I will answer them before they even call to me. While they are still talking about their needs, I will go ahead and answer their prayers!* (Isaiah 65:24 NLT).

What a wonderful Daddy in heaven He is!

Chapter 5

DADDY, CAN WE SPEND TIME TOGETHER?

I was fourteen years old when my father separated from my mother–and effectively from me–and moved into his own apartment just a few miles from our home. I don't remember many details of the separation, but I can't forget how little I saw of my dad after that–even though I wanted to spend time with him.

But a subsequent incident made things much worse.

A few months after he left, he told me how much I had disappointed him by never coming to visit him.

Me? I had disappointed *him*?

Here I was, a fourteen-year-old kid still too young to have a car or driver's license, and my father, who had taken next to no initiative to spend time with me, blasted me for our lack of time together.

My father's exit from our family had a profound effect on me. It conditioned me not only to believe that Dad didn't want to spend time with me, but also that dads in general don't care all that much about spending time with their kids.

I'm happy to know (now) that I came to a very wrong conclusion.

Since those heartbreakingly difficult years, I've learned there are many good dads out there, and I've learned that one of the things that makes them so good is that they take the initiative to spend time with their children. Somehow, these "good" dads got enough of a dose of wisdom and maturity to know how important it is to spend time with their children.

How can you quantify the spiritual and emotional nourishment a child receives from spending time with his or her daddy? How can you place a value on the affirmation dads give their kids?

In truth, you can't do it.

You can't quantify it. You can't assign a value to it. In fact, it is priceless.

But I will say this. Such affirmation, *from possibly the most important person in a child's life,* lays the foundation stones of maturity that will help that child develop into a happy, healthy, and confident adult.

But, of course, that's not all. It also lays the groundwork for a healthy, accurate impression of that individual's Daddy in heaven.

He Wants to Spend Time with You

Maybe you grew up in a home where your daddy wasn't there at all, and because of that, you didn't get to spend time with him. Or maybe your daddy was home and cared for all your physical needs, but never showed much interest in spending time with you.

You might even go so far as to say, "David, I didn't have a good dad. I didn't have a good role model. He didn't seem interested in me at all and I really have nothing positive to say about our relationship. In fact, I think my perception of God is messed up because of it."

The bad news is that an absent or distant, non-communicative earthly father can indeed leave us with a highly distorted picture of God. But the good news is that you have a Daddy in heaven who wants more than anything to spend time with you. And maybe even better news is that He is so committed to you that He will move heaven, earth, mountains, and whatever else He has to in order to make sure you understand that. He is very real and very present, not some kind of ghost in the sky you can't personally get to know. He wants to be everything to you, emotionally and spiritually, that your earthly dad may not have been for you.

Do you have a difficult time wrapping your heart and mind around that kind of "Daddy God"? It took me a while to get there, too, but I'd like to share what I've come to learn about my Daddy in heaven. He not only created me and provides for my physical needs, He also *enjoys* being with me. He *enjoys* it when I just hang out with Him so we can each share our souls with one another. He craves an intimate Father/child relationship.

And, whether you are at this moment able to process this truth or not, He wants exactly that kind of relationship with you.

Our Daddy God's Main Interest
A friend of mine once told me about watching an old home movie shot when he was about five years old. The movie showed the visit of some family friends and followed him as he went around to the guests, proudly showing them his "Flippy the Frogman" action toy. One guest in particular seemed especially interested in the toy and in my friend. She took Flippy from him, took a good long look at it, and then handed it back to him, smiling at him and talking to him as she did so.

My friend then told me about the next few seconds of the movie. He took Flippy to his dad, no doubt hoping to get the same reaction. But his father took the toy from his hand, put it down, and then completely ignored his son.

My friend didn't specifically remember the incident, but what he saw in those frames helped him to make sense of a lot of his life. "I did feel unimportant and insecure over many, many years," he told me, "and I still do sometimes."

The things an earthly father does to show his children that he's truly interested in them as individuals, in the things they like to do, in what they think, and in what they have to say, add up over time. But so do the words and actions that communicate his lack of interest in a strong, intimate father/child relationship.

Oh, how important that we dads never allow ourselves to fall into the trap of believing that caring for our children's physical needs, as loving an act as that may be, is enough! Kids need to know that their daddy truly cares about them—and that he is actually interested in them as individuals.

If you were fortunate enough to live in a home where your dad teamed up with your mom to care for you, what material things did you want from him but didn't always (if ever) get?

- A hefty allowance?
- Gifts and presents?
- Help with college?
- A new car (or at least a nice used one)?

Now think about some of the "relational" things you craved from your dad when you were a kid—the things money can't buy. Did your dad provide these things for you?

- The *I love yous?*
- Genuine hugs?
- Real conversation?
- An opportunity to work together on projects?
- Walks together?
- Encouragement?

I'd be willing to bet that once boys and girls become adults, most of us (and by a large margin) look back on our childhoods at home and realize that we wanted, more than anything else, those things that centered around an intimate relationship, full of connectedness and a sense of belonging. We wanted the communication, personal interaction, and words of encouragement and affirmation that showed us how much daddy loved us and wanted to spend time with us and connect with us.

In other words, we wanted and needed to know that our daddy was interested in us.

Connectedness, which comes from a deep knowing and which provides an incredibly resilient foundation, can come in only one way: time spent. That's where a deep sense of belonging, rooted in security and well-being, gets created. This is true for children and their earthly daddy as well as for us and our Daddy in heaven.

It's a marvelous fact that God as your heavenly Daddy wants to just "be" with you. But maybe more importantly, He knows that you have a need to "be" with Him. You're His beloved child and He is deeply interested in you and everything about you, right down to the smallest details. He wants to share Himself with you on the most intimate level. And He wants you to share yourself with Him.

A Daddy's Delight

If there's one thing about me that I hope you have figured out through the first four chapters of this book, it's that I love my daughters. But now I want to take that a step further. Not only do I love them, but I also *love being with them*. I not only love my kids, but I also enjoy them. It isn't just duty or obligation or "the right thing to do." It is sheer delight.

Can you guess my favorite time of each day? It's when I get to just hang out with Belle and Diana, to play with them. That normally happens either first thing in the morning after they get up, or last thing at night before they go to bed…and if I'm lucky, both.

It would seem the feelings are mutual.

When Belle was a year and a half old, even though she couldn't talk, she could really communicate. She talked with her eyes. They widened when she was surprised, narrowed when she got angry or upset, smiled when she felt happy, and closed when she cried hard.

She talked with the sounds she made. She gurgled with glee and happiness, shouted just for the heck of it, talked in her own cryptic language that only she understood, sighed for reasons only she understood, screamed with excitement or frustration, cried when she grew unhappy or needed something, and "sang" along with her favorite songs.

She talked with her hands, too, moving them about when she spoke in the cryptic language. When she sang, she clapped those little hands and kept rhythm. As the drowsies came upon her, she would rub her eyes.

She talked with her body. When we washed her face, she squirmed. When she heard music, she wanted to dance. When we played with her, she would roll away from us or toward us.

And when Belle wanted some concentrated "daddy time," she became a cute little expert with her non-verbal cues. Crawling over to me, she would grab my pants leg, pull herself to a standing position, and bury her head between my knees. Pulling on my pants leg was an assist to get her where she really wanted to be–up close to my face.

Even though I couldn't always understand her, even though I might be really busy doing something "important," I was happy–delighted, actually–to turn my attention fully toward my precious daughter who had gone to such lengths to gain an audience with me.

Fun "Daddy Time"

Like other men I've known, I don't have many fond memories of time spent doing fun things with my dad. My chances to do fun things usually came with someone else's father. I would go water-skiing with my friend Matt's dad, Dr. Tallman, and I'd go snow skiing with my friend, Wade, and his dad, Warren.

To this day, I'm grateful that God brought these and other men into my life to teach me the importance of just being together having fun.

When Belle showed me that she needed her "Daddy time," often she didn't want to talk. She just wanted to sit and have some fun playing with Daddy. She loved crawling up into my lap with her alphabet board, dumping out all the letters, and then choosing them one-by-one under my watchful eye. She'd place the letters in the right place, all the while awaiting affirmation from me that she had placed them where they belonged. She would squeal with delight when I made a big production out of the fact that she had chosen a letter and put it in the right place.

I may not squeal, but I feel my own sense of delight when we have a chance to play.

Believe me, since I'm in my fifties, it can be a bit more of a challenge to get down on the floor to play with Belle. But, once again, I know this isn't about me but about her. I know that when I get down on the floor to play with my daughter, or let her up onto my lap so we can have some fun, I'm showing her just how much I love her and delight in being with her.

Think about all the things people do just to be with one another. For a parent and child, it can be silly, seemingly unproductive, "mindless" activities–like tea parties, fun games, or just watching cartoons together. For two male friends, it might be fishing or hunting or watching sports together. For a married or committed couple, it could be going to dinner or watching a movie together.

It took me a while to understand, but I've come to know my Daddy in heaven well enough that I know–not just *believe*, but *know*–that He loves me affectionately and deeply and truly values and enjoys spending time with me. He loves it when I just come near Him because I need my "Daddy time," and He's always available for me. When I say 'just come near Him' what I mean is sitting quietly, without any other distractions, and intentionally being with Him– listening for His voice while I talk to Him and while I read His words to me in the Bible.

But my heavenly Daddy also loves being with me when I'm doing "fun" things. While the Bible doesn't use the word "fun," I've come to believe with all my heart that my Daddy God loves spending time with me when I'm simply enjoying myself. In other words, I'm aware that He is with me all the time–no matter what I'm doing. Whether it's sports or hobbies or hanging out with friends, my heavenly Daddy really enjoys seeing me laugh and smile. What

I'm doing at the time doesn't much matter, just as it doesn't matter what Belle and I are doing, as long as I get to spend time delighting in her. What matters is that we're together, spending time savoring one another's company.

He Comes Down to Our Level

Belle, no longer an infant now, recently started asking me to have tea parties with her. So, at those times, being a loving dad and all, I put my "important stuff" down and go outside with her onto our back deck. We set up her little blue plastic table and arrange all her princess teacups and saucers, as well as the teapot, sugar, creamer, and little spoons. And then we have a father/daughter tea party. I put on my best British accent (you know those Brits and their tea!) as we sit and pour water for each other and talk about anything and everything, whatever is on her mind.

Do you really think that all on my own I would want to have a tea party in my backyard? Umm, not so much.

Sitting and sipping isn't the most fun thing in the world for me to do. But a tea party with Belle? Well then, yes! I just want to be with my little girl, doing what she enjoys so we can be together. Bottom line, it's not just about what David Gallagher likes or doesn't like. It's about Belle. It's all about the little girl that a wise and gracious God has brought into my life. It's about meeting her where she lives and spending quality time with her at her own level, doing what she likes to do.

We men are naturally "wired" to be productive, to do manly things that yield visible results. At a glance, having a backyard tea party with Belle might not seem very productive–and certainly not very manly. But what it does do is lay a foundation, brick by brick– or, perhaps, sugar cube by sugar cube– of a connected relationship that will continue to grow over time. I know that as Belle matures, our tea parties will help her to grow in the strength and confidence and security of knowing who she is and *whose* she is. Those little tea parties will help her to get rooted in a healthy, loving, personal relationship with arguably the most important person in her life–her daddy.

Children want to relate to their daddies at eye level, and that means that we must either stoop low, get down on the floor with them, or pick them up and bring them to our level. That is where the best quality communication and intimacy take place. I like to call the practice of getting eye-to-eye with my kids "leveling." Are you leveling with your children? Are you meeting them at eye level by bringing them up to where you are or by lowering yourself to where they are? Practice your love for them and develop intimacy by getting eye-to-eye with them.

That's also our Daddy God's heart for you and me. He just wants to be with us. He wants to spend time with us and He wants us to spend time with Him. And He's shown us in the most amazing way that He's not above coming down to our level to make it happen. You can hear the wonder in King David's voice when he tells the Lord, *Your right hand sustains me; you stoop down to make me great* (Psalm 18:35).

Our Daddy God levels with us.

The most incredible, incomprehensible example of a father coming down to his children's level took place when our Daddy God, the Creator of the universe, became a man so that He could be with us–so that we could spend time with Him in intimate fellowship. Jesus "leveled" with us when He came down to earth to live with us and be with us. He wanted His kids to know without any doubt how close He wants to be to them. How close He wants to be with them.

From the very beginning, we were meant for close, intimate fellowship with our Creator God. But we could do nothing, in and of ourselves, to make that happen. Just as I have to reach down to my little daughter to enter her world, so our Daddy in heaven had to lovingly reach down to us. And He is still reaching down to us.

When My Daddy Seeks Me Out

I once went away on a weekend men's retreat with twenty-four other guys. One afternoon, we all went our separate ways for a time to find our own sanctuaries somewhere on the grounds of the massive ranch hosting the retreat. I found a nice spot under the shade of a huge, beautiful oak tree. I set up my folding chair and sat down. As I sat there, my Daddy in heaven began speaking to me.

Just above me, up in the branches of the tree, I saw two limbs–one dead and barren of leaves, and the other alive and covered with greenery. My Daddy, as only He can, nodded toward those two limbs and spoke to me right then and there.

David, do you see that dead limb lying there across the other branches, how it is completely disconnected from the rest of the tree?

"Yes, I see it."

Well, that dead branch is you. You have unplugged yourself from Me for quite some time, and now you're dead inside. You're in such a bad way right now that if even the slightest wind of adversity or difficulty were to blow, you would be completely and totally removed from the tree.

I didn't enjoy hearing those words, but I knew they came from a loving Daddy God who longed for me to reconnect with Him.

David, it's time to tap back into Me as your Daddy. I would never force you to do that, because that wouldn't be love. It's up to you, but I'm here, waiting and ready to receive you. Connect yourself to Me once again in an intimate relationship and allow Me to feed you, support you, love you, listen to you, and speak to you. Allow Me to bring you back to life. I hate seeing you suffering and almost dead.

It wasn't as though I had fallen into any kind of serious sin. I was working in ministry and living a "good" life. But my Daddy God knew something was missing: the closeness and intimacy He wants to share with me as His child. So He sought me out and found me, sitting under an oak tree. He knew that I desperately needed to hear from Him…even if I didn't realize it at the time.

I can't imagine the anguish an earthly daddy goes through when his child goes missing. I know that when I lose track of one of my girls, even for a short period of time, I immediately launch out on a quest to find her. As the seconds turn into minutes, I can become more and more alarmed. Why? Because I love my girls and don't want any harm to come to them. At their young and vulnerable ages, their Daddy needs to know where they are at all times.

My Daddy God knows where I am at all times. He never loses track of me. And yet, when I "go missing"–when I allow other things to take the place of spending regular, intimate Daddy/son time with Him–He'll go to all kinds of lengths to search for me until I get back to where I belong. He wants me to return to that secure place where we spend intimate time with each other, the kind of time that both of us crave.

Because He's Your Daddy

I love Diana and Belle just because they're my little girls.

Period.

I don't love them because they give me anything or because I get some kind of material benefit from having them around. I don't love them because they've "proved" themselves worthy or because they have accomplished great things that make me proud of them. Belle and Diana are still too young to "prove" themselves, but even if they never become star students or gifted athletes or highly paid executives or great ministers, I'll still love them and want to spend time with them just as much as I do now. Why?

Because they're my daughters.

But let me take that a step further. As my daughters grow up, if one of them goes astray and somehow builds recklessly or carelessly on the foundation I have attempted to lay for her–even if she departs from the path I have tried to teach her to follow–I'll still love her and want to spend time with her, just as much as I do now. And if one of my daughters were to rebel against her mom and me to the point that she stopped speaking to us, I'd still long to have that relationship restored and the communication re-established. In fact, I'd go to great lengths to make that happen.

Only a parent with the right kind of heart can really understand this kind of love. I've known parents whose children have drifted so far from them that even the most basic communication has ceased. Their child's actions and attitudes and words have caused these parents unimaginable heartache, and it seems that reconciliation would require a major miracle. These moms and dads lie awake at night in tears, longing for their son or daughter to return home. There's nothing they wouldn't give just to be able to spend time with their children, like they once did.

Why do they feel that way? Why do they find it impossible to simply cut the cord and move on? Because that child—no matter how wayward, rebellious, ungrateful, or self-destructive he or she might be—is still their son or daughter. Truly, there is *nothing* he or she can do to make that love go away.

Do you know what? That is just the kind of love our Daddy in heaven has for each and every one of His kids.

When we fail, when we make terrible choices, when we sin (meaning when we miss God's intended target for our actions, words, and choices, something every one of us does routinely), and even when we openly rebel against Him, our Daddy in heaven still loves us and still longs to spend time with us.

Sadly, we all too often project onto our Daddy God our own reactions to failures and mistakes. We think that He is like us and we wrongly believe that He thinks like we do. Fortunately, much of the time we are wrong. We engage in the too-human thinking that if we have failed or hurt someone, then that person won't want anything to do with us—or might even be plotting retribution against us. So we do the only thing that seems logical at the time: we turn away. Have you ever done this with God? Turned away from a heavenly Daddy who you're sure feels so disgusted with you that He wants nothing more to do with you? I'd be willing to bet that almost all of us have gone down this rocky road at one time or another. I certainly have.

But what a waste! That whole line of thinking is so *human,* not divine. We tend to hold grudges and hang on to our anger. We refuse to forgive and sometimes seek vengeance. How far that is from how our Daddy God thinks about us or acts toward us when we fall! Listen to how King David put it:

The Lord is compassionate and gracious, slow to anger, abounding in love.
He will not always accuse, nor will he harbor his anger forever;
he does not treat us as our sins deserve or repay us according to our iniquities (Psalm 103:8-10).

David tells us that God refuses to repay His children for their sins—as they *deserve*—for two reasons. First, His capacity for love expands infinitely beyond our own. And second, He loves us as *His children* and wants to shower us with His boundless love and compassion. Or as David goes on to say:

For as high as the heavens are above the earth,
so great is his love for those who fear him;
as far as the east is from the west,
so far has he removed our transgressions from us
(Psalm 103:11-12).

Our Daddy God *always* wants to spend time with His kids, and as hard as it may be for us to fathom, He wants even more to spend time with us after we've blown it. Even though our human thinking may tempt us into believing that He's angry with us and no longer wants to be near to us, the amazing truth is that it's during those times after we've fallen that our Father in heaven wants more than ever to spend time with us. When my little girls have fallen and skinned their knees, I don't want to be anywhere else other than right there with them to pick them up and to bring healing and relief to their pain. When you and I fall and skin our hearts, our Daddy God doesn't want to be anywhere else other than where we are to pick us up and to bring healing and relief to our pain.

It's as if He's saying to you, right now, *Yes, I still want to spend time with you. I want to talk to you and listen to you, because I love you. I don't want anything to come between us.*

The Bible insists there is nothing we humans can do to earn God's love or forgiveness. Those are His free gifts to His kids, and He has given them to us gladly. Our only part in that grand, heavenly bargain is to run to Him–run straight into His loving arms, where He showers us with His love and forgiveness. Resist the temptation to think there is some *thing* you must *do* to "get back into His good graces." He did it all when He died for your failures and mistakes (your sin) on the cross. He has already done all the doing. Just be with Him.

Accept No Substitute

Sadly, too many of us trade spending time with our Daddy God for "doing" things for Him (also known as "doing religion"). We go to church, maybe even serving as a Sunday school teacher or an usher. We might even do the more "spiritual" things like singing with the worship choir on Sunday mornings or serving on some time-intensive church board. And if we're feeling *really* devout, we might serve once a week at a homeless shelter or a soup kitchen, or volunteer to help people in a hospice or a shelter for battered women. I believe many of us "do" this and that because we believe that serving others in the name of the Lord will somehow make us more worthy of gaining from God whatever it is we think we want or need.

Please don't take this the wrong way. I know many people who practice these and other acts of kindness and compassion out of a sincere heart for God and a genuine desire to serve the needy and suffering souls that our Daddy in heaven cares so deeply about. He loves to see His kids following Jesus' example and reaching out to the not-so-fortunate among us.

But in the midst of all that service, we absolutely can't forget to stop long enough to actually spend time with our Daddy God–and know that it's also okay to stop and rest and do nothing. Doing things for others in the name of the Lord can certainly energize our souls and draw us closer to our Father, but they should never substitute for actually slowing down so we can enjoy intimate, soul-nurturing time with our Daddy in heaven.

Jesus understood better than any of us just how important it is to invest time with our Daddy in heaven. As His earthly ministry picked up steam, the demands of the crowds felt overwhelming, and He knew the crucial importance of taking a break, getting away from all of those loved-but-needy people, just to spend some alone time with His Daddy. Luke the physician reports, *Yet the news about him spread all the more, so that crowds of people came to hear him and to be healed of their sicknesses. But Jesus often withdrew to lonely places and prayed* (Luke 5:15-16).

Wow. Jesus *often* withdrew.

Jesus knew He needed to continually get His soul restored. He knew He needed a regular re-energizing interlude with His Heavenly Dad. A quick shot of caffeine or a bottle of energy drink just wouldn't cut it. His source of power was His Father in heaven, and there could be no substitute. So Jesus regularly removed Himself from all the busyness of His ministry and the never-ending problems of needy people around Him, just so He could spend time alone with His Heavenly Dad.

Jesus never questioned whether His Daddy in heaven wanted to spend time with Him. He knew whose Son He was, and He knew that His Daddy God always had time for Him. Do you know whose son you are? Do you know whose daughter you are?

He's Waiting for You

Because of what Jesus has done for us, we have the same kind of access to our Daddy in heaven that Jesus had. Just as my daughters know they can come to me whenever they need or want some "daddy time," so I know that when I need some "heavenly Daddy time," all I have to do is approach Him. I do so in much the same way my daughters approach me when they want to spend some special alone time with me.

They just come.

They don't wring their hands, get anxious, or wonder if they've behaved well enough or finished all their chores before they approach me.

No, they just come.

And when I come to my heavenly Daddy, I hear the same answer every time:

Of course I want to spend some time with you, David! You're my son and I'm your Daddy, and I always look forward to our time together.

Why not spend some time with your Daddy in heaven, right now? He's got time. He always has time for His kids.

Chapter 6

DADDY, I'M TIRED

By and large, my little Belle is a fun, sweet-natured little ball of energy who gives me and most everyone around her a great deal of joy. But like any child, she has those other times, the ones when she makes it abundantly clear that she feels hungry, uncomfortable, frustrated…or tired.

I can't begin to count the number of times when Belle was a baby and I watched her in the middle of playing or crawling around or just conducting "baby business" when, quite suddenly, she would begin to become irritable, impatient, or even frustrated, either with another child or with me or with her Mommy. Sometimes she would vent her frustration on a toy. At other times she would just stop whatever she was doing and begin to rub her eyes. And then there were those times when she would become so sleepy that her coping mechanisms would disappear completely and she would go into full-bore meltdown mode.

As her Daddy, I know Belle well enough and have seen this scenario played out enough times to know that at times like these, she needs to take a break. She needs to get some rest. Without realizing it, Belle has communicated to me one simple message:

Daddy, I'm tired. I need rest.

So what do I do next? Because I understand and appreciate her need for rest, far more than even she does, I scoop her up in my arms and take her to a place of rest–better known as her crib.

To Be at Your Best, Get Some Rest

When I was eighteen years old, my friend Brian and I drove from Oregon to California for a few days, just for a change of scenery. (If I remember correctly, that change of scenery may have involved a couple of girls, but the mind conveniently grows hazy after decades.)

On our way home, Brian sat behind the wheel of his 1947 GMC pickup truck as we headed north back toward Oregon on Interstate 5. We'd burned the midnight oil for several days, and both of us felt exhausted. (Okay, yes, now I do remember that the scenery involved a couple of girls. But don't get the wrong idea. We did burn the midnight oil, but we also remained gentlemen.) Totally worn out, I slumped in the passenger seat and dozed off. Unfortunately, Brian also felt exhausted, and he joined me in a little catnap...with his truck zooming along at sixty miles per hour. He jerked awake just as we headed for the ditch on the right side of the highway. Brian swiftly steered left, and the truck swerved back across all three lanes, before flying off the pavement and hurtling down a long embankment and into the grass median.

It's a miracle the truck didn't roll—and that no one was in the other three lanes we had suddenly careened across.

To this day, I thank God that what could have turned into a tragic accident instead became merely our own version of Mr. Toad's Wild Ride. A few thrills and chills, but no broken bones or gashed foreheads. I've come to see this incident as an example of how all of us need regular rest in order to be at our best, whether physically, mentally, emotionally, or spiritually.

Fatigue due to a lack of sleep and rest can lead to a dangerous loss of concentration and alertness, triggering mental mistakes. And as every NASCAR driver, train engineer, jet pilot, and ship captain should know, the smallest mental mistakes can be very, very costly. It has been estimated that fatigue plays a significant role in about 100,000 auto accidents and more than 1,500 deaths each year in the United States alone. The list of well-known accidents due to fatigue is long and infamous.

If I mentioned the song title "Blue Suede Shoes," who comes to mind? If you know the song at all, probably you'd respond, "Elvis Presley." But the only reason "Blue Suede Shoes" is connected in most people's minds with Elvis Presley is because of a car accident caused by a driver falling asleep. Carl Perkins actually wrote the song and made it into a monster hit. But while he and his band were on their way from Virginia to New York to appear on NBC's The Perry Como Show, Perkins' friend and driver fell asleep at the wheel and collided with a poultry truck, ultimately causing two deaths and putting Perkins in the hospital for several months. While Perkins recuperated, Elvis Presley had the opportunity to sing his hit tune on The Milton Berle Show, and from that moment on, "Blue Suede Shoes" became forever associated with "the king."

Sleeplessness also causes a myriad of physical health problems. Medical experts tell us that a chronic lack of sleep can help cause or exacerbate any number of physical issues, including heart disease, high blood pressure, strokes, and diabetes.

Knowing all of this should be more than enough to convince us to make sure we get enough sleep!

Getting the Rest We Need

As human beings living in mortal bodies, our need for regular rest never ends, no matter how old we get. Our heavenly Daddy knows this. He knows we need rest. He knows when our bodies are screaming, "I need sleep!" And He knows when life's pressures, combined with a lack of rest, simply become too much for us.

King David went through a really stressful and distressing time when his own son, Absalom, turned on him and tried to take him down. He cried out to God in Psalm 3:1-5:

O Lord, how many are my foes!
How many rise up against me!
Many are saying of me,
God will not deliver him.
But you are a shield around me, O Lord;
you bestow glory on me and lift up my head.
To the Lord I cry aloud
and he answers me from his holy hill.
I lie down and sleep;
I wake again, because the Lord sustains me.

He remembers that we are frail and weak human beings with a long list of limitations. He knows we can't keep juggling half a dozen balls in the air for hours on end without any break. And knowing all this, He's made a way for us to get the rest we need. Our Daddy in heaven knows how to sustain us when we are frazzled, tired, and anxious.

I believe our Daddy in heaven wants His children to live long, productive, joyful lives, and for that to happen, we need rest. Sadly, however, too many of us don't get enough rest, and that deficit leads to untold problems not only with our bodily health, but also with our relational health. A lack of rest can cause all sorts of difficulties in our interpersonal relationships, whether with our spouses, our families, our friends, and even with our Daddy in heaven. When we get tired, we typically become irritable and impatient, and sometimes that irritability and impatience leads to relational meltdowns.

By the way, that's true for children of *all* ages.

My daughters, like most children, can be handfuls when they're tired. But here's a little secret. I can be, too. Tiredness can cause any of us to vent our frustration on the things and people around us.

Fatigue can lead to objects getting thrown, unkind words getting spewed (even four-letter ones that we don't typically utter), and a host of other less-than-becoming exhibitions that would diminish or disappear…if we just had enough rest.

I doubt any man or woman in history has not fallen victim at some point to the undesirable effects of a lack of rest. None of us can be at our best when we fail to get enough rest, even when we work to meet every other known need. We can eat the healthiest foods and get plenty of quality exercise, but if we don't get the rest we need, then we'll have a really tough time being what our Daddy in heaven intends for us to be.

Rest for Our Bodies

When I was twelve years old, I had a chance to climb Mount Hood with my Boy Scout troop. At 11,250 feet above sea level at the summit, Mt. Hood is the highest peak in Oregon, my home state. While it isn't exactly K2 to climb, it's not a leisurely stroll, either. Far from it!

We climbed the route that begins at Timberline Lodge, slightly less than a six-mile round trip. In the approximate three-mile climb to the summit, you ascend about 5,450 feet at a 35-degree slope. It's a strenuous climb in the best of conditions, but my fellow scouts and I planned to start our ascent around midnight. I don't especially like getting cold, but there we were, about to climb Oregon's highest peak during the most frigid part of the day.

This, friends, is what a lot of people in Oregon call "recreation." It felt a lot more like sheer torture to me.

Despite the icy temperatures, we continued to climb all through the night, and as the slope grew increasingly steep, I grew increasingly tired. After climbing for six or seven hours, I had moments when I felt so physically exhausted that I didn't think I could keep going. In hindsight, I know that if had I tried to manage that climb alone that night, I never would have reached the summit.

Fortunately, good friends surrounded me, along with even better scoutmasters, all of whom encouraged me and helped me to keep going. Not only that, but our adult leaders kept a sharp eye on us to make sure we stopped from time to time to get a few minutes' much-needed rest before we continued.

I've often thought how my climb up Mount Hood that night reflects in many ways the rest of my life on earth. I've pictured life as a long journey in which we face uphill challenges of all kinds. If we're going to rise up and do what God has called us to do and become what He wants us to become, then we need to take a break periodically from the grueling climb to get some rest—sometimes desperately needed rest.

Do you feel physically tired as you read this? Have you become aware that you need some time to recharge? If so, ponder the benefits of stopping so you can get a break from your own ascent, whatever it may be. Also consider how important it is to your Daddy in heaven that His kids slow down to get the rest and sleep they need.

Most believers have no problem accepting that God created them and loves them. They know He cares about them on so many levels and wants to provide for them. But I'm willing to bet that very few of us have thought much, if at all, about the truth that our Daddy in heaven is acutely concerned about something so "worldly," so "mundane," as physical rest from our daily grinds.

I'm convinced our Daddy God cares about our getting all the physical rest we need. In fact, the Bible contains several stories of God providing physical rest for His weary people.

Three Weary Heroes

Moses grew exhausted as the Israelites faced off against the Amalekites in battle (Exodus 17:10-13). The leader of God's people stood on a hill overlooking the battlefield, and as long as he held his hands skyward, the Israelites won. But when he grew so tired that he had to lower his arms, the situation quickly deteriorated for God's people.

Enter Aaron and Hur, who provided Moses with a stone to sit on while they stood on either side of him, holding up his hands when he grew too tired to do it himself.

Also consider King David, who nearly lost his life in a fierce battle with the brutal Philistines.

David grew so exhausted during the battle that he soon would have become easy pickings for a Philistine soldier named Ishbi-Benob. But one of David's men, Abishai, came to the king's rescue, killing Ishbi-Benob and saving David's life (2 Samuel 21:15-17).

Finally, remember that Jesus Christ Himself, the God-man, grew tired and needed rest. In the fourth chapter of John's gospel, we read how Jesus and His disciples traveled through a place called Samaria. *So he came to a town in Samaria called Sychar,* John writes, *near the plot of ground Jacob had given to his son Joseph. Jacob's well was there, and Jesus,* **tired as he was from the journey,** *sat down by the well* (John 4:5-6, bold added).

Does it seem odd that our Lord Jesus, God in the flesh, became tired and thirsty from His lengthy journey? Does it surprise you that He needed to sit down and rest after a long, grueling walk? If so, remember that while Jesus was fully God, He also was fully human. That means His body needed both rest and water. A local woman who came to the well to get water for her village met His need after He asked her for a drink.

Do you see the common theme in each of these stories? In each case, these men—Moses, David, and Jesus—had pushed themselves to a point of physical exhaustion, and in each case, God provided others to come to them to help them find rest in their weariness. Whether they needed some physical restoration, assistance in their work, an ally in their defense, or just a helping hand, none of them had to go it alone. Their Daddy God provided each of them with the help they needed.

As Belle's and Diana's daddy, I know that in order for my daughters to remain physically healthy, emotionally strong, and spiritually vigorous, they need regular rest and sufficient sleep. My Daddy in heaven knows the very same thing about me. He created me in such a way that my body, soul, and spirit all interrelate, and He knows that when one of them gets out of whack, the others are sure to follow.

In the Old Testament, God not only allowed for physical rest, He commanded it by instituting the Sabbath. He considered rest so important that He made it part of the Law of Moses, the set of rules and regulations He gave to His people as a guidebook for living.

God, our all-loving, all-wise Daddy in heaven, designed His beloved creations in such a way that our bodies must have rest in order to get restored and rejuvenated. In Old Testament times, that rest took the form of the Sabbath, the seventh day of the week, when His people were directed to observe a 24-hour shutdown from all their labors.

God created the Sabbath because He wants you and me to rest so that we can live longer, healthier, and more productive lives. As Jesus once said to a group of self-righteous Pharisees, *The Sabbath was made for man, not man for the Sabbath* (Mark 2:27). God has given each of us, not just permission to slow down and get regular rest from all our busyness, but also has set aside a day to actually get that rest.

Your Daddy God already has told you He wants you to rest. Are you honoring Him, and the body He gave you, by getting the rest He knows you need?

Rest for the Soul and Spirit

I was fourteen years old when doctors diagnosed my father with terminal leukemia. He had separated from my mom and moved out of our house just six months before doctors informed him that he had an acute form of the disease.

His departure from our home in 1974 already had taken a big toll on me, and the addition of his illness led me to a place of extreme emotional fatigue. Doctors had basically given Dad a death sentence, and it seemed that I had received a death sentence of my own.

Not long ago, my mother and I talked about this dark time in our lives. She told me about an incident I couldn't remember, probably because I hadn't wanted to. One day as I walked home from school, a neighbor found me, stumbling along with labored steps and weeping uncontrollably. I had hit an emotional wall. My earthly dad, missing in action for months, was about to disappear from my life forever. My father's departure from our home had already left me in terrible inner pain over the separation and lack of a father/son relationship, and now he lay dying in a hospital bed. As a teenager, I lacked the resources to deal with this kind of deep pain, and I began sliding toward an emotional meltdown.

King David captured exactly how I felt when he wrote:

Be merciful to me, Lord, for I am in distress;
my eyes grow weak with sorrow,
my soul and body with grief.
My life is consumed by anguish and my years by groaning;
my strength fails because of my affliction,
and my bones grow weak.
(Psalm 31:9-10)

Very descriptive words from a man clearly in the midst of intense emotional and spiritual pain!

His authentically human words resonate with so many of us.

At the time of my father's illness, I didn't recognize—and couldn't really articulate—what I needed to comfort me.

But in hindsight, I know Who did.

It was Someone far greater, more caring, and infinitely more available to me than I could possibly have understood. My heavenly Daddy was paying close attention to me—and He knew I desperately needed emotional rest.

I see now, looking back, that He put very caring people in my life. His presence was with me because He was present in the people He surrounded me with.

I think of my high school counselor, Mrs. Oberteuffer. I worked for "Obie," doing office tasks and receiving extra high school credit.

I remember my pastors, Earl and Wanda, who so wisely cared for me during this time.

I will always remember the kindness of my two sisters, Debbie and Kerry, and my mom, Gerry, who cared most of all. But there were others too. Friends, neighbors, and other family members who stepped into my life with a smile, a kind word, or some sort of practical help.

I was never left alone.

My Daddy in heaven made sure of that.

While King David certainly understood this kind of sorrow, he also knew where to go to find relief. He fled to his heavenly Daddy's loving arms. He made one simple request of his heavenly Daddy: "Be merciful to me, for I am in distress." He cried out to God to give him the peace and rest he needed in order to survive at this low point of his life. He pleaded for God's mercy to lighten his crushing load of emotional and spiritual exhaustion.

Have your eyes ever grown weary after shedding countless tears? Has deep sorrow ever so consumed you that it left you completely laid out, exhausted, and depleted? If so, you're in great company. Human beings all over the world and throughout history have felt the same way. It's part of what it means to be human on a planet devastated by sin.

The good news is that you have a Daddy God who wants to give you what you can't manufacture for yourself: real peace and genuine rest.

Daddy Knows Best

I can't say that I delighted in handling Belle's frustration and occasional meltdowns when she was an infant. I wouldn't name those times as the most enjoyable part of being her daddy. In fact, I didn't even like seeing this transformation as it progressed, any more than I liked hearing her cry when she felt hungry or in need. But because I loved her and wanted to do everything necessary to make sure I meet her needs, I did whatever had to be done.

And that included putting her down for a nap.

Belle needed me, as her daddy, to recognize when she grew tired. She needed me to help her (or more accurately, *make* her) do what she so often couldn't or didn't want to do for herself. She needed rest.

Make no mistake, Belle didn't like it, fighting tooth and nail against the very thing she needed most. She wailed. She would sometimes throw herself around. She would shed a stream of tears. Even so, I would gently settle her in her crib, turn off the lights, shut the door, and make things in the house as quiet as possible. Gradually–or sometimes rather suddenly–the wails and whimpering ceased. And it's a funny thing. When she would awaken from her nap, she never seemed to remember feeling upset with me for forcing her to rest. In fact, she usually woke up feeling like a million bucks, ready to go after it all again.

For most adults, a chance to steal away for a nap during busy and trying times feels like finding extra change in the coin return of a vending machine. We grown-ups do like our naps, and they can work wonders in recharging our batteries, if only for a busy afternoon.

Belle didn't quite see it that way. She saw a nap not so much as a chance to rejuvenate her tired body, but as a harsh sentence condemning her to spend time in a fortress-like pen, complete with vertical bars to prevent escape.

As Belle's daddy, I didn't relish these moments of naptime struggles. But I've come to see a very sweet side to her desperate struggle to avoid going to her crib for a nap. I've realized that she fought the process, even though she could barely hold her eyes open, because she was afraid she would miss out on something happening around the house while her eyes remained closed. She tried desperately to stay awake because she'd been in our home long enough to know that something's always going on, and she didn't want to miss any part of it.

Energetic little kids use up a tremendous amount of energy, and that energy needs to get regularly replenished. But small children tend to want to push through their tiredness so they can continue to do the things they love to do.

Really, are we adults that much different from my beautiful-but-tired-and-cranky little girl? I doubt it. I've seen it in my own life too many times to count: the demands of work, of being a good husband and father, and of handling the crises that life inevitably brings, wear on me. These things conspire to bring me to a point where I begin to feel physically and emotionally exhausted. Yet, even though all signs point to my need for rest, I push myself and then push myself some more. Finally, I have no choice but to slow down, if even for a short time, and get some rest.

I've learned that my Daddy God knows how to slow me down, and, despite my own protestations, make me get some rest.

Wandering a Wearying Road

Many years after a neighbor spotted me wandering the street, crying uncontrollably, I once again found myself physically exhausted and emotionally spent. This time I wandered down a much different road.

As a thirty-one-year-old, when I ventured out of the calm and safe harbor of a regular job with a regular salary and benefits to start the television program *Night Light*, it was a huge leap of faith for me. For seven years, I worked extremely hard, building the business with a staff of about six people. It appeared to be paying off. We seemed to be really going places.

That entire time, though, I put myself through great emotional strain. We never knew–day-to-day, week-to-week, or month-to-month–where our contributions would come from or how much they would total. I labored with the heavy burden of people's livelihoods hanging over me. It all drained me, probably more that I realized at the time.

Then the drain expanded from the emotional arena alone to encompass the financial.

In that seventh year of my venture of faith, after building something I was proud of and felt sure would grow into something *big*, one of our most important corporate partners pulled their support. We had depended heavily on this organization; it had equipment we needed and personnel that helped us with our work. More than that, the organization believed in what we were trying to do. By the third year of the partnership, however, the organization just hadn't received the financial returns it needed in order to continue with us. So, just like that, the relationship ended.

A few weeks after that blow, everyone could see the writing on the wall. Our little organization had lost whatever financial stability it once had. The hemorrhaging had started.

By this time, I felt spent in every way.

Emotionally frazzled. Mentally flat lined. Physically fried.

I had been running nonstop on the treadmill for more than six years–and didn't know how to get myself off. I pushed and pushed until I just couldn't push any more. One sleepless night turned into two. Two turned into four. And my physical and emotional stamina wasn't getting stronger or better.

Without realizing it, every part of me cried out to my Daddy in heaven, "I'm tired. I need rest!" We finally acknowledged that we couldn't continue our venture and pulled the plug, I felt a keen sense of disappointment in letting others down.

But I also felt relieved.

I had arrived at a point where I knew I needed rest and peace–and my Daddy God knew it too. Of course, He'd known it all along.

And, being the loving Daddy He is, He intended to make sure I got the rest I needed, even if it meant closing down the beloved little company I had started.

My physical, emotional, and spiritual well-being–all of which suffered during this trying time–were more important to my heavenly Daddy than the little venture I had begun. My Daddy God, despite my own desires and protestations, despite my own frustration and disappointment, despite the fact that I struggled and cried (just like little Belle), had done just what He knew needed to be done.

He put me down for a nap.

Our Ultimate Place of Rest

God knows when His kids need a break, when they need rest from physical and emotional upheaval. He knows how difficult it can be for us to get the rest and peace we need. He also knows that the toughest thing we must do, sometimes, is to let go–let go of our dreams, let go of our companies, let go of our professions, let go of our relationships, let go of our identities.

Our identities?

Yes, in the sense of who we have made ourselves out to be. I'm speaking here of the image we have created in order to feel a sense of self-worth in this world–the sort of esteem we draw from other people's perception of us. And oh, how difficult it can be when we realize we have to let go and allow our identities to rest in our Daddy God alone!

"But Daddy," we cry out. "This is *who* I am! This is *what* I am! If I let go of *that*, then who am I?"

I'll tell you in the simplest possible terms who you are. You are simply and wholly and completely a son or daughter of your heavenly Daddy. That is it. And that should be enough.

Can you let go of the things that you hold? Can you let go of the things that hold you? Can you let go of the things that have falsely, but powerfully, become your identity? Can you rest and find peace in simply being a son or a daughter of God? Because at the end of the day and at the end of your life, in spite of whatever accomplishments you have or haven't achieved, you are simply and only your Daddy's son or daughter. Period.

Do you remember when you were a child and didn't have a care in the world? You went off to school and that kept you busy enough. Apart from class time, you had recess, PE, and sports. Then you came home and ran out into the neighborhood, maybe joining a game of pick-up football, basketball, softball, or volleyball. You felt free, really free, with hardly a care in the world.

Did you realize that such a place of freedom and rest still exists? God our Daddy wants us to find that relief and refreshment in Him, even while we live on this earth.

Your Daddy in heaven knows you need rest and peace, and He knows the very best place for you to find them. Just as I encourage my daughters to head for bed, and even carry them there when I know that's where they need to be, so too, our Daddy God knows when we need to slow down, get next to Him, and enjoy true rest and peace.

So if you feel tired and weary today—whether physically, emotionally, spiritually, or a combination of all three—remember that your Daddy in heaven wants you to draw close to Him and rest. Remember our faithful shepherd Jesus, *who makes me lie down in green pastures...leads me beside quiet waters...and restores my soul* (Psalm 23). And then ask your Daddy God to restore and refresh your body and your soul by drawing you away from the things that have worn you down...and toward Himself.

He is, after all, the Prince of Peace.

Chapter 7

DADDY, CAN WE TALK?

As a baby, Belle loved to talk.
Well, all right, maybe that term could be more precise.
Her communication consisted more of gargling, gurgling, giggling, and gaggling sounds, than any recognizable words

Even so, *she* believed she was saying something. That much was obvious. I could see by the look on her face that she really believed she was uttering something important, or at least something fun. She always made me smile when she talked to me, and as a daddy who still had a lot of kid in him, I'd get down to her level and try to talk back. I had a lot of fun speaking to her using my own baby talk. I know she understood me perfectly.

Of course, Belle's gibberish sounded different from mine. I did my best to mimic her, and my "words" vaguely echoed hers. But big differences existed between my own baby language and hers. As a baby, she had her advantages!

Our eyes would lock and we would speak to each other in these other-worldly sounds. Belle would say something unintelligible to me and I would gurgle something equally unintelligible back. On and on it went.

Even though we really couldn't understand each other, in some strange way, we communicated. Our eyes spoke to each other, as did our facial expressions and voice inflections. Though we didn't communicate "verbally"–at least, not in the same way my wife and I speak to one other–we interacted as a loving father and a deeply loved daughter. And though she may not have understood the particulars of what I "said," she did understand what I most wanted her to know: that I loved her enough to take the time to communicate with her.

How's that for a funny, crazy picture of a man embracing his childlike side? Belle and I had a lot of fun in our conversations, bonding as a daddy and his daughter. And I think those interchanges provide a pretty good picture of what caring daddies, the earthly kind as well as the heavenly kind, love to do.

As I wrote this chapter a very interesting thing kept happening. I would intend to type the word "heard" but it kept coming out "heart." It was really strange.

Or then again...maybe it wasn't. When you and I are heard–genuinely listened to and valued by another–that result goes right to our heart. I believe that our Daddy God wants us to know that He hears us. And when we know *that*, we will also know that we have His heart. And He has ours.

Daddy, Are You Listening?

While he lived in our home, my dad had a big La-Z-Boy-type recliner, his equivalent of an imperial throne, presiding over our 1,200-square-foot suburban American palace. My siblings and I remember how Dad would come home from work every day, take his place on his throne, and put the daily newspaper in front of his face, as if to wall himself into his own little fortress.

We got the message. Dad had closed the doors to his throne room, and he didn't want to be disturbed. Whether he intended that message or not, I remember believing that he didn't want me or my siblings to bother him as he read the paper or watched television. So I didn't say much to him, and he didn't say much to me.

I paint this picture of my early home life, not to cast my earthly father in a negative light, but to illustrate the sad fact that too many fathers loom in their homes as larger-than-life authority figures. They reign, but they don't relate. They pay the bills and provide for their kids' physical needs, but they don't consistently engage with their children on any meaningful level. They don't talk much with their kids or listen to them when they want to discuss their daily lives or talk over something important. Though such dads probably would never come right out and say it, their actions and their attitudes toward their children communicate the old-school line of thinking that children should be "seen and not heard."

The sad fact is that most dads who operate this way are only doing what was modeled for them. My own dad had no idea how to relate to us kids because he didn't have a good example modeled to him when he was growing up. But whatever the reason (or excuse) might be for such behavior, it is a shameful way to treat children. Parents who ignore the little ones God has entrusted to their care do more lasting damage than they can begin to imagine. I believe boys and girls can begin to feel frustrated, aggravated, and devalued when their moms and dads don't listen to them. The old-school "seen-and-not-heard" style of parenting didn't work well "back then," and it works no better now.

Kids *need* to be heard. They need to know that their parents value them, that their moms and dads want to hear their thoughts. They need their parents to affirm them by showing genuine, consistent interest in what they say, in what they think, and in the things they like to do. If parents don't make it a priority to talk to and listen to their children, *then someone else will.* Our kids may seek the self-worth we should be giving them by looking for it in all the wrong places, by all the wrong means, and often with all the wrong people.

I've seen it time and again in the spiritual lives of many of my friends. They love God and want to please Him, yet they have a difficult time praying, simply because they can't fathom that He really cares about what's on their hearts and minds. After all, their own dads didn't; so why should God, the Creator of the universe? King David mused in Psalm 8:4, *What is man that you are mindful of him, the son of man that you care for him?* Taking it another step, we all can often wonder when it comes to God, "Who am I that you are mindful of me? Who am I that you would care about me?" How can I possibly matter to God?

I'm willing to bet that those who struggle most in this area grew up in homes where their parents—and especially their fathers—didn't seem to take much interest in engaging them in meaningful conversation. They consistently ran into the paternal attitude, "Hey, as long as you have food in your belly, clothes on your back, and a roof over your head, then I've done my job."

As an adult, can you think of anything more aggravating, frustrating, or hurtful than being in a personal relationship with someone you care deeply about—especially an important, familial relationship—but feeling as if the other person doesn't have any real interest in listening to you?

I mean, *really* listening.

Think back to a personal relationship you've had with someone who didn't seem to put a lot of energy into really listening to you when you had something to say. It could be your dad or mom, maybe someone you considered a close friend, or maybe even a spouse. Sure, you knew the person heard the words coming out of your mouth; but you couldn't help but think that the effort it took to process those words seemed like a burden to that individual. Certainly, it didn't appear to be anything like the privilege that true love or genuine friendship brings.

How did that make you feel? I used the words "aggravating" and "frustrating" to describe how it feels when a close family member or friend doesn't listen to you. But now, let me take it a step further. I suggest that the lack of truly engaged listening on the part of that person probably made you feel as though they didn't especially *value* you.

There really is nothing more important in a love relationship than communication. If that sounds like a cliché, then so be it. When healthy communication flows in both directions, then the relationship not only lives, it thrives. But when the communication gets neglected or blocked, the relationship shrivels. And unless big changes get made, it might even die.

That's yet another way we grown-ups resemble little children. All of us want to feel loved, valued, and important. We want to know that we're worthwhile and that our lives really matter to those closest to us. We need to feel confident that our loved ones value our thoughts and the contents of our heart. We want to know that our loved ones will take the time and the effort to just listen to what we have to say– even when it doesn't come easy.

Here's the great news. Even if your earthly dad was physically present in your life but not around much emotionally or socially–or even if he wasn't present at all–you still have a Dad to talk to. Your Daddy God has always had a plan and a desire to fully interact and engage with you. You are His beloved child! King David touched on this life-giving truth when he wrote, *Though my father and mother forsake me, the Lord will receive me* (Psalm 27:10).

I've thought a lot about that verse over the years. If Daddy God has "received" me, He will not ignore me. I will never be a seen-but-not-heard child of God! The fact is, He has not only received me, but He *keeps on receiving me every day,* so that He can have a wonderful, life-giving, vital relationship with me. He wants an intimate relationship in which I can talk to Him and He'll not only listen, but also offer me meaningful feedback and dialogue.

Remember, you are your Daddy God's child. He wants you to know that you are of incredible value to Him. He knows you need to be heard, and He wants that too. And best of all, He wants to listen and give you His full, undivided attention.

Into Your Daddy's Heart

From the time Belle and Diana became part of our family, I made it a huge part of my role as their daddy to talk to them and to listen to them. And when I say "talk to them" and "listen to them," I don't mean just hearing what they say and making sure they hear me; I mean really engaging with them on a deep, emotional, daddy/daughter level.

Why do I do that? Well, I love my girls, and I enjoy speaking with them. I take joy in the fact that we can just sit and talk, and I truly enjoy our time together, discussing anything that's on their little hearts. In other words, I do it simply because I want to.

But that's not all there is to it. I talk to my daughters and listen to them because I want them to know that they mean the world to me. I want them to know their daddy's voice. I talk with them and I listen to them because I want to be a daddy who has a big place in his little girls' hearts.

At the risk of repeating myself...*no love relationship survives long without good communication.*

Two people cannot truly bond with one another in love without enjoying good habits of communication.

Think about the beginning of your relationship with your spouse or a significant other. You probably can remember spending many hours together, just talking. You passionately wanted to know everything on her (or his) heart and mind, and you spent countless hours just talking...just listening...just asking questions...just finding your way into his (or her) heart.

If you get nothing else out of this book, please get this: your Daddy God wants to find His way into your heart and He wants you to find your way into His. He wants a deep, lasting, loving, and caring relationship with you, one in which you share with Him a trusting Father/child relationship. He wants you to converse with Him about anything and everything that's on your heart or mind.

When we first come into a relationship with God through Jesus Christ, we have a hunger to know more about Him. And so it's natural to talk to Him, to read His written Word, to spend time just getting to know Him. And this is no one-way relationship! Our heavenly Daddy longs to listen to us, to hear what we have to say to Him. And get this: He's even prepared for the hard talks. In fact He relishes those—because you only have hard talks with those you trust. Whatever you have to dish out, He can take it. (Not to mention that He already knows it!)

Talking to Your Daddy in Heaven

One morning, Belle sat alone at the breakfast table, finishing her last few bites of French toast. Her mother and I had left the table a few minutes earlier, after we finished eating. We then got busy with post-breakfast cleanup and a few other projects.

A little while later, I returned to the breakfast table and found Belle still sitting there, all by herself. I like to stay on the lookout for opportunities to grow my relationship with my daughter. This certainly seemed like a good one, so I seized it.

I walked over to the table, pulled out the chair next to Belle, and said to her, "Do you want to spend some time talking to Daddy?" She smiled broadly and responded with an enthusiastic "Yes!" Maybe she just felt bored that morning, or maybe she thought a conversation with me sounded better than sitting by herself. It really didn't matter to me. I just saw the moment as an opportunity to spend some quality time, conversing with my daughter.

I decided to engage Belle by asking her some questions about our recent return trip to Kenya and our hotel stays during the journey. I asked her about some of the highlights of the trip and felt a surge of delight when I saw her eyes light up as she recalled some of our experiences. At the time, at age two-and-a-half, Belle couldn't yet converse like an adult, but that didn't stop us from engaging deeply with one another as we discussed our trip. (I remember being amazed at some of the details this little girl could remember.)

To this day I'm always tickled at how naturally my daughters and I can talk with one another. It warms my heart to see that it obviously means so much to them that I would take the time to sit and chat with them. They seem comfortable and at ease talking to their daddy. They talk and I listen; I talk and they listen.

That's just the way it should be between a child and a loving daddy. And it's very much the way our Daddy in heaven wants it to be between Himself and His kids.

The thing we call prayer—an act that sometimes seems so otherworldly, so holy, so mysterious—is simply talking to our Daddy God and allowing Him to talk to us. It's as simple as my daughter and me talking with one another and engaging with one another on a deep, emotional level as we explore what the other is thinking or feeling.

Or at least, it should be.

God designed prayer, talking to your Daddy in heaven, to be as natural as talking to your best friend. It should feel easy, relaxed, comfortable, and safe. We should be able to converse with Him about our feelings, thoughts, and desires, what we want and need Him to do for us, and how much we love and admire Him. We also should be able to talk with Him about the things that might be putting a strain on our relationship with Him (more on that later).

But we humans like to complicate things, don't we? We tend to make prayer into something our Daddy never intended for it to be. It doesn't come easily to many of us, and often it doesn't feel relaxed. Why? Possibly because we imagine prayer has to be "formal," and it takes a lot of work to "get it right." Some of us, raised around the old King James Bible, may even toss in archaic words like "thee" and "thou" to make our prayers seem more "holy."

Most of us feel like we should somehow get our act together before we even think of talking to God.

And worst of all, perhaps, prayer sometimes doesn't feel "safe" to us, mostly because we're not quite sure how we could dare to approach the almighty Creator of the universe.

Because of these things, we tend to worry about details like what posture we should take when we pray. Should we kneel or stand? Is it okay to sit? What about bowing the head and closing the eyes? Is it better to pray at the altar at our church? Should we start by reciting the Lord's Prayer, or reading from some book of ready-made prayers?

The world has many religious traditions concerning prayer, many of them very beautiful and based on the words of the Bible. But I don't believe God feels as concerned with our posture or location when we pray as He does that we're actually talking to Him on a real, personal level. I don't believe He longs for us to recite already-prepared prayers as much as He wants us to speak to Him in the same way a little child speaks to his or her daddy.

Whenever it's possible, I want to talk to my little girls any time they want to talk to me. And when I speak with them, the last thing that concerns me is whether they're sitting, standing, lying down, or running in circles. I just want to have a conversation with them so I can share my heart with them and so they can share their hearts with me.

I believe their Daddy in heaven feels exactly the same way.

Daddy Always Hears

As Diana's and Belle's daddy, I have the privilege of watching them grow and learn more and more every day. But I also have to observe the "dark side," those times when they make wrong choices. Yes, even little kids like my two young daughters can make wrong choices! Those wrong choices can include their actions, their attitudes, and of course, their words.

At times I overhear the girls saying things to one another that I know they wouldn't say if they knew I was listening. They don't seem to realize that just because they can't see me, doesn't mean I don't hear every word. Maybe this is because children don't quite have that volume control thing down, or maybe it's because moms and dads just seem to develop a talent for hearing things that their kids didn't intend for them to hear. But on many occasions, I've heard them speaking...well, "very freely" to one other. More times than I care to remember, in fact, I've heard them saying hurtful things to each other, often prompting me to walk into the room to give them one of those "parentisms."

"What did you just say?"

I ask the question with what I hope is the right touch of sternness in my voice. At that moment, they don't volunteer what they said or who said it. Instead, a dead silence envelops the room. I encounter a grand reluctance to report the words that one has just said to the other. Why? Because they made the uncomfortable discovery that Daddy had overheard, and that the words he heard didn't make him happy. Time for me to be a teaching daddy...

...just like my Daddy God is for me.

Hearing my daughters say things they shouldn't say has reminded me of something we all need to know about our Daddy God: He hears us and listens to us, even when we'd rather He not.

It's true that your heavenly Dad is a loving, available Father in heaven who wants to spend time with you and converse with you. But frankly, this talking-and-listening Daddy God can be like the proverbial two-edged sword.

Because He listens to us all the time, He doesn't hear us only when we talk to Him directly in prayer.

He hears every word we say. All the time.

He hears us when we say unedifying or unkind things to others. He hears us when we curse at a driver who cuts us off in heavy traffic, when we mutter something unloving or rude about our spouse, when we spread gossip about someone, when we tell an off-color joke. He hears us when we gripe and complain, when we're having a bad day, or when things haven't gone the way we'd prefer.

In the ninth chapter of Mark's gospel, we read a story describing what happened when our Daddy God in the flesh, Jesus, heard words that His disciples didn't intend for Him to hear. One day, as He and the twelve were on their way to a town called Capernaum, He "overheard" them in the middle of an argument about which of the twelve of them was the most important. Once they reached

Capernaum and settled into a house for the night, Jesus asked them: *"What were you arguing about on the road?"* (Mark 9:33)

Dead silence.

Whenever I read this passage, I can't help but think of the looks that Belle and Diana give me when I walk into their room after hearing them talking to each other in ways that make their mommy and me unhappy. The disciples never would have had such a discussion had they known that Jesus could hear them; but Jesus, as the perfect representative of their Daddy in heaven, heard every ugly syllable.

But here's something else I love about my Daddy God. Although He hears every word I say, He doesn't throw them back in my face, and He doesn't throw me under the bus. Instead, He uses these times as teaching moments, just as Jesus did with His disciples. Instead of verbally chastising them, He used the very things they'd been saying as the basis for a critical lesson. He sat down with them and taught them this simple kingdom truth: *If anyone wants to be first, he must be the very last, and the servant of all* (Mark 9:35).

I'm beyond grateful that my Daddy God hears me when I speak to Him. And, in a different way, I'm grateful that He hears me even when I say things not meant for His ears. He's a heavenly Daddy who wants His kids to speak in ways that build others up and not tear them down, words that bless and don't curse, words that humbly seek the best for others. And even though I don't enjoy His correction, I know that He always acts for my good…and His.

That's what my Daddy's discipline is like. It's not always pleasant; in fact, at times it's very hard to take. The writer of the book of Hebrews made this discovery long ago, when he wrote,

> *They (our fathers) disciplined us for a little while as they thought best; but God disciplines us for our good, in order that we may share in his holiness. No discipline seems pleasant at the time, but painful. Later on, however, it produces a harvest of righteousness and peace for those who have been trained by it.*
> (Hebrews 12:10-11).

Sometimes God's discipline involves more than just a simple "teaching moment." But the Bible teaches that our heavenly Daddy loves us so much that He'll do whatever it takes to help us to get it right. And so I pray, "Thank You, Daddy God, for hearing me, even when I say things I'd rather You not hear!"

He Gets to the Heart of the Matter

When I was twelve years old, I opened my heart to my Daddy God by accepting Him through faith in His Son, Jesus Christ. I can't help but think that my first attempts at talking to my new Daddy in heaven were nothing more than "baby talk," like Belle's first attempts to talk to me. But to this day, I'm absolutely sure that He wanted to hear from me, as well as talk to me.

Not long after I opened my heart to my heavenly Daddy, He began speaking to me about some things He wanted to change in me. He left no doubt about His intent. But at the same time, I recognized those words as coming from a Daddy who calls me His own, leaving no doubt that He loved me and had a massive interest in everything about me.

God began speaking to me by awakening my conscience to some of the not-so-great things about me. The first thing I remember Him talking to me about was how I treated others, especially the kids I considered my friends. I was a typical twelve-year-old who often didn't act in thoughtful ways toward others. My words and actions could be downright mean. But that began to change when my heavenly Daddy began to speak to me about how I treated others.

Before long, I knew I had to go to my best friend, Matt, who had suffered the worst of my bad behavior (the fact that he is still my best friend is nothing short of a miracle; he will have a ton of jewels in his celestial crown for putting up with me). I had to ask him to forgive me for how I had treated him. In tears, I confessed my unkindness to him and asked him to forgive me.

That was a big milestone for me, but it didn't mean I instantly became perfect in how I treated others. I haven't reached perfection in that area of life, or in any other area. But my Daddy in heaven never fails to speak to me to let me know what He wants to change in me, even when I don't especially want to hear it.

Your Daddy God loves you in the same way. He wants to have two-way conversations with you, which means you need to be prepared for those times when He has something to say that you really don't want to hear. He knows your personal "sticking points" and wants you to be free of those things that hold you back from all that He has for you. Sticking points are where your Daddy knows you get stuck. He doesn't want His kids stuck anywhere. He wants us to keep moving and growing.

When my Daddy in heaven speaks to me about needed changes in my life, He doesn't hem and haw. He doesn't sugarcoat things. He's gets right to the heart of the matter, speaking to me honestly and directly; many times gently, and many times in a firmer and harder-to-miss Daddy voice. And He'll do the same with you.

When We Miss the Mark
It never feels pleasant when someone tells you that you've gone wrong somewhere. It feels even less so when your heavenly Daddy is the One doing the talking.

But one of the many great things about my Daddy God is that He will never leave me without hope. While with one breath He may tell me, "You're falling short of what I have for you," in the next breath He tells me, "You're still My son, and nothing you've said, done, or thought will change that. I love you more than you can know, so let's spend some time together and talk about what we need to change in you." Our Daddy God is never more willing and available to speak with us than when we mess up or when something in our lives doesn't please Him. And here's what I love about Him when I do mess up: He doesn't criticize me or scorn me and then walk away leaving me alone to figure things out and make the necessary adjustments. He sticks right beside me and gives me what I need to see those changes take place.

When you and I are suffering because we know we're in a spiritual place, our heavenly Daddy never intended for us, that's when we become vulnerable to another "father."

The father of lies.

He swoops into our lives, attacking, accusing, and mocking. He makes us question whether we really are one of our Daddy God's kids. At those times, you need to listen carefully to your Daddy God as He begins speaking the truth to you about who you are... and about whose you are. When you fail, your Daddy in heaven doesn't give up on you in disgust, and He doesn't turn you over to your accuser to be destroyed. He doesn't crucify you in the midst of your spiritual pain. He was crucified so you wouldn't have to be!

When you fall, when you're down on yourself and think of yourself as a failure, your Daddy God simply calls you to Himself and invites you to talk with Him. When you accept that invitation, He'll ask, "My daughter (or my son), where are your accusers? Where is the chorus of voices that want to condemn you?" And then He'll say, much as Jesus did in John 8:11, *"I don't condemn you. Go in the freedom of knowing you belong to Me and leave your mistakes and failures behind you."*

An Always-Available, Always-Listening Daddy

Belle isn't at all shy about letting me know when she wants to talk with me. Sometimes, in fact, she wants to carry on a conversation in places that most adults would consider less than optimal.

When Belle is in the bathroom, at times she'll call out for me to come in, sit a spell, and talk with her. When I walk in, I see her sitting on the toilet and motioning me to sit down next to her. So I take a seat on my own "potty chair," which is the stool she stands on to wash her hands in the sink.

At other times, Belle will be sitting at her little child-size plastic table eating. She'll look up at me, smile, and say, "Sit here!" I don't know about you, but when an adorable toddler issues such an invitation, I find it hard to say no.

But as much as I love spending time conversing with my daughters, there are times when I can't do that. I am just one man, subject to the confines of a twenty-four-hour day and a seven-day week. I face limitations of time and energy, and as much as I'd like to be available at all times to chat with my girls all day long, I can't always do it.

Not so with our Daddy God! He is never too busy to spend time with us, just talking and listening.

How can a God who created the universe, who holds *everything* in His all-powerful hands, care so much about such insignificant specks of dust placed on a tiny blue dot on the outskirts of the cosmos? He must have too much on His plate to worry about just one of over seven billion people who live on this planet!

As a man with a finite understanding of God and His creation, I won't pretend that I fully understand it. But I know beyond any doubt that the same God who created all things also loves little ol' me so much that He promises to make time to talk to me and listen to me. And I know that He makes the same promise to you.

Our Daddy in heaven is available to His children 24/7, anytime and anywhere. Whether it's near a burning bush or a blooming bush, on an ark or in a park, on a mount or when you're down for the count, God is always there for you and ready to engage in some great Daddy/child interaction.

Why don't you make His day and grab some of that time right now? In the process of making His, day, you'll be sure to make your own day, too.

Chapter 8

DADDY, ARE YOU ALWAYS THERE FOR ME . . .?

When Belle was a tiny baby, I would sometimes stand over her crib in the quiet of the night and adoringly watch her as she slept. I would study all her features, from her curly hair to her chubby cheeks to her impish nose to her beautiful, ebony skin. In those moments, I just couldn't imagine looking down at anything else as beautiful as my precious daughter.

Something else felt special to me about standing over her and watching as she slept. I loved the idea that Belle was at peace in a home where her Daddy loved her deeply, provided for her faithfully, and protected her from any threat the outside could bring her way. I loved it that she could lay there so completely free of fear and worry…just because her Daddy was there for her.

God has spoken such words over me, too.

He speaks to me about how He adores me as His son, even with all my wrinkles, warts, pimples, and flaws. I can't fathom it! He also makes it clear He wants me to rest and relax in the knowledge that He's always there for me, even in my darkest nights, protecting me, picking me up, and healing and teaching me.

I know He wants you to have that same assurance and confidence.

An Always-Present Daddy

In the inevitable dark times of life, in those desolate, desperate moments when we can't seem to see an inch in front of our faces–in those times, it can seem especially difficult to fathom a heavenly Daddy who is always there for us, committed to be present with us.

The truth is, however, our Daddy God does some of His best work in the darkness.

Life changes for me when I stop trying to fight the surrounding night and simply rest in Him. Just because I can't see Him doesn't mean He can't see me. He doesn't need night vision goggles.

I'm not the first of my heavenly Daddy's kids to figure out that truth. King David, who lived through some very dark periods of his own–far darker than most of us will ever face–once wrote:

If I say, "Surely the darkness will hide me and the light become night around me," even the darkness will not be dark to you; the night will shine like the day, for darkness is as light to you (Psalm 139:11-12).

I identify with this psalm. I understand these feelings. Maybe you do, too.

I understand what it feels like to be emotionally and spiritually spent, consumed with life's difficulties…all the while asking "why?"

I couldn't understand *why* my earthly dad left Mom and me, and then why he made very little effort to see me.

I didn't understand *why* Dad had to die of leukemia, before we had a chance to reconcile. I didn't understand *why* the lights on the set of my dream television show had to go dark.

I didn't understand *why* my wife fell so ill that she came close to dying, leaving me pretty much on my own for ten months to care for our two-year-old daughter.

I didn't understand *why* any of these things happened, and I still don't know why some of these trials came my way. But my Daddy God, who knows me better than I know myself and who superintends and is fully aware of everything that comes into my life, remained right there with me through it all. And He did so even when I couldn't feel His presence and wondered where He was in my suffering. My eyes may not have been able to see because of the dark but it didn't mean He wasn't standing right over me the entire time.

Just as I'm always present for my daughters, even when they're sound asleep and doing nothing but being the apples of my eye, so my Daddy God remains present in my life. Even when the darkness blinds me. Even when I feel weary to the bone from the demands of life.

My heavenly Daddy is there. Always.

The psalmist wrote of his Daddy God's presence, *You hem me in behind and before, and you lay your hand upon me* (Psalm 139:5). In other words, God will never let me go anywhere or do anything without His hand of protection remaining upon me. He follows me so closely that I can't escape His touch or even His sight.

My Daddy God's presence has greatly reassured me over many years and in many life circumstances. I am not and never have been alone. And I never will be alone, because my Daddy God never changes. When seemingly everything in my life changes, He does not. When everything around me rocks and churns and spins and sways, He remains steady, immovable, my divine anchor in the storm.

He Knows Us and What We Need

If you're the parent of more than one child, you may share in my amazement at how two children from the same home with the same mom and dad develop such different personalities. Even though I'm not Diana's or Belle's biological daddy, and can't attribute my DNA to their unique personalities (thank goodness for their sake!), my two girls are growing up in the same environment. But they are so very different from one another.

Diana ...
- sleeps well (and a lot);
- has inimitable dance moves that most grown women envy;
- loves to come home and do her homework;
- gets very emotional and cries at the drop of a hat;
- is a talented performer with both singing and acting;

➤ is an organizer with a need to have everything neat and orderly.

Belle ...
➤ sleeps not-so-well (and not-so-much);
➤ has the cutest dimples on her lower back;
➤ has a scar on her left forearm from her BCG (Bacillus Chalmette–Guérin) vaccination;
➤ didn't walk until she was twenty-one months old (what a blessing for an older mom and dad!);
➤ loves erasing pencil more than writing with pencil;
➤ is not an organizer and is good at making messes and leaving them behind.

I know all these things about my daughters, not because I'm the most observant or insightful man in the world, but because I want to know them. I want to know everything I can about Belle and Diana because I love them on a level I once thought impossible. I want to know their strengths and weaknesses, the things that make them laugh, the things that frighten them. The list is too long to finish. A daddy who loves his children deeply will try to know all he possibly can about them.

And that's the kind of loving heavenly Daddy we have. God knows us intimately and infinitely *beyond* intimately. Plain and simple, He knows *everything* about us. Nothing about us remains hidden from Him.

I could devote many pages to the things my Daddy in heaven knows about me, but let me note just a few examples that really jump out at me.

He knows that I was a skinny, small, late-blooming boy with freckles I didn't like.

He knows that my earthly father cringed when he came to watch me at Little League games as I stood in the outfield and watched the butterflies rather than the guy at bat.

He knows how my broken relationship with my dad caused me many years of pain and fear.

He knows how terrified I felt of commitment because of what happened in my own home as I grew up.

He knows how I wanted to become a pop singer, even traveling to Hollywood to try and "make it big."

He knew how scared and anxious I felt as I drove away from Portland with all of my worldly possessions (a couple of suitcases) to go to a Bible college in Texas.

He knows how excited I felt when I asked Rachel White to marry me in 1998, at around 10 p.m. in front of a roaring fire in the lounge at Skamania Lodge in Washington State.

He knows how hard I took it when my television career came to an end, and how, in order to make ends meet, I took a job picking up garbage on construction sites.

He knows how excited we felt to establish Open Arms International in a room out of our home in Portland.

He knew Rachel and I could not get pregnant, and He knew when we were ready to receive our first two rescued babies and become Mom and Dad to them.

My heavenly Daddy knows all these things about me because He cares enough to want to know. Because He wanted to know my strengths and weaknesses, He knows. Because He wanted to know what frightens me, tempts me, angers me, and hurts me, He knows. Because He wanted to know my little personality quirks, He knows.

He *knows*.

Someone might say. "Okay, David. So God knows everything. That's kind of the definition of God, isn't it? But what does that have to do with Him being there for you in every life circumstance?"

Just this. His desire to know everything about me makes my relationship with Him intensely personal. It's one thing to acknowledge that God cares for His people and is always there for them; it's quite another thing to say, with absolute confidence, that *my* Daddy in heaven is there *for me* when I need Him most.

The Bible tells us repeatedly of God's adoring love for His church, for the group of people who have committed their lives to Him through faith in His Son, Jesus Christ. But let's keep this in mind: none of us are just faces in the crowd to our Daddy God. We're individuals for whom He gave everything to make it possible for us to join His family. He loves each of His kids with a passion that even the most adoring earthly daddy can hardly begin to understand.

How could it get any *more* personal?

He Knows What's Going On "Inside"

I recently met Joseph Onkuyo. In our first meeting, he told me about his remarkable father. His dad is now in his late eighties and Joseph told me, "To this day, my father can look at me and know exactly what is going on inside of me. He gives me this penetrating look as if to peer into the deepest part of my soul and know everything that's happening."

That's an uncommonly special kind of love and insightfulness! That's a dad who so deeply knows and loves his son that nothing can stay hidden. To be able merely to look at his son and just *know*...well, that's a kind of connectedness that many married couples don't share.

But our Daddy God is just like that. He knows us so completely that He understands our thoughts before we even think them. At all times, He can accurately peer into the deepest recesses of our souls:

You have searched me, Lord, and you know me.
You know when I sit and when I rise;
you perceive my thoughts from afar.
You discern my going out and my lying down;
you are familiar with all my ways.

Before a word is on my tongue you, Lord, know it completely (Psalm 139:1-4).

Joseph would likely tell you that sometimes he doesn't feel completely comfortable with how well his father knows him. I get that. Most of us would never want even our closest friends or loved ones to know *everything* that goes on inside us. We feel fairly certain that if they actually knew, they'd walk away from us in disgust and never have any more to do with us.

It sometimes makes me squirm when I ponder how my heavenly Daddy sees everything about me, especially those things I'd like to remain hidden. A big part of me doesn't like the idea. When awful things go through my mind, it makes me uncomfortable. I sometimes wish He didn't know when my motives go wrong, when utter self-centeredness and ugly human pride take over.

But at the same time, the fact that my Daddy God knows everything about me feels incredibly reassuring. Despite all the ugliness inside me, I know He still loves me as His own son. He doesn't give up on me or lower the boom when I think terrible thoughts, when I want to hang on to anger and bitterness, when my words and actions flow out of my own selfish motivations and pride.

And so I love praying, along with the psalmist: *Search me, God, and know my heart; test me and know my anxious thoughts. See if there is any offensive way in me, and lead me in the way everlasting* (Psalm 139:23-24).

For the first time in my life, when I was in my early fifties, I began to feel a deep and prolonged bitterness, anger, and unforgiveness toward some people who had hurt me. I had always thought of myself as a loving, not-easily-angered kind of guy who never holds grudges. But that changed when a tough set of circumstances triggered some real ugliness inside me.

I fought an intense inner battle. I didn't like my feelings toward these people. My anger tore at me from the inside out, and in time

I came to a point where I didn't even like myself.

God not only saw what was happening inside me, He knew about it long before I did. And He loved me enough to expose those immature, ugly, poisonous seeds germinating in my heart. But He didn't want me to try dealing with them by myself; He wanted to be right there with me, touching me with His healing hand. Despite the ugliness in my soul, my Daddy God remained constant in His love for me. He walked with me as I worked my way through the ugliness.

It grieves God to see our thoughts heading off into dark, ugly places, but as our Daddy in heaven, He'll never jump ship. He'll never leave us to go it alone. He'll stick by us through it all, and He'll not only heal us and give us a sound mind, but He'll also use those dark times to set our hearts and minds back on the right track.

He Sees Our Failures and Imperfections

As a teenager, I went out on a few casual dates with a young lady named Janice. I liked her and thought she was attractive. But while we enjoyed one another's company, the relationship never became serious.

Then I met Janice's best friend, Mandy. Right away, I decided I wanted Mandy to become my new "best friend." (Translation: I wanted to start dating her.)

I started taking journeys in my mind, hatching and plotting schemes, hoping that the ultimate destination would lead to a good connection with Mandy. I concocted a plan whereby a not-so-charming coworker of mine, Brad, would get matched up with Mandy and they and Janice and I would go out on a double date. I knew Mandy would never have an interest in Brad, so I saw it as a way to get closer to Mandy without arousing Janice's suspicions. It took me a while to manipulate the circumstances, but I finally managed to arrive at my intended destination. Mandy and I started dating.

As a teen, I didn't have the guts or the maturity to honestly communicate my true desires and motivations. Maybe we can cut some slack to an adolescent, but what happens when an adult does a similar thing? What happens when that adult's friends and family members take note of the foolish and sometimes destructive path? What happens when the people closest to that person see the character flaws and the sinful behavior that results? Will they immediately reject us and turn away from us?

Sometimes, they do.

Too many of us learn from an early age that love is conditional, based on our ability to perform.

We learn that we must act and speak and behave "just right." We learn that we have to "earn" love.

And yet, all of us crave unconditional love. We want others to love us despite our flaws and imperfections. We want them to want to know us as we truly are, but love us despite our shortcomings. We want them to love us just because they do, and not because of anything especially loveable in or about us.

That's the perfect love of our heavenly Daddy. He loves all of His kids unconditionally, without strings or conditions. God loves us in spite of ourselves, and will never give up on us or turn His back on us when we choose to journey to dark or sinful places.

Certainly, God wants us to obey His guidelines and boundaries as outlined in the Bible, because He knows that they lead to a healthy, successful life. Following His directions keeps the lines of communication open between us. But even when we fail to follow God's laws–and none of us perfectly obeys on this side of eternity–His love for us remains uncompromised.

The Bible insists that *love covers over all wrongs* (Proverbs 10:12). It also says that our Daddy God is *love* itself (1 John 4:8). Put these two verses together and you have God, the embodiment of love, covering over all our wrongs.

My Daddy God reminds me a lot of the dad I once saw in an old, dimly-recalled movie. His son had messed up badly and when

Dad arrived on the scene, he helped his son clean up the mess, gave him a good "talking to" (good dads, including our Daddy God, use their kids' bad decisions as teaching moments), and then put his arm around the boy's shoulders and said, "Come on, let's go home."

Home is where it's safe, where you're loved, where you're protected. Dad is there! And when, not if, we mess up, our Daddy God is there to pick us up, forgive us, heal us, and then bring us home. And there we can rest in His presence.

He's There for Us When We Fall

When Belle was about two-and-a-half years old, she stood one day on a large plastic lid, the kind that goes on storage tubs. When the lid started slowly sliding out from under her on the tile floor of our bathroom, she reached out and gripped the door frame in a desperate attempt to keep from falling.

"Daaaaaadddddyyyyy!" she cried out in a near panic. Fortunately, I stood nearby and managed to catch her before she hit the floor and hurt herself.

Our Daddy in heaven sees everything about us, and that includes those times when we're about to hit the floor – and get hurt. Whether we fall fast or slow, He knows and hears our cries. He wants us to remember that no matter what happens, He is within earshot and can catch us before we crash.

The New Testament epistle of Jude closes with an amazing promise: *To him who is able to keep you from stumbling and to present you before His glorious presence without fault and with great joy—to the only God our Savior be glory, majesty, power, and authority, through Jesus Christ our Lord, before all ages, now, and forevermore! Amen* (Jude 24-25).

What a magnificent promise! And yet, as most of us know from personal experience, our heavenly Daddy, as much as He loves us, doesn't always catch us before we hit the ground. That's a tough one to understand. It helps to remember that we live in a fallen, evil world, and that it won't always be this way. But for now, even the children of our Daddy God will find themselves exposed to trouble and evil.

When we choose to give ourselves to God, however, we receive a supernatural and divine protection that covers and helps us more than we will ever fully recognize in this life. Even so, sometimes we'll still stumble and fall. But whenever that happens, our Daddy God is right there to pick us up, hold us, and teach us.

Our Daddy God has made it clear that no matter what we may face in these physical, mortal bodies of ours–be it suffering, pain, dementia, or even death itself–there is no evil force in all of creation that can pluck us from our eternal place in His family. *That* is the stumbling He keeps us from. He protects us from those obstacles that can threaten and affect our spiritual, eternal destiny.

All parents, divine and human alike, must grapple with the reality that kids *will* have falls, near-falls, and all other kinds of mishaps. Sometimes those things hurt, and sometimes they leave scars. Truth be told, there's only so much parents can do to keep their kids from falling and hurting themselves. A friend of mine, in his youth, suffered a bizarre succession of injuries over the course of several years. These included four broken arms, a broken toe, a broken thumb, twice a broken nose, and a shattered elbow.

I know this family, and I know that my friend had parents who loved him very much. But he just kept hurting himself!

Sometimes I'm close enough to my girls to catch them before they fall–but not always. There are still times when these little ones will hit the floor or the ground in a sudden fall. Even so, there is one constant in our home: I'm always there for them. And I will always be with them during the healing process…and during the learning process that often follows.

Jesus faced similar dynamics as He dealt with His disciples day after day. They could often act like impetuous, childish little kids. One of them, Peter, once cried out for Jesus to keep him from falling, much like Belle cried out to me (Matthew 14:24-33). The disciples had been crossing the Sea of Galilee in a boat when they spotted Jesus walking *on the water toward them.*

How often do you see someone walking on water? I never have. The disciples hadn't, either. Understandably, they concluded they must be seeing a ghost. Jesus immediately calmed their fears (as any good Daddy would), calling out to them, "Take courage! It is I. Don't be afraid."

In other words, "I'm right here with you. I know your fear. Let me calm your nerves."

Peter immediately jettisoned his fear in exchange for some bravado. "Lord," he said, "if it's You" (note, he wanted to make sure!), "tell me to come to You on the water."

"Come," Jesus answered.

Peter then took a step of faith that hadn't even occurred to any of the other disciples. He stepped out of the boat and began walking toward Jesus. On the water! But since he wasn't a ghost, either, and he knew flesh and blood really can't walk on water, once more he lost his nerve. He looked away from Jesus and toward the things that frightened him. He saw big waves and felt strong wind. And immediately, he began to sink. He started falling into the dark water on which he had just been walking.

"Lord, save me!" Peter cried out. And in that instant, Jesus reached out and took Peter by the hand. Jesus knew Peter's fear. He knew his predicament. He was right there, present in the trouble. And He lifted him up.

You won't find Peter's grave at the bottom of the Sea of Galilee.

"You of little faith," Jesus then said in a memorable teaching moment. "Why did you doubt?"

What could Peter say in reply?

"I didn't think you knew?" No.

"I didn't think you were nearby." Nope.

"I wasn't sure I could trust you?" Nah.

And so Peter said nothing. Exactly the right response, for once.

Those three shouted words Peter used can come in handy. He said, "Lord, save me!" When we face crises in our marriages, our families, our jobs, our finances, our health, or in our personal relationship with the Lord, we need to exercise our own vocal chords:

Daddy God, save me!

Or maybe it sounds more like Belle's cry: "Daaaaaadddddyyyyy!"

While the long arm of the law or the long arm of the search and rescue team doesn't always comfort us or even reach us, we need to remember that "the long arm of the Lord" is always there for us. Our Daddy God is real; He's powerful, and He's always nearby, available to render us aid whenever we need it. Our heavenly Daddy is always at the ready to touch us, take hold of us, rescue us from falling–or pick us up and embrace us after we have fallen– whenever we call out to Him.

A Strong Promise

Remember this amazing promise to God's own people: *Be strong and courageous. Do not be afraid or terrified because of them, for the Lord your God goes with you; he will never leave you nor forsake you* (Deuteronomy 31:6).

While the terrifying *them* in this verse may differ from the "them" that confronts us today, the principle remains the same. God is always there with us, holding us tightly through all the trials and difficulties that life on a fallen earth can bring our way.

And because He knows us thoroughly and is always present with us, we can be at peace. At peace like my daughter Belle is as she sleeps so soundly in her crib beneath my loving watch.

No matter what tomorrow may bring, no matter what life may throw across our path, no matter what transpires in this unpredictable world of ours, our Daddy God will always be there.

Chapter 9

DADDY, WILL YOU HOLD ONTO ME?

A few years ago as we waited in Schiphol Airport in Amsterdam, The Netherlands, for a flight back to the United States, Belle was playing near an elevator. When the door suddenly opened and a group of people appeared, it seemed to terrify her.

She raced over to me with uplifted arms, crying out, "Daddy, up! Daddy, up!"

We still had to ride in that scary elevator, but Belle wanted to be held before she would even consider going in.

Did her fear make a lot of sense? Maybe not. But her reasoning really didn't matter to me at that moment. I just knew she needed me to hold her so she could get through the short, frightening ride, and I felt more than happy to oblige.

My daughters often want me to pick them up and hold them, in all kinds of situations and for all kinds of reasons. Sometimes they want to be held because they feel scared or nervous. Sometimes they want to be held because they don't feel well. At other times they feel upset or sad. Occasionally they just want to be close to Daddy. I never get tired of that one!

Recognizing how often my daughters want me to hold them has made me think about what I sometimes need from my heavenly Daddy. I've learned that He not only takes joy in caring for my physical, spiritual, and emotional needs, but He also knows how to make His presence felt in my life by actually "holding" me when I need or want Him to.

We have few guarantees in this life, but Scripture makes certain that we can count on trouble. Jesus clearly tells us, *In this world you will have trouble* (John 16:33). Because we are humans living in a fallen world, we will have times when we're hurting, disappointed, distressed, or overwhelmed by fear and anxiety. At these times, we need to find peace and safety, the kind found only in the loving embrace of our heavenly Daddy.

In the midst of difficult and frightening situations, our fear and discomfort can get the better of us. And though we may feel breathless and at a loss for words, if we can find enough air to say anything at all, we would do well to utter something as simple as, "Daddy, up!"

A Loving Daddy's Embrace

Something within all of us makes us crave our daddy's approval. You may have grown up in a home where Dad gave you little positive affirmation or affection. Even so, you still have an instinctual need for a father's love, through both spoken words and tender acts of affection.

It doesn't matter if you're a grown man or woman or a boy or a girl, the loving embrace of a daddy's arms is a tremendously powerful thing. When we've been embarrassed or humiliated, we want to run to our dad and bury our face in his neck and shoulders, knowing he will love us and accept us unconditionally. We want to feel the embrace of Daddy's powerful arms when something frightens us or we get in trouble, knowing that he can protect and defend us and fight off any attacker or threat. We want Daddy's arms around us when we've accomplished something important, believing he will rejoice with us fully and give us a hug, a pat on the back, and loving words that express his deep pride and joy.

In all these moments, only the warm embrace of Daddy will do. Yes, we also need those warm embraces from mom, but it just feels different when our fathers lovingly put their arms around us. Maybe it's the strength of those arms. Maybe it's the safety they convey. Or maybe it's something else entirely. Whatever it is, when we run to our dads for that kind of affection, we communicate a single message: "I don't want to be alone in this moment. I want to share it with my dad, the most important guy in my life."

A daddy's embrace reinforces for us a sense of perfect contentment, ultimate safety, powerful protection, shared emotion, and a deep sense of belonging in this world. The child who grows up with a demonstrably loving father, a man who shows his love through hugs and other signs of physical affection, most often develops a profound sense of connectedness in the world. And that child usually grows up to be an emotionally and spiritually healthy adult.

A lot of people have a tough time thinking of God as a heavenly Daddy who wants to be that kind of a Father–and more–to us. But that's who our Daddy in heaven is. He's a heavenly Dad who not only loves and provides for his people but who tends his flock (you and me) like a shepherd:

He gathers the lambs in his arms and carries them close to his heart; he gently leads those that have young (Isaiah 40:11).

Think of it: your Daddy God wants to take you into His powerful, tender arms and hold you when you need it, or even when you just want it. Do you believe this?

Believe He Wants to Hold You

A while back, Belle went through an illness that lasted several weeks. Rachel and I suffered through that time, right along with her. It was terribly hard on both of us to see our little girl suffering and not be able to do anything to make her feel better. We did everything we possibly could to help her recover quickly, but nothing except the passage of time did her any good.

During that time, Belle didn't sleep well. She's never been a great sleeper, but those few weeks felt like months. As Rachel and I slept, Belle would get up in the middle of the night, demanding attention. On several occasions when Belle stirred from her sleep, I stealthily slipped out of bed (so as not to disturb Mommy), and carried my hurting daughter into the family room, the home of Daddy's recliner. I would grab a nice, soft blanket, lay Belle against my chest, pull the blanket up over her, and recline the chair.

When I did so, Belle fell asleep quickly. She clearly found great comfort in her daddy's arms.

Around this time, I felt a great deal of stress in my own life. One night as I held Belle, my own Daddy in heaven used the moment to gently and lovingly speak to me.

David, I know you're going through a rough time right now. But do you know that I'm holding you right now, in the same way you're holding Belle? Do you know the tender care and love you feel for your daughter, especially when she's sick and suffering? That is the same tender care and love that I feel for you as My son.

My Daddy God let me know that nothing could keep Him from giving me the assurance and rest that only His strong, loving arms could provide. I heard Him saying to me,

You don't always have to be the "grown-up" and the strong husband and father that everyone, including yourself, expects you to be. Right now, in this moment, just rest in My arms. Be the son to Me that you always have been and always will be. I know you're not feeling well. I know things are tough right now. But it's all okay, because I have you in My arms. Now rest, My son. I've got hold of you.

In that moment, with my beautiful daughter sleeping in my arms, I rested and soaked in my heavenly Father's love. That night, with God's peace surrounding me, my Daddy God's incredible words came rushing back to me:

In peace I will lie down and sleep, for you alone, Lord, make me dwell in safety (Psalm 4:8).

Whoever dwells in the shelter of the Most High will rest in the shadow of the Almighty (Psalm 91:1).

I hated it that my daughter Belle had fallen so ill that she couldn't get to sleep on her own. Her daily suffering broke my heart. At the same time, though, I took great joy in being able to hold her and comfort her and help her to get the rest her little body so desperately needed. And in those trying days, Daddy God showed me that He feels exactly the same about me, but on a level far deeper than even I, the father of a sick little girl, could imagine.

I can't claim to fully understand the love my Daddy in heaven has for me or His strong desire to just hold onto me when I need it. But I know it's true. I know that when joy fills my heart, He feels that joy right along with me. I know that when I'm hurting or feel confused, in a very real way He feels my pain right along with me. And I know that when fear or worry stalks me, He understands that fear and anxiety and comes alongside me to calm my troubled heart.

I know all those things—but there's one thing I've learned about my Daddy God's deep desire to hold onto me when I know I need it.

Sometimes, it's just a matter of running to Him.

Courage to Say, "Daddy, Up!"
Because I love my daughters, I often take the initiative to pick them up and hold them. Sometimes I do this because I know that if I don't, they might get hurt by something I see coming their way. But at other times, they make it very clear that they want or need to be held. Either way, I'm always ready to gather them into my arms and just hold them.

Daddy, up!

It makes me sad to realize that many of our Daddy God's kids feel reluctant to seek out His embrace. Some have a difficult time believing that the Creator God is also a heavenly Daddy who wants to lovingly embrace His kids. Others allow human pride to push them to lean solely on their own strength. They permit their independent spirit to convince them that it alone can get them through the often ugly times we face on earth.

For both of these groups, I'd like to present a quick look at the life of a man who knew very well how much he needed his Daddy God's touch. I'm talking once more about King David, one of the strongest, toughest, most courageous men who ever lived. If you're not familiar with David's story, understand that he faced a lot of tough, challenging, and extremely frightening situations. Consider just a few examples:

> Before he became king of Israel and even before he had any real experience as a warrior, he volunteered to fight a nine-foot-six, well-armed, battle-tested professional soldier named Goliath. And he did so, armed with nothing more than a leather sling and a fistful of small stones.
> He remained loyal to his deranged king, Saul, who on more than one occasion, out of sheer jealousy, tried to kill him.
> He went into battle time and time again, wielding swords and spears, getting sprayed with the blood of his attackers–and perhaps his own blood as well.

By God's grace, David survived these and many other scary episodes. And it's the mature, survivor David who gives us a beautiful word picture of a heavenly Daddy who is always available, always willing to honor a request for some real "Daddy time":

I waited patiently for the Lord; he turned to me and heard my cry. He lifted me out of the slimy pit, out of the mud and mire; he set my feet on a rock and gave me a firm place to stand
(Psalm 40:1-2).

Few men have ever been in David's league. He was a true man's man, tough when he needed to be tough, brave and courageous when he needed to be brave and courageous. But most people remember him today as a "man after God's own heart," a man who instantly recognized a situation when he'd gotten in over his head.

In times of trouble or danger, this man's man was more than willing to cry out to his heavenly Daddy, "Daddy, up!"

No matter how tough, independent, and determined you are, are you willing to cry out to Daddy God? When you need help or deliverance, or just some time being held, have you trained yourself to cry out, "Daddy, up"?

All of us will face times in our journey through life when we'll need our Daddy God to come near, pick us up, and hold and comfort us. And when that time comes, we all will need that small amount of courage and humility that it takes to forget ourselves, look past our own situation, and cry out to our heavenly Father:

"Daddy, up!"

And when you cry out to your Daddy God in that way, you can be sure He'll answer you and give you what you need. The "God of all comfort" knows how to deliver that comfort with oceans of both tenderness and fatherly affection.

Do Your Part to Close the Gap . . . and Be Patient
I love it when Belle and Diana run to me to be held. That they sometimes do so when they feel afraid, upset, or sad doesn't bother me in the least. But even the best of us earthly dads have our limitations, don't we? We don't always know why our kids want us to pick them up and hold them. And sometimes, whatever we're doing at the time seems more important than a child's cry to be held.

But whenever we run to our Daddy God, He is there for us, arms open wide to receive us and hold us. It doesn't matter to Him why we need to be held. Maybe we've done something unwise or foolish, or perhaps something beyond our control has flattened us or threatens to undo us.

Or maybe we just want our heavenly Daddy's touch.

I've learned something important about my heavenly Daddy and His willingness to hold me when I need it. Sometimes, it's a matter of me making the first move. Just as my daughters sometimes have to make the first move, so too, I must be willing to make that move. I, too, need to run to my Daddy God when I need Him to hold me.

In other words, I must be willing to close the gap.

I believe that's one of many kernels of truth we can take from the amazing story of the Prodigal Son, a parable Jesus once told to illustrate our heavenly Father's deep love for His children, regardless of what they have done. The young man in the story had done everything he could to distance himself from the love and security of life provided by his earthly father. He took his inheritance early–a deeply shameful thing in the time of Jesus–and then left home, thinking he would find true happiness and fulfillment away from his daddy's home.

But this young man soon learned that wild living costs a lot of money. He tore through his inheritance with blinding speed, and before he knew it, he found himself flat broke and abandoned by the kind of "friends" who stick around only while the party rages on. In a desperate bid just to survive, he took a job feeding a pagan farmer's pigs, the worst job conceivable to a nice Jewish boy. He soon became so hungry that the pig slop he fed the hogs started to look good to him.

With no options left to him other than death, the chastened young man decided to return home, hoping against hope that his dad would at least take him on as a hired hand. He couldn't even dream of a life anything close to what he'd enjoyed before, but hey, at least he wouldn't starve to death.

It's amazing what great good a little desperation can sometimes do for us.

After the foolish boy hit rock bottom, he finally started making his way back home. Along the way, he rehearsed a speech he planned to deliver to his father, begging for a job and disavowing any claim to sonship.

What a surprise awaited him!

Instead of an angry, bitter father, he found a daddy so delighted at his return that he joyfully embraced him and welcomed him back: *his father saw him and was filled with compassion for him; he ran to his son, threw his arms around him and kissed him* (Luke 15:20).

This story can teach us a lot about the consequences of making unwise decisions that distance us from our heavenly Daddy. But it also instructs us about closing the gap that our poor decisions caused. We have to decide, as the prodigal did, to leave our mess behind and return to our Father. That takes a certain amount of humility. It takes a willingness to admit our pride and foolishness. And it takes a willingness to admit to ourselves, "I really don't know best. My Father knew all along. If I want to live, I need to return to Him."

Have you ever reached that place? Are you there right now? It might just be a good time to consider the prodigal's example and close the gap.

When Daddy Seems a Million Miles Away
But what about those times when we end up, through no apparent fault of our own, in one of life's deep, dark, filthy places–and Daddy God seems nowhere near? What about those times when life in this fallen world puts us in a place where we desperately need our heavenly Daddy to pick us up, clean us off, and then just hold us… but He seems to be off on a vacation somewhere?

All of us sometimes find ourselves in these terrible places, and our Daddy God seems to be a million miles away. We wonder why He seems so far from us. We ask why He allows us to go through such terrible suffering. Aren't we our Daddy God's kids? Isn't He all-powerful and all-knowing? If He chose to, couldn't He spare us from spending time in those dark, dank, scary places?

Where are His hugs when we need them most? Even Jesus cried out, *My God, my God, why have you forsaken me?* And David himself asked, *Why are you so far from saving me, from the words of my groaning? O my God, I cry by day, but you do not answer, and by night, but I find no rest* (Psalm 22:1-2 ESV).

Does God run out of hugs?

It might surprise you to read this, but I believe that when God allows us to spend time in these dark places, it's one of the most loving things He does. He wants us to more acutely feel our need for Him and to know where to turn when we're in just the place we don't want to be.

Our Daddy God wants us to depend on Him for absolutely *everything*. But He also knows we're prone to wander, especially when we feel content and comfortable. We find it all too easy to take His hugs for granted, and to act as though we don't always need them.

Have you considered the all-important virtue called "patience"? For reasons we can't always understand, our Daddy God often allows a gap in time between our trouble and His deliverance. From our point of view, He leaves us too long in that dark place before He finally picks us up and puts His loving arms around us. Sometimes when we cry, "Daddy, up!" we have to remain patient and wait for Him to respond.

We have to wait.

Just like all of God's kids throughout history.

The author of Psalm 10 pointed to this truth when he wrote, *Why, Lord, do you stand far off? Why do you hide yourself in times of trouble?* (Psalm 10:1). This lament reveals an obviously frustrated man, a man who wonders where God had gone off to in his suffering. When you read the entire psalm, you see that he's being treated unjustly and he wonders if God even sees what's going on.

Have you ever wondered something like that? Have you wondered why your Daddy God seems AWOL when you're suffering, when you need more than anything else to feel His strong embrace? I believe we find the key in David's words: *I waited patiently for the Lord* (Psalm 40:1, bold added).

David knew his God was always there for him. He knew when to cry out to his heavenly Daddy to come to his aid. But he also knew that he sometimes had to wait. He might not have understood why, or even appreciated it much, but he believed that God would eventually be there for him…and that he would somehow be a better man for the wait.

King David's Daddy God is the same mighty Lord who loves you and promises to hold you today. Whatever your circumstances, and no matter how long you have to wait for His intervention in your life, don't give up on the truth: He *will* lift you up. He *will* take hold of you, even as you travel through your difficulty. So keep crying out to Him, "Daddy, up!" Wait patiently. Know that He *will* be there for you. Even when your fears try to tell you He won't.

Across the Finish Line

"One minute I was running; the next thing there was a pop, and I was down."

Derek Redmond, an athlete from the United Kingdom, was describing to a news conference what had happened to him in the 400 meter semifinals at the 1992 Olympic games in Barcelona.

Derek, twenty-six, had waited for this race for four years. Back in 1988, in the South Korea games, his dreams of Olympic gold had evaporated after an Achilles tendon problem. In that race, he had waited until a minute and a half prior to the starting gun before he finally admitted to himself and to the world that he couldn't do it. He simply couldn't run.

In November of 1990, he underwent surgeries on both Achilles tendons, which made five surgeries in all. But he worked and worked, trained and trained, and he came back. In the first two rounds at the Barcelona Olympics, he recorded his fastest time in five years. At long last, he was finally in position to fulfill his dream–to qualify for the finals in the Olympics.

"I really wanted to compete in my first Olympics," he told the news conference. "I was feeling great. It just came out of the blue." Halfway around the track, Derek lay sprawled out in lane five. This time, it was his hamstring.

Struggling to his feet, Derek began hobbling around the track. All the other runners had crossed the finish line and headed into the locker room. But the last runner hadn't finished. He continued to run.

Jim Redmond, Derek's Dad, was sitting high up in the stands and had witnessed his son's collapse. Breaking all the rules, the forty-nine-year-old machine shop owner ran down the steps and leaped onto the track. "You don't need credentials in an emergency," he later reflected. At the final turn, Jim Redmond caught up with his son and put his arm around him. Derek leaned into his Dad's shoulder and sobbed. But they kept going. A race official attempted to intervene and get Jim off the field. It was a futile attempt.

With Derek's left arm around his father's shoulder for support, they crossed the finish line…together. By rule, Derek was disqualified, and to this day Olympic records state that he did not finish the race. But that didn't stop the 65,000 fans in attendance from showing their appreciation for what they had just seen. They stood as one, giving Derek–and Jim–a thunderous, standing ovation. (You can view the race on YouTube, but be warned–you will shed tears.)

In a post-race interview Jim said, "Whatever happens, he had to finish. And I was there to help him finish. I intended to go over the line with him. We started his career together, and I thought we should finish it together."

Nothing can keep a loving daddy away from his children when they need his attention. No one could keep Jim Redmond from rushing to his son's side when he needed comfort or from helping him finish what he had started.

Our Daddy God operates in the very same way.

No wonder the apostle Paul likens our lives of faith to a competitive race (1 Corinthians 9:24-25). Each of us knows from personal experience that the race we run, the one called life, is filled with all sorts of obstacles and hurts. And when (not if) we get tripped up or hurt as we run the course, we have a choice to make:

Do we just lie down and give up, figuring that it just wasn't meant to be?

Or do we count on our Daddy God and call on Him to come alongside us, pick us up, and give us the help we need to finish? Do we count on the fact that His arms are strong enough and long enough to hold us through anything and everything life throws our way?

During those difficult times, times when we just don't have it in us to go any further, our heavenly Daddy comes to our side, lovingly puts His arm around us, comforts us, and dries our tears. And then He encourages us to continue on until we finish whatever He has for us.

Even if He has to gather us up in His arms and carry us over the finish line.

The Lanes of Your Life

Take a moment with me now and picture an Olympic running track. Pretend with me that each lane represents one decade of your life. Lane one is from birth to ten years old. Lane two is eleven to twenty years old. Lane three is twenty-one to thirty years old and so on. My question is this: *Which lane were you in when you suffered a serious blow that took you down?*

Which lane were you in and how old were you?

Running the "human race" as we are, there are events in life that interrupt our journey and take us down. We work hard, do our best, but then something unexpected and unforeseen knocks us to the ground. Was it abuse of some kind in lane one when you were six years old? Was it bullying in school when you were twelve years old in lane two? Was it not getting accepted into a certain graduate school when you were in your early twenties in lane three? Was it not getting the job promotion you were expecting at age thirty-five in lane four? A divorce in lane five when you were forty-two? And on and on. Death, divorce, job loss, abuse, illness, relationship issues, or unseen trouble of some kind taking us down at various times in our lives. We get knocked down and don't know if we'll ever be able to get up. Maybe it happened a long time ago and we still haven't gotten up off the ground. If we do get up, it will be a long, slow, painful limp to the finish line. Maybe we'll get there, but maybe we won't.

Just as Jim Redmond vaulted out of the stands and onto the field to help his son—letting nothing and no one stop him when he saw his boy go down hurting—our Daddy God isn't going to let anything keep you from crossing the finish line. He doesn't sit idly by and expect you to go it alone—especially when you're hurting. The very same Daddy God who was with you when you started this journey called life has determined that He will be with you right to the end.

When He comes alongside you, lean into Him and find your comfort and strength there. After all, He started this race we call "human" with you, and He's going to see you right through to the end.

Chapter 10

DADDY, CAN YOU GET ME WHERE I NEED TO GO?

Travel with Diana and Belle is always an adventure.

For near-distance travel in a car, it's the mad dash to get the car seats in place, figure out whose seat belt is whose, and then make sure each girl gets safely secured and buckled in. Then we have to make certain we've set the child-proof locks on the rear doors. And, finally, we have to put a plastic bag in the seat pocket in front of Diana, as she is prone to getting carsick (let's just say she has been known to nail Mom and Dad all the way from the back seat).

We had an even more complicated adventure as we prepared for our first trip from Kenya to the United States with Belle, then only four months old. Because Belle was a citizen of Kenya, Rachel and I had to go through the pain(s) of getting her a passport. In addition, since a Kenyan court had committed her into the custody of Open Arms International, we needed to seek permission from the court to take her out of the country. We had to gain written approval from the Kenyan government–and even had to surrender a title deed to a piece of Open Arms' property as security that we would return with Belle.

All this to say, it sometimes requires a lot of time and effort to get our daughters to their intended destination.

Such Gallagher family road trips provide another example of how our young daughters depend on Daddy and Mommy for everything. Our girls depend on Rachel and me to determine where we're all going and how we plan to get there.

I know that as my daughters grow and mature, they'll depend on Rachel and me less and less to get them where they need to go. They won't need Mom and Dad to take care of every small detail. They will make their own plans, do their own travel arrangements, and just *go*.

I have mixed feelings about that coming day.

On one level, it's exciting to think of our girls growing up and learning to depend on themselves.

But on another, I never want them to think that I'm unavailable to give them some direction and help when they need it. I want them to know that Daddy's ear will always be there to bend when they don't know for sure where they need to go or how to get there.

Here's the bottom line. I don't want my girls to ever get lost in life. I don't want them to wake up one day wondering where in the world they are or how they got there. I don't want them disoriented and trying to work their way back to a place they know they should be.

I think my Daddy God feels the very same way about me. In fact, I know He does.

I know He has taken great joy and excitement in seeing me grow from a newborn baby Christian who had no clue about leading the life He wanted me to lead, into a spiritual "teen" who more often than not stumbled and fell as he made his way through life, and then into a man of God who has learned to make daily use of the wisdom He's imparted to me over the years.

But no matter where I am in this ongoing process of growth, my heavenly Daddy constantly reminds me that I still need to depend on Someone much bigger than I am to get me where I need to go, whether physically, emotionally, or spiritually.

Great daddies don't leave their kids on their own to figure out their direction in life—even after the little ones aren't so little anymore. I wouldn't do that with my daughters, and I'm thrilled that my Daddy in heaven doesn't do that with me, either.

A Personal Roadmap

When my best friend Matt and I were both twelve years old and in sixth grade, we started a Bible study for our classmates in the basement of Matt's house. We would invite our friends over, and then we'd share God's Word and what a relationship with Jesus was all about—or, at least, we shared what little we knew about those things.

When Matt and I hosted our Bible studies, we had no idea that one day we'd work together as middle-aged men in Open Arms International. We had no real clue as to where God was taking us or how He would get us there. Yes, we excitedly talked about our dreams of sharing God's love through Jesus with residents of various countries. But neither one of us intentionally followed any particular path that we believed our Daddy God had laid out for us.

Sometimes, we can all look back at the winding paths our lives have taken and see God at work in very real ways. He's taking us on an incredibly blessed journey, very often without our even recognizing it. Hindsight, as the old saying goes, is always 20/20.

And when Matt and I look back today on how God brought us to our current place, it's crystal clear to both of us that our Daddy God not only had a plan for where He wanted us to go, but that He also had drawn up a wonderfully detailed roadmap for how to get us there. Our Daddy in heaven has guided us and carried us—and continues to guide and carry us—exactly where we've needed to go in life.

How cool is *that*?

A Book Full of Examples

The Bible is chock full of examples of how our Daddy God directs and guides His kids, so that they will end up where He wants them to be, doing what He wants them to do.

I think of Noah, the landlocked man who received from God what must have seemed like crazy instructions. God told him to build a huge boat that would take him, his family, and who-knows-how-many animals to God-only-knows where (Genesis 6-9).

Or consider Abram. God told him to pack up his family and all his earthly belongings, leave his homeland and all he'd ever known, and head out to a new home that God would later show him (Genesis 12).

Then there's Moses. God gave him clear instructions to leave Midian and return to his birthplace of Egypt so he could lead the people of Israel out of their long captivity (Exodus 3).

For a more New Testament flavor, take a look at Matthew 2 and read how God instructed Joseph, Jesus' earthly dad, to take Him and His mother, Mary, to Egypt–and to stay there until God gave them the "all-clear" to return home to Israel.

Finally, I think of the apostle Paul, whom God instructed, *Now get up and go into the city, and you will be told what you must do* (Acts 9:6).

In every one of these cases, God told His children to do something very specific–without offering to hand them an entire itinerary. He just spoke some version of, "Go, and I'll tell you more when you need to know." Our Daddy God had an amazing plan for humanity and He used these men to fulfill His purposes. He worked in profound ways to get these people, and many others whose stories appear in Scripture, just where He wanted them to be.

He did the very same thing for me. When He told me to go to Bible college, I listened to Him and went. He later told me to go to Africa, and again I listened and went. And because I listened and was willing to step out and go, He has blessed me and used me in ways I never could have imagined.

What about you? Do you believe God has a specific path He wants you to follow? Many of our Daddy God's kids have a difficult time believing that He has a specific place He wants them to be in this world, much less a path that He wants them to follow to get there. But I can say with absolute confidence that He has both.

For you, too.

You might say, "But I'm not a Noah. I'm not an Abram, Moses, Joseph, or Paul. I'm not! I'm not anyone but me. So who am I to think that God has a path for *me* to follow, like He did for those great people?"

Of course you're not any of those people. Neither am I. You're the one whom God so fearfully and wonderfully made you to be, and no one else. He values and adores the *you* He has created. I wonder, though, if sometimes we might do better to focus less on who we are, as important as that is, and focus more on *whose* we are.

Clearly, not many of Daddy God's kids are called to do great things like save humankind (Noah), or become the father of a great nation (Abram), or lead an entire nation out of slavery (Moses). And He chose only one man to fill the role of our Savior's earthly father (Joseph), and only one man to serve as His first key messenger to the non-Jewish world (Paul).

But you have one thing in common with all those men, and it's this: you're a child of a loving heavenly Daddy who has a plan and a path on earth for you. You're one of God's kids, and He has promised you, *I will instruct you and teach you in the way you should go; I will counsel you with my loving eye on you* (Psalm 32:8).

There it is, in black and white! If you have been adopted into God's family through faith in Jesus Christ, then He wants to guide you and speak to you about where He wants you to be on this planet. And He'll most certainly do it too…*if* you're willing to listen.

Where do you think your Daddy God wants you to go? If you don't know, then it's probably just a matter of asking and listening, and then being willing to move–even when the instructions don't seem to make complete earthly sense.

Reluctant to Travel

Rachel and I know a wonderful couple from the United Kingdom who recently entered their retirement years. Both worked as educators. He as a former principal or head teacher, and she as an ECD (Early Childhood Development or nursery school or kindergarten) teacher.

Stan and Karen have a real heart to train and equip our teachers at Open Arms and thereby help our students to learn better. They have visited our Village in Kenya a number of times and have spoken with Rachel and me about the possibility that God might want them to come out and work with our school and our teachers for substantial parts of the year.

We remember the day when, for the first time after their several previous visits, they talked to us about the possibility of spending more time at the Village. Toward the end of our discussion, Karen brought up one major consideration. "There is just one thing that would hold us back," she said. "It's our daughter. She is fragile, and with her health challenges, she is very dependent on us–especially emotionally–and needs us."

Sandy, their daughter, was born with medical challenges that have affected her in various ways throughout her life. To meet her and talk to her, though, you would be hard-pressed to suspect any significant challenges. She has remained very close to her parents but has lived very independently at various times in her life.

Before I responded to Karen's concerns, I asked for her forgiveness for what I was about to say, especially if it seemed in any way out of line. I also said that I didn't want my comments to come off as self-serving, because we would, of course, feel thrilled to have them come to work with our school on a more permanent basis.

Then I asked my question.

"Karen," I said, "is it possible that Sandy doesn't need you as much as you actually need her?"

Karen's eyes instantly filled with tears and so did her husband's. I knew I had struck a chord–or rather, God's Spirit had. I learned later from mutual friends that their daughter had been encouraging them to take the step and come to Kenya. She didn't depend on them nearly as much as they'd thought–or maybe hoped.

Far be it from me, *very* far, to pass any kind of judgment on this wonderful couple, or to dare to declare the "right" decision in regard to their coming to work with us. If it were my decision to make, I'd have them here with us right now, simply because I know they would be such wonderful assets to our school. But it's *not* up to me. That decision is between them and their Daddy God, and my role in that decision-making process is simply to pray for them and ask the Lord to move them where He wants them to go.

Have you sensed your Daddy in heaven prodding you toward launching out in some way and doing something out-of-the-box and beyond-the-ordinary for His kingdom? There may be times when you would willingly embrace such moments. But there may be other times when you feel afraid. Or frozen by life circumstances. Or locked up by inertia. In other words, I wonder how many of us are a lot like Moses when he heard the voice of his Daddy God speaking from the burning bush.

God gave Moses a clear calling and a plain path toward following that calling. Moses would have the very great honor of traveling back to Egypt, linking up with his brother Aaron, confronting Pharaoh, and then leading the people of Israel out of captivity and into their own promised homeland.

We might like to think that all the great heroes of the faith we read about in the Bible believed and trusted in their God so deeply that they answered His calls without reservation. But it wasn't always like that, even when these men quite literally *heard* the voice of their Daddy God calling them to greatness. Just crack open your Bible to Exodus 3-4 and read about God's call to Moses. When the Lord miraculously appeared to him and told him to "go," Moses hesitated. Instead of eagerly accepting the assignment, he offered up every excuse he could think of to persuade his Daddy God to send someone else:

➢ *I'm not qualified* (Exodus 3:11).
➢ *No one will listen to me* (4:1).
➢ *I'm not a good enough speaker* (4:10).

The Bible tells us that the Lord wasn't happy with Moses (4:14)– in fact He got angry–but at the same time we see God getting upset with His child, Moses, we also see a picture of a heavenly Daddy who remained incredibly patient with His appointed deliverer. God knew exactly what He was doing and exactly who He was choosing. God firmly let Moses know that he was the man He had called. He also let him know that He would always be with him and that He would perform great miracles through Moses, big enough to get the people of Israel out of Egypt and on their way to the Land of Promise.

This story should remind us how intimately our heavenly Daddy knows us. Before He ever appeared to Moses in the burning bush, He knew how He'd wired this man (only the One who so lovingly made us could possibly know us that well). He knew about Moses' shortcomings, about his fears and anxieties, and He knew beforehand that this future man of faith didn't see himself as worthy to follow such an amazing and life-changing path.

Moses' Daddy God is the same Daddy God who loves you today, every bit as deeply as He loved Moses. He has an incredible path mapped out just for you. He recognizes your reluctance and your fears about launching out into the unknown. He knows all about your strengths and weaknesses and that you don't always see yourself the way He sees you.

Have you reached a point in life where you believe God may be calling you to get up and move on to a different place, but you aren't so sure if your earthly circumstances (or your own shortcomings!) will allow it? If you have, then let me suggest something: do what Moses did. Honestly share your concerns, your fears, and your own feelings of unworthiness with your Daddy God.

Your heavenly Daddy is incredibly loving and patient and He wants you to talk with Him about anything troubling your head or your heart. If you come to Him with a heart and a mind truly open to whatever He has in store for you, He'll calm your fears, ease your anxieties, and comfort you with the promise that He'll never leave you to follow your new path on your own.

Provisions for the Journey

As I said earlier, my dad passed away when I was sixteen. He didn't leave me or my siblings with any kind of inheritance, and left my mother with only the small house that we had grown up in, along with the mortgage. I knew from the time I was a teenager that life would be more challenging for me than for some of my friends and acquaintances.

In the years after Dad's death, I got to witness, up close and personal, just how faithful my heavenly Daddy is in fulfilling His promise to *meet all [my] needs according to the riches of his glory in Christ Jesus* (Philippians 4:19). I didn't always know where my Daddy God was taking me in life, at least not very far in advance; but as I look back, I can see how He made sure I had *everything* I needed for *every* step of my journey.

It started with my physical needs. After my Dad's death, I began to receive Social Security benefits, which went a long way toward paying for my university education. I also got hired for several good part-time jobs that helped me pay my bills and college expenses.

I could fill this book with stories of how my Daddy God faithfully provided for my physical needs and for the physical needs of my brothers and sisters in Him. I could recount story after story of how He came through at just the right time to make sure His kids had what they needed in order to continue on in their journeys and get where He wanted them to go.

But as important as the physical provisions are, God doesn't stop there. Not even close! Our heavenly Daddy knows that the path we're on can get pretty bumpy. He knows we'll encounter all sorts of obstacles, some of which might make us feel like reversing course and going back to what we might see as a more comfortable place.

And He's more than happy to provide desperately needed strength and encouragement for our souls and spirits to enable us to continue.

When the Path Gets Rough

My nephew, Ryan, had a vision. He wanted to get a group of guys together and climb Mount Kilimanjaro in Tanzania. Because of the proximity of the Open Arms Village to neighboring Tanzania, the group would come to Kenya and spend a few days serving the children and community around our Village, and then go on to Tanzania for the big climb.

Four men ended up making the trip, including my brother-in-law, Nick. I'd never seen Nick so nervous as he was in the weeks of preparation leading up to the climb. By the time he arrived at Open Arms Village, however, he exuded an air of relaxation and confidence.

After spending almost a whole week with us, the guys took off for their Kilimanjaro adventure. I well remember how I prayed for them at least two or three times during the course of the climb. After it ended, I learned why the guys–and especially Nick–needed those prayers.

The rigorous climb demanded far more of them than they had expected. The thin air caused Nick some serious breathing difficulties. On two nights during the climb, he stayed awake all night, unable to sleep, because he couldn't catch his breath. For the first time in his life, he suffered panic attacks because of his inability to breathe.

As the group neared the summit, something quite unexpected happened. The weather changed, for the worse.

A surprise snowstorm blanketed the top of the mountain, so the four had to alter their course. The new path they took had much more difficult ups and downs than the one they had planned to take. In some places, the path narrowed to as little as eighteen inches wide, with sheer drop-offs of hundreds of feet. A layer of ice on these narrow paths made the climb all the more treacherous and frightening.

Nick later said that on the last night of the ascent, he felt so "done" with the rigors and anxiety of the climb that he seriously considered remaining in his tent while the others climbed on to the summit.

But then he realized that quitting would mean staying behind, by himself, in ten-degree temperatures. He couldn't bear the thought of being left alone–in his mind, left alone to die. So he summoned every bit of strength and courage within himself and then continued on with the others to make the final ascent.

I'm glad to say their adventure had a happy ending. All four climbers safely made it to the summit. I don't doubt they'll be telling their stories for the rest of their lives. But it didn't happen without some angst and drama, without some real scares and opposition.

All four of the men later realized that much of the opposition that threatened to keep them from reaching the top came from inside their own heads. In fact, they realized that nothing they had experienced could have stopped them from making it to the top… except themselves.

It isn't always easy to get where we want to go, and sometimes it's even tougher to get to where our Daddy God wants us to go. The terrain can grow difficult and the climb can become steep, and the weather can change in a blink of an eye. We can feel discouraged and start thinking we'd be better off giving up and reversing course.

But our heavenly Father knows us, and He knows exactly what we need in order to get us where we need to go.

Daddy God is an absolute master at giving us what we need to continue with the journey He has set before us. He will *never* leave us alone to make that journey by ourselves, although quite frankly, it can feel *exactly* as though He does. Regardless of our feelings, He goes with us every step of the way:

- When clouds of fear come, He gives us rays of confidence and reassurance.
- When clouds of nervousness or anxiety come, He gives us rays of peace.
- When clouds of discouragement come, He gives us rays of courage.
- When clouds of sadness come, He gives us rays of joy and happiness.
- When clouds of weakness gather, He gives us rays of strength.
- When clouds of poverty come and we are under-resourced, He gives us glorious rays of provision.
- When clouds of doubt come, He gives us rays of belief in Him and in ourselves.

My Daddy God has given me a picture of how He wants to provide for me as I head wherever He wants me to be. As Belle and Diana's father, I am 100 percent committed to doing everything I can to making sure my girls have everything they need–physically, mentally, and, as far as it depends on me, spiritually–to get where their heavenly Daddy wants to take them in this life.

And I know my Daddy in heaven has the same commitment to me.

But Daddy, It's Dark Out There!

Belle and Diana don't much care for the dark (except when I transform from Dad into the "tickle monster" once the lights go out at night. That can be exciting and a little scary, but in a fun way). I suppose they're like a lot of children. For reasons I mostly understand, kids don't like being in the dark, even when the time comes to go to sleep.

Truth be told, most of us grown-ups don't much like the dark either. At least, we often don't function well in it. Being in the dark disorients us. We can't see where we are and we don't know whether to keep moving forward, turn one direction or the other, turn around and head back where we came from, or just stand still. We can also hurt ourselves in the dark when we trip over unseen obstacles that are in our way.

Our world is filled with darkness–both literal and figurative. And as our Daddy God's children, it's important for us to understand that we will often have to navigate our way through the dark as we follow the path He's laid out for us. To get to where He wants us to go, we often have to travel through some very dark stretches.

Jesus Himself told us to get prepared for the dark, not only because *men loved darkness instead of light, for their deeds were evil* (John 3:19) but because *each day has enough trouble of its own* (Matthew 6:34). So long as we live in these mortal bodies on this fallen and deteriorating planet, we will face dark, difficult times, even when we remain faithfully on the path God has led us to follow.

Many of God's kids struggle to believe that He stays with them during difficult, challenging times. They reason that if God really were with them, especially when they walk the path He's asked them to walk, then they wouldn't or shouldn't have to endure such trying circumstances.

Not so. This is one of those cases where our limited human logic fails us and falls short. The Bible makes it very clear that God's most trusted servants had to walk some pitch-black paths–even Jesus, His own Son. That's why thousands of years ago, Isaiah wrote:

Let the one who walks in the dark, who has no light, trust in the name of the Lord and rely on their God (Isaiah 50:10).

I can't speak for others, but I take great comfort in the fact that my Daddy God has told me ahead of time that I'll face times of darkness. Forewarned, as they say, is forearmed. Since I know I'll face difficulties, I am more likely to prepare for them. But more than that, I think it's because my heavenly Daddy has promised to be with me as I make my way through the darkness. He'll be my eyes when my own can't see anything ahead of me or around me.

Our heavenly Daddy stays right by our side in the darkness, giving us direction, guiding us, and protecting us:

Even though I walk through the darkest valley, I will fear no evil, for you are with me; your rod and your staff, they comfort me (Psalm 23:4). Knowing that my Daddy God will never leave me, not even for a moment, as I walk through life's darkest shadows brings me great peace and assurance. It also continually deposits into my heart and mind a sense of dependency on my Daddy, especially when I have to walk through the most painful and scary times.

With Us for the Distance

Author Kevin Leman tells how his daughter, Hannah, once needed to fly from their summer home in New York State to Tucson, Arizona, where the family spent the school year. Hannah wanted to spend a week with a friend in Tucson before the rest of the family moved back home. But there was a problem. The rest of the family couldn't yet take the trip, and Kevin didn't want his nine-year-old Hannah to fly alone. So here's what he did–in his own words:

When the flight attendant found out what I was doing–spending an entire day flying from Buffalo to Tucson and then immediately back to Buffalo, just to chaperone my daughter–she couldn't believe it. "Why didn't you just put her on the plane?" she asked "We chaperone kids much younger than her all the time. Don't you trust us? We do a good job."

I replied to her, "It's not your job - it's mine."[1]

I can easily identify with Kevin Leman's feelings. As Belle and Diana's daddy, I see it as my job to "travel" with them. I love my daughters deeply, and I'd never think of turning a blind eye or a deaf ear to them. If they need me for direction, I'm there. If they're reaching out for a little physical or emotional support, I'll be reaching back. If they just want someone alongside them to share their journey, I'll do my best to be available.

That's what a loving, caring daddy does.

It's not just my *job* and my *responsibility* to remain available for my daughters on their life journeys; it's something I *want* to do. And it's something I don't want anyone other than me to do. I want them to know that I am with them for the distance, through the difficult times and through the joyous times alike.

We can count on our heavenly Daddy to give us direction and to show us where He wants us to be. And we can count on Him to give us the provisions we need for the journey. But far more than that, we can rely on Him to walk with us every step of the way, regardless of terrain or conditions.

Our Daddy God takes this responsibility *very* seriously. So when He tells us in His life manual, the Bible, that He will "never leave us or forsake us," He means it. He is with us for the distance, whether during the joyful, happy times, or the painful, difficult, challenging times.

In one of the less-quoted books in The Chronicles of Narnia series, C.S. Lewis provides a potent picture of this divine truth. Shasta, the boy in *The Horse and His Boy,* has taken a path that has grown dark, cold, and miserable. He calls himself "the most unfortunate boy that ever lived" and starts crying. In the pitch dark, he can see nothing–and then he hears someone or somebody walking alongside him. He gets the impression it must be some huge beast, which frightens him all the more. At last he learns the beast is a lion, Aslan Himself, a symbolic figure of Christ. The Lion and the boy have a remarkable conversation in the dark, and just as Shasta begins to feel less afraid, Aslan vanishes. And so Shasta finds himself on the desolate road again, heading to...where? He doesn't know. But if the Lion got him there, he figures, it must be all right.

The next day, Shasta gets another surprise. Traveling with a group of friends this time, he finds himself walking gingerly along the edge of a precipice–and realizes with a fright that he had done the same thing the night before without knowing it. *But of course, he thinks, I was quite safe. That is why the Lion kept on my left. He was between me and the edge all the time.*

As you travel your own God-ordained path, the Lord remains between you and the edge all the time. You are quite safe. And He will get you to where you need to go. Every time.

Just ask Him.

Chapter 11

DADDY, WILL YOU HELP ME TO FEEL BETTER?

Like most infants and small children, both Diana and Belle have suffered their fair share of illnesses and health problems. These have ranged from the little colds and cases of the sniffles, all the way up to scary bouts with more-stubborn sicknesses. Diana, for example, once went through an outbreak of painful, itchy, fluid-filled bumps that turned out to be the result of some kind of staph infection. None of us had any fun with that one.

The worst health issue Belle ever faced was truly a nightmare.

No child or parent should ever have to endure it–something far more trying on her mommy and me than anything we could have dreamed. And she suffered with it from the moment she came to live with us.

Belle was born to a nineteen-year-old street girl addicted to alcohol, glue (glue sniffing is the "high" of choice for many street children in various parts of the world), and only-God-knows what else. I highly doubt whether Belle's biological mother gave much thought to what she was doing to the little life growing within her, because she continued using glue throughout her pregnancy.

It had a devastating effect on baby Belle's physical being. Belle was *born* an addict.

If you want a horrifying experience, go watch a drug addict suffer through withdrawals as he or she tries to get "clean." But watching this little girl, just twenty-nine days old when we took her in, go through withdrawals felt horrifying, frightening, and heartrending, all at once. For the first two or three months Belle lived with us, she had to endure awful "episodes" as her little body tried to purify itself from the poison inside. This happened like clockwork, from 5-10 a.m. and from 5-10 p.m. *every day.*

Rachel and I felt a nauseating sense of helplessness as the daily cycles washed over our little girl. We couldn't do much for her in her suffering except be there for her, hold her close, comfort her, and try to reassure her. We did the best we could, for an infant who had no understanding of what convulsed her little body, to show her that she would survive, that her daddy and mommy would stay close, and that she would be okay.

It's hard to describe the pain and anguish I felt as I watched my little girl suffer the way she did.

But let me add something else to that statement: it's just as difficult to describe the joy I felt at the privilege of being the one who got to embrace her during those awful times. As wrenching as it felt to watch her writhe and convulse in pain, I also experienced a profound sense of my fatherly calling in those moments.

As trying as caring for sick children can be, Rachel and I do it for the simple reason that we love our daughters, and because that is what loving mommies and daddies do.

And it's what our all-loving Daddy God does for His kids too.

When I think about how much my wife and daughters need me when they don't feel well, I'm reminded of how much we all need our heavenly Daddy when we're suffering and sick, whether physically, emotionally, or spiritually. And I also think about how committed He is to coming to the aid of His children whenever they suffer. Rachel and I would never stand idly by while our girls suffer, muttering to ourselves, "Boy, we sure do hope they get better."

Daddy God doesn't do that either.

Daddy God's Heart for the Sick
As a loving daddy who hates seeing his loved ones sick and

suffering, I think I have some understanding—limited as it may be—of my Daddy God's heart of compassion for His kids when they suffer with disease and sickness.

Your Daddy in heaven knows when you don't feel well. He knows when you feel sick or weak, and He knows when you fall behind mentally, emotionally, or spiritually. He knows, and He is able and eager to reach down to you and comfort you in your suffering. He wants to place His healing hand on you to make you feel better.

I'm so thankful that our Daddy God has not left us without a clue as to how He feels about us when we don't feel well. And that He hasn't left us without a glimpse into His caring heart for our suffering. Would you like to see your Daddy God's heart for His children's sickness and pain, for *your* sickness and pain? Then take a look at what His Son, Jesus, came to do as He revealed His Daddy in heaven to humanity:

Jesus went through all the towns and villages, teaching in their synagogues, proclaiming the good news of the kingdom and healing every disease and sickness. When he saw the crowds, he had compassion on them, because they were harassed and helpless, like sheep without a shepherd (Matthew 9:35-36).

You might have reached a point in your life where you need to make a fundamental decision about what you believe about your heavenly Daddy. Do you believe in a detached Creator, a god who made you and more or less meets your physical needs, but is somehow not terribly concerned with how you've felt lately? Or do you believe in a loving, concerned Father in heaven, a God who loves you as His very own child and who is deeply, passionately concerned with what's going on in your body, in your mind, and in your emotions?

I have chosen, with absolute assurance, option number two.

Just believe it: your Daddy God not only *can* heal you and make you feel better, but also He *wants* to do it. I know I believe this, and it's not only because my Father in heaven has told me so in His

Word, the Bible. It's also because I've experienced it in a very real and personal way.

He hasn't just told me; He has *shown* me.

Miracles of Physical Healing

I will never forget that first time we brought Belle to the United States. The memory of that trip remains burned into my mind but not just because of the joy we felt in giving our loved ones a chance to meet our daughter, hold her, and hug her. I'll also never forget it because of the wrenchingly difficult period we had to endure while we were there.

We had been in the U.S. about a week when our phone rang one night around 10:30 p.m. My best friend, Matt Tallman, was calling me from Kenya. Matt and his wife, Cheryl, had chosen to give one year of their time to serve with Open Arms. Matt haltingly told me that they had gotten some very bad news that day about Belle's recent blood test, performed at Moi Referral Hospital in Eldoret.

The test showed that our little girl was HIV positive.

I can't adequately describe the feelings that washed over me when I heard the phrase "HIV positive." It felt alien, surreal, like a horrible dream. I just couldn't process what I'd heard. *It can't be true,* I thought.

In reality, though, I just didn't want it to be true. I couldn't bear the thought of my little girl beginning her life saddled with such a cruel illness. *Belle already has been through so much in her young life,* I thought, *and now this?*

And yet, at the same time, I knew that this horrible disease was a terrible reality for far too many children born in Kenya. I had to face the awful possibility that Belle, born to a drug-addicted street mom and who had spent her first twenty-nine days living on the mean streets where AIDS is a terrible reality, was indeed HIV positive.

Of course, we wanted a second opinion, so we called our friend, Dean Moshofsky, a Portland, Oregon-area pediatrician. We asked him if he could make arrangements for Belle to get tested in the U.S. Dean quickly got us a referral to Providence St. Vincent Medical Center, near our home, and we took Belle in for her tests.

Over an excruciatingly difficult nine days, we spent more time than ever before praying over our little one and asking God to heal her. We wanted nothing, absolutely nothing, *more than for Belle to receive a clean bill of health.*

Finally, after what seemed like an eternity, Dean called. When we heard his voice greeting us, we each took a deep breath and put ourselves through a quick final preparation for the news. Prepared for the worst and hoping for the best, we listened intently as he began reciting the test results: "David and Rachel, the lab tests indicate that Belle is HIV negative. There is no sign of the HIV virus."

Instantly, overwhelming joy and excitement poured over our souls, mixed with deep relief. We praised our Daddy God's name and we thanked Him for the test results, and for what we saw as an example of miracle healing.

To this day, Rachel and I remain convinced that we, and Belle, experienced an incredible miracle, straight from the hand of our loving heavenly Daddy. We believe that God laid His healing hand on our daughter and reversed Belle's HIV status.

Skeptics, especially those from the West, might say, "I'm glad you got your good news, but more than likely, the test done in Kenya was simply faulty. The doctors there just got it wrong."

I fully understand such skepticism. I've spent enough time in Kenya to know about the inadequacies of the health care system there. At the same time, however, I know that the western-funded and managed HIV/AIDS program in Eldoret, where Belle got her first lab test, is highly respected. Tests from the AMPATH labs, founded and overseen by Dr. Joe Mamlin from Indiana University, have been consistently reliable.

I choose to be a believer rather than a doubter and a skeptic. Because I believe in my Daddy God in heaven, and because I know that He loves me and my family and hears my prayers, I am convinced that He intervened on our behalf and did what even the best doctors and facilities in modern medicine could not do.

After reading about Belle's brush with HIV, you may think, *It's great that God healed your little girl, David, and I'm happy for you and for her. But I've been sick for years, and God hasn't healed me. Does that mean He doesn't care about me as much as He cares about your daughter?*

The quick and entirely true answer to the question is, "Absolutely not!" Your Daddy in heaven loves you with all His heart, and He knows and cares about the fact that you don't feel well. He knows and cares about your suffering. And He will, at exactly the right time, do something about it. In the meantime, though, choose to be a believer and not a skeptic–even in your suffering. And trust your Daddy God that He knows what He's doing and when He's doing it. You may get the taste of heaven on earth or it's possible that you'll get the taste of heaven in heaven. Either way, remember that heaven–and healing–is coming. Your Daddy God will see to it.

Waiting for Daddy God's Healing Touch

A dear friend of ours named Tara Lepp works with us at the Open Arms Village. She also has an amazing story of receiving the touch of her Daddy God's healing hand.

Beginning in 1987, Tara began suffering from a terrible illness that went undiagnosed for more than two years. She suffered from severe fatigue and at one point spent four days in a hospital, undergoing tests for seizures. In addition to the extreme fatigue, weakness, and seizures, she suffered intense pain throughout her body, as well as vertigo and double vision. That made walking so difficult that she had to use a cane just to keep her balance. For an entire month she lay bedridden.

Several times, doctors thought they had diagnosed Tara's illness, but each time, the diagnoses turned out to be incorrect. Then, on October 3, 1989, after visiting with a specialist, she got the correct diagnosis: multiple sclerosis, an incurable neurological disease.

Tara's debilitating battle with MS lasted approximately seven years. In the fall of 1991, she faced a tough decision: return to work or lose her job. Tara couldn't afford to be unemployed, but she also lacked the physical ability to work full time. She soon reached a point of desperation and did what she had done from the beginning of her challenges: she cried out to her Daddy God for help.

Leaders at her church anointed Tara with oil and prayed for her, while friends from around the world also prayed for her. Those praying friends included someone who also had been diagnosed with MS, but who had been miraculously healed.

Tara did not receive an instantaneous healing; the process occurred over several years. But in His perfect (albeit sometimes incomprehensible) timing, Tara's Daddy God touched and healed her body.

Today, many years since her illness, Tara remains healthy and is doing great. She spends six months out of every year living in Kenya, working with us at the Open Arms Village. To this day, Tara says with certainty that her Daddy God miraculously healed her and restored her.

And I, for one, believe her–and heartily agree with her.

Does this happen all the time? I wish it did, but I know it doesn't. I don't believe that God *always* heals us (at least, in the here and now), any more than I believe that our Daddy in heaven never miraculously heals the sick and hurting. The last thing I want to do is raise false hopes. But I do want to raise real hope in the truth that nothing is impossible for God. And I know that my Daddy God loves to bring hope to people who don't have any hope.

But what about those times when we cry out to God for physical healing, and don't get well? We've prayed fervently and unceasingly for our Daddy God to heal us, and our friends and loved ones have faithfully supported us and interceded for us. But after weeks, months, or even years of reaching out to our heavenly Daddy, we still struggle with the same physical problem. Many of us have had to wrestle with exactly that kind of tough reality.

I've known many precious believers in the Lord whose prayers for healing got answered, sometimes immediately, sometimes over an extended period of time. But I've also known many others whose prayers for healing seemed completely fruitless. They continued on in their physical pain and sickness, and in the midst of their suffering, they began asking the obvious question: *Why doesn't God heal me, right here and right now?*

I don't have an ironclad answer for those kinds of questions. I honestly don't know why God sometimes instantly delivers His children from their pain and suffering, while at other times He seems to wait...if He heals them at all in this life.

I do remember that Jesus once got in big trouble with the people of His hometown when they insisted that He heal the sick of their community, just as they'd heard He'd done with the suffering residents of Capernaum. Do you know what He told them that got them so angry? He said to them: *There were many in Israel with leprosy in the time of Elisha the prophet, yet not one of them was cleansed—only Naaman the Syrian* (Luke 4:27). He didn't try to explain it. He just said it. And Luke tells us that the enraged crowd tried to throw Him off a cliff.

I don't know why God sometimes heals and sometimes doesn't, but I do know this: our Daddy God loves us more deeply than we can possibly imagine, and He has promised that He will heal us, that one day He will make us completely whole. God has promised that all sickness, and the pain and suffering that comes with it, will someday have no part in His children's lives.

The apostle John, in his vision of the end times in the book of Revelation, wrote: *And I heard a loud voice from the throne saying, "Look! God's dwelling place is now among the people, and he will dwell with them. They will be his people, and God himself will be with them and be their God. He will wipe every tear from their eyes. There will be no more death or mourning or crying or pain, for the old order of things has passed away"* (Revelation 21:3-4).

Whether you are six or sixty, whether your most major health challenge is a sniffle or some terrible form of cancer, when you know your Daddy God, you also know that one day you'll be all better. The day is coming when everything about you–your physical body, your mind and emotions, and your eternal spirit–will be made healthy and right. Once and for all. Forever.

In Kenya, on the wall in the entry to the local government hospital, you will find this saying, "Doctors Treat but God Heals." You may receive your healing in the here and now through the hands of some of God's most gifted servants, doctors, and nurses. Or you may receive it through a direct, supernatural touch from your Daddy God Himself. But even if your body is not healed and made whole in the here-and-now, take comfort in knowing that it will happen when you enter God's eternal kingdom.

He Knows and He Cares

I also know another thing about our heavenly Daddy: He knows when we're hurting physically, mentally, emotionally, or spiritually. And though His healing may not come exactly when we want it to or even how we want it to, we can cry out to Him at all times, knowing that He hears our prayers and sees our tears.

And like any great daddy, He loves wiping those tears away and comforting us in the midst of our suffering.

Whether our greatest source of discomfort comes from physical, emotional, or spiritual sickness, the one thing we all desperately want and need is our Daddy God's comfort in our affliction. And that's exactly what He promises us:

Praise be to the God and Father of our Lord Jesus Christ, the Father of compassion and the God of all comfort, who comforts us in all our troubles, so that we can comfort those in any trouble with the comfort we ourselves receive from God (2 Corinthians 1:3-4).

Whatever the span of time between your suffering and your healing–no matter how long it is–don't believe for one minute that your Daddy God doesn't care about you. He remains present and attentive–caring for you and holding you in your suffering– just like I did for my little girl when she suffered through her withdrawals.

Where are you hurting? Is there some disease or injury that seems to consume your entire being?

Believe that your Daddy *can* make you feel better and wants to make you feel better. And ask Him to comfort you in your suffering.

Comfort for Your Mind and Emotions

By now you know that I didn't grow up in the happiest of homes.

My parents didn't get along well and oftentimes engaged in some ugly verbal altercations. I remember it as if it happened only yesterday, hearing the awful shouts of my parents as they yelled at one another in their bedroom. Sometimes, my brother and two sisters and I would sit or lie down on the floor outside their bedroom door and listen to their arguments.

I hated hearing my mom and dad fight. It caused my stomach to churn and tie up in knots, out of fear for what might happen next. And I know my siblings felt the same way.

Many children grow up with far worse than that, I know. We could all tell a few stories, couldn't we? It's a heartbreaking reality that many children today carry painful emotional and mental scars due to terrible things they had no choice in or control over. More children than we'd like to believe have their tummies tied up in knots and their souls traumatized because:

- ➢ A family member or friend touched them inappropriately.
- ➢ They grew up not knowing where they would get their next meal.
- ➢ Either their mom or dad, or maybe both, went AWOL from their lives.

> When they returned home from school, their mom or dad, maybe under the influence of drugs or alcohol, would heap verbal or physical abuse on them.

As I have already noted, my own early home life left me with wounds that I carried into adulthood, wounds that my Daddy God has worked with me over the years to heal. Over time, He's brought me to wholeness.

Sadly, trauma to one's soul doesn't occur only during childhood. Many adults feel their stomachs getting tied up in knots and their souls traumatized because:

> Someone they love has abandoned them or been unfaithful.
> They don't know how to make their unhappy marriage any better.
> They've lost a job and don't know how to provide for their family.
> They have a serious ailment and doctors can't do anything to help them.
> They, or someone they love, is physically impaired, injured, or disabled.
> A fire or natural disaster has ruined their home and destroyed their worldly possessions.

In and of themselves, emotional trauma and sickness can feel agonizing. But if those ailments don't get healed, if they don't get dealt with effectively, they can negatively affect other aspects of our being. They can lead to any number of physical problems (high blood pressure, heart problems…it's a long list), and they can lead to spiritual problems that can impair our ability to relate properly to our Daddy God and to other individuals.

Your Daddy God knows all too well how bad things can get for us emotionally and mentally.

Elijah, in 1 Kings chapter 19, was literally running for his life. Eventually exhausted, he crawled under a scrawny tree in the desert and told God he'd had enough, and he asked God to take his life, right there on the spot. Have you ever come to the place where you just didn't think you could go on any farther? Where things looked so bleak that you just wanted it all to end? God knows.

Here's what He did for Elijah, because He knew that His discouraged servant wasn't finished with his earthly assignment. An angel touched him and told him to get up and eat for food had been prepared for him.

The angel said to Elijah, "Get up and eat, for the journey is too much for you." So he got up and ate and drank. Strengthened by that food, he traveled on (verses 7-8).

And God will do the same thing for you. He knows when your journey has become too much.

He knows exactly what you need to give you the strength to keep going.

Let's get personal for a moment. You know you're not at your best when you feel stressed, heartbroken, worried, or hurting. You know that those emotional and mental hurts affect your body, your relationships, and the way you see your relationship with your Daddy in heaven.

I want to assure you that your Daddy God cares about your emotional and mental health. I want you to know that your Father in heaven wants you to be at your very best. He knows about your anxieties, fears, and heartbreaks, and He cares. And while He uses wise and learned men and women to help individuals suffering from damaged emotions and minds move toward inner peace, He also promises to *personally* walk with you through all the life-rattling trenches that leave you feeling as though you just can't go on.

Earlier I quoted Psalm 23, one of the most amazing promises in the Bible to God's kids, reminding them where to find inner peace as they make their way through their sometimes-difficult lives. I think it bears repeating here:

> *The Lord is my shepherd; I shall not want.*
> *He makes me to lie down in green pastures;*
> *He leads me beside the still waters.*
> *He restores my soul;*
> *He leads me in the paths of righteousness*
> *for His name's sake.*
> (Psalm 23:1-3 NKJV)

Our heavenly Daddy gave us these words of comfort because He wants us to know that He cares when life throws more at us than we can handle. He knows that our souls can get so down that we begin running on fumes. And He promises to walk with us through even the worst difficulties, as well as their emotional and mental aftermath, and to fill us up again. He promises, in other words, to restore our souls.

Healing for Spiritual "Sickness"

As I've looked back on my life, I've concluded that I have a gift for "making the deal." I just seem to have a bent and something of a passion, for buying and selling things and making a profit doing it.

This ability became clear even as a young boy. I loved bartering, trading, buying, and selling, and my friends became my best "customers." When I was around ten years old, my mother caught me (yes, caught–I distinctly remember that I didn't want her to know I was doing it) selling my toys to the neighborhood kids out of my bedroom window. I don't remember the aftermath–I'm sure I blocked the painful consequences out of my mind–but my siblings tell me that Mom made me go back through the whole neighborhood to collect my toys and offer "refunds." Knowing myself as I do, I don't doubt that I hated breaking the deals I'd made.

My ability and love for wheeling and dealing followed me into adulthood. I'd buy things at what looked like a bargain price, and then sell them for several times more than what I paid for them. Over time, my success fueled my passion. In my free time, all I could think about was going out and buying stuff to resell. Over time, this hobby became more of an obsession than a nice pastime.

Eventually, I realized my buying and selling had gotten out of control. I never spent money I didn't have, so thankfully, I stayed out of financial trouble. But my desire to buy and sell gripped my heart, and thus my attention, and became the most important thing in the world to me. My relationships with people started to suffer, because rather than spending time with them, I was out hunting for the next great bargain. But worse than that, my relationship with my Daddy in heaven suffered because I didn't have as much time for Him as I used to.

Please don't misunderstand. God created us to live on this planet, and part of that life includes work. There is nothing wrong with buying and selling things to earn money. If you can buy low and sell high, more power to you. But it becomes a serious problem—a spiritual disease, really—when you allow your work or passion to control you or to master your heart. When anything controls you more than you control it, it indicates a serious problem. At that point, it morphs into a spiritual sickness that needs a healing touch from your Daddy God.

When we so focus on our work, whether it's our day job or our off-hours hobby, that we lose sight of heaven and our Daddy God who lives there, then we become distracted from what He says is important.

And when that happens, our point of focus becomes an idol. We trade life for death.

My obsession with buying and selling became a spiritual sickness that was damaging my soul.

Of course, this is nothing new. It's been happening since the dawn of time. King David, who had his own seasons of spiritual sickness, wrote of how his transgressions against God made him physically sick and weak:

> My wounds fester and are loathsome because of my sinful folly.
> I am bowed down and brought very low;
> all day long I go about mourning.
> My back is filled with searing pain;
> there is no health in my body.
> I am feeble and utterly crushed;
> I groan in anguish of heart.
> (Psalm 38:5-8)

Most of us probably don't feel our spiritual illness as acutely as David did; but when we realize that something in our lives doesn't please our Daddy God, we should certainly sense something out of balance. We know we're not well, that something has gone missing between ourselves and our heavenly Dad.

The apostle Paul in Galatians 5:19-21 lists some areas in people's lives that point to spiritual sickness. He mentions several sins, including sexual immorality, idolatry, hatred, jealousy, fits of anger, selfish ambition, and drunkenness.

Let's refer to the sins in Paul's list as "symptoms" of spiritual sickness. When one of Daddy God's kids engages in any of these behaviors or thought patterns (there are many more; we're very creative in how we sin), then that person gets sick spiritually and needs God's forgiveness, cleansing, and healing.

Has your Daddy God recently brought to your attention an area in your life which needs His touch…His correction…His discipline? Or have you known for months, maybe even years, that some kind of sickness within you requires the cleansing and healing of your Daddy in heaven?

If you and I knew each other better, and you were to sit down with me and confess those areas of your life, I'd be honest with you.

I'd affirm what God's written Word tells us, that you need God to heal you and forgive you and remove those things from your life. But here's what I wouldn't do. I wouldn't get in your face, judge you, or write you off as a hell-bound sinner.

Your Daddy God won't do that, either.

If you are allowing a distance to grow between you and God, He will let you know—and He has a million ways to do it. If you are falling short or veering off onto a wrong, destructive path, He will let you know that, too, and seek to bring you back. But at the same time, He also reminds *all* His kids that *there is now no condemnation for those who are in Christ Jesus, because through Christ Jesus the law of the Spirit who gives life has set you free from the law of sin and death* (Romans 8:1-2).

When your Daddy God comes to you and lets you know that you have a sickness in one or more areas in your life, He does so because He loves you and wants to make you completely well. He doesn't want anything to control you or to cause even the smallest separation from Himself. To make sure that you are pure, clean, and spiritually healthy, He'll go to almost any lengths.

As a daddy who would do anything I possibly can to make my wife and daughters well when they feel sick, I get that. I love my wife and kids more than I can put into words—and my attention never gets more focused on them than when they become physically, emotionally, or spiritually sick. And there is nothing I wouldn't do to see them healed and well.

There are limits, however, on what I can do to help. But my Daddy God has no such limits.

He isn't bound by any kind of limitations. And not only that, but He's made a way for every one of His children to enjoy a lifetime of spiritual health.

Time to Get Spiritually Healthy

How do we get spiritually healthy? How can we get rid of the loathsome diseases that keep us spiritually enslaved? These questions lead us back to Jesus, our Daddy God in the flesh.

Don't they always?

God has given us eternal life and forgiveness through Jesus Christ, who gives us life and has set us free from the law of sin and death (Romans 8:2).

The apostle Peter pointed toward our Daddy God's ability and desire to heal us spiritually when he said, *God anointed Jesus of Nazareth with the Holy Spirit and power,* enabling Him to go *around doing good and healing all who were under the power of the devil, because God was with him* (Acts 10:38).

When you realize that you have some kind of spiritual illness, remember that your Daddy God has already given you everything–everything–you need to make you well. Run to Him. Get into His presence, knowing that He knows you, loves you, and wants you to be 100 percent whole.

Chapter 12

DADDY, I'M GROWING AND CHANGING; WILL YOU HELP ME THROUGH THE CHANGES?

As a twelve-year-old, I felt very excited about rising through the ranks of the Boy Scouts. I loved Scouting because it taught me (and so many other young men) all kinds of life skills with countless life applications.

Each new skill required a Scout to master some regimen of tasks, just to show himself worthy of a glorious merit badge, the symbol of being tested and proven. Earning each new merit badge felt like an adventure, in and of itself. Some badges came easy; others took far more time and effort.

One vivid memory from my Boy Scout days really stands out. I had worked hard to earn what is now called the Wilderness Survival merit badge. Earning that badge meant going out into the great outdoors and "surviving" by subsisting on whatever nourishment nature could provide. You had to be able to demonstrate that you had the requisite skills to survive on what nature alone could provide in the way of food, water, and protection from the elements.

My buddy Wade and I together tackled a portion of the merit badge requirements on the fringe of a small wooded area adjoining land belonging to Alpenrose Dairy in Portland, Oregon. Our "guide" for this experience, and the one who would administer the test of skills for the merit badge, was Wade's Dad, Warren, an assistant Scoutmaster.

I remember it as though it happened yesterday–pulling moss off trees, boiling it, and eating it. Who knew you could actually eat that stuff? But before we could dine on the amazing natural bounty we found, we had to build a fire.

And on that part of the adventure, I fell miserably short.

When the time came to build the campfire so we could boil water and eat the moss, Warren handed Wade and me our quota of two matches apiece. That was it. If we didn't get our fire going with our pair of matches, we would disqualify ourselves for the day and would have to repeat the exercise at another time.

Those who have camped in the western part of the Pacific Northwest might guess one of the biggest obstacles to getting a campfire started: the weather. Wind and rain love western Oregon, year round, and this day was no exception.

I carefully but purposefully lit my first match, doing my best to protect the small flame from the elements. But almost as if the wind and rain had deliberately conspired against me, *Whoosh!* a small gust of wind–nothing more than a puff of air, really–almost immediately blew out the match. Now I had just one match left. "Oh boy," I thought. "My odds of succeeding have just dropped by 50 percent. Now it's all or nothing with just one chance left." All I could hear playing in my head was "Come On Baby Light My Fire." With no margin for error, I proceeded carefully.

I struck the second match and watched it ignite beautifully. Feeling a rush of confidence, I leaned down to light the kindling I had so carefully cut and arranged. And then it happened again. *Whoosh!*

Seemingly out of nowhere, another puff of wind extinguished both my little flame and, it seemed, my chances at earning the coveted merit badge. It almost felt as if the wind and rain were laughing at me.

I felt utterly dejected and defeated, and it seemed like the "survival" part of the experience had turned into "dying." Neither

Wade nor I were in any real physical danger that day, of course, but my spirit had wilted in the dampness of the day.

Warren saw the look of despair and despondency all over my face and refused to let it win. He decided, right then and there, to help me, regardless of the rule book.

Warren looked both ways and over his shoulders to make sure he saw no unfriendly eyes. Then, with one smooth stroke of his hand, he reached inside his jacket pocket and brought out a lighter. He handed it to me and said quietly, "Get your fire going." One quick click, and a flame leaped up that even the cockiest, most determined puff of wind couldn't blow out. I leaned down, got a couple of pieces of kindling ablaze, and soon had my fire.

My campfire experience was one of my earliest glimpses into the nature and character of my Daddy God. Through Warren, I learned something new. As a growing young man, I had begun learning how to survive in the wilderness. Unfortunately, my first test hadn't gone well. It would have ended miserably had I not received outside help from someone older, more experienced, and better equipped than I was to handle the cold and rain. I learned an important lesson that day about my Scoutmaster and his unwillingness to see a young man's hope extinguished along with two smoldering matches–and about the grace of God.

I think it's safe to say that all of God's kids have encountered life experiences that have the potential to teach us something important, something that can cause us to change and grow in a positive way. And I also think it's safe to say that all of us have blown opportunities for growth and learning, or have seen them get blown away by outside forces–like the wind on my matches. We tend to think, *All is lost! I've wasted my opportunity!*

That's when our Daddy God comes through for us, giving us what we need to change and grow into what He has made us to be.

Over the years, my Daddy God has used many life experiences to teach me important things about Himself. Sometimes I learn those lessons on the spot, but at other times He reveals some important truth about Himself only in hindsight. But however He does it, He reminds me that all is *not* lost. He knows where the hidden lighters are, and He sends the Warrens of this world to deliver them, just when I need them most.

No matter what kind of lessons or change or growth our Daddy God takes us through, He'll never abandon us to go it alone. He'll always give us whatever we need to get us to the next crucial stage in our growth.

Too windy? Too rainy? No problem for Him. He always knows when two matches just won't be enough.

In Times of Change

I'll never lose my amazement at how my daughters change as they grow. As they've grown from infancy to childhood, we've had to transition from feeding them formula to feeding them solid food. Part of that transition required them to learn how to feed themselves…a sometimes entertaining and most often messy change.

The most readily visible change in my daughters, of course, has been their physical growth. It has been a joy for me to see them grow bigger–and it amazes me that they do it so fast! Rachel and I regularly need to shop for clothes and shoes because the girls outgrow the old ones so quickly. I know that they will continue to grow physically, so I know–especially with two girls–that we have many shopping trips in our future!

Of course, Mommy and Daddy will play another big part in their girls' growth in that we will continue to teach them to do things they don't yet know how to do, just as we've already taught them. I'm talking basics-of-life stuff here, such as eating and going to the bathroom.

The "potty training," as we call it, started when Belle was two-and-a-half years old and for Diana when she came into our home when she was three years old. While the adventures of potty training were fairly involved and a sometimes messy part of raising our daughters, it also marked positive change, both for them and for Mommy and Daddy.

If you're not a parent, you may not get this, but something as basic as potty training represented an exciting time of change for Belle and Diana–and for Rachel and me. Over time, and with some patient teaching, they grew in confidence as they discovered they could go to the bathroom on their own. They didn't need our help! Rachel and I considered it a positive change: no more diaper changing and no more having to help out our daughters every time they needed to use the toilet. That's worth a "Hallelujah!"

Though some of the changes in our growing daughters can be a bit unpleasant, Rachel and I both take great joy at the privilege of being there to help our girls do things they can't do for themselves. We love teaching them new things they otherwise wouldn't know.

As I've navigated through some of the changes I've personally gone through over the years– some exciting and enjoyable, others harder to handle or even painful–I've learned that my Daddy God wants to play the pivotal part of being my source of comfort, wisdom, and teaching. Just as I *want* to be the one to help my daughters through their times of change, so my Father in heaven *wants* to be the One who helps me navigate through my own seasons of change.

The Pitfalls of "Good" Change

My longtime pastor, Ron Mehl, was an amazing man. Pastor Ron passed away in the spring of 2003 after a long battle with leukemia, a much longer fight than any of his doctors expected. Though Ron took possession of his eternal home more than a decade ago, I still remember so many lessons I learned from him. One of those lessons involved knowing how to handle success and God's many blessings.

Positive changes can bring some happy, desirable elements into life. These include enhanced self-esteem, greater confidence and optimism, and stronger faith in our Daddy God's trustworthiness. But if we're not careful, these kinds of changes can also challenge our humility and give us an out-of-balance sense of self-importance.

We've all heard it said of this or that man or woman that success has "gone to his/her head." I know of many people who failed to keep their heads out of the clouds and their feet on the ground simply because they lost sight of the Source of their success. Their failure to remember Him allowed them to somehow see themselves as exalted and overly important. They forgot the apostle Paul's pointed question: *For who makes you different from anyone else? What do you have that you did not receive? And if you did receive it, why do you boast as though you did not?* (1 Corinthians 4:7).

I think success should put people on their knees–filling them with humility and gratitude toward God and toward those who contributed to their success. When you refuse to take all of the credit for success and positive changes in your life, you will feel very uncomfortable standing too long in the spotlight. When you're on your knees in humility before God, it's easier to keep your head out of the clouds and your feet on the ground. In fact, it's really tough to kneel and *not* keep your feet firmly on the ground.

That didn't ever seem to be an issue for Pastor Ron. I remember seeing a small sign prominently displayed on his desk that bore just one word. It faced him, to serve as a reminder of what God wanted him to be about: *Others*. Ron likely would have told anyone who listened that he needed that daily reminder. He wanted to remember that the work he did was about God and others and not about him or his own personal success.

Over the thirty years he served as its senior pastor, Beaverton Foursquare Church (Beaverton is a suburb to the west of Portland, Oregon) grew from a congregation of dozens to one of more than 6,000 (not including children in Sunday School!). That kind of growth certainly qualifies as a success and as a mightily positive change in ministry. But Pastor Ron never allowed the church's growth to go to his head. In fact, he once had the opportunity to take his citywide radio program national. After thinking and praying about the offer, he decided against it; not because he believed a national radio program would fail, but because he believed his show should be heard only in the area where his church was located. He believed it should be broadcast in the geographic area of his pastoral calling and where people could easily attend his church.

Pastor Ron never allowed his success to go to his head. Instead, he allowed it to drive him to his knees. And from that posture, he could listen well as his Daddy God reminded him, over and over again, that the positive changes he saw through his work weren't about his personal success or accolades. Much to the contrary, they were about giving his Daddy God the credit and about serving Him and others.

Human nature being what it is, Pastor Ron stood out to me as an exceptional example of being wisely circumspect about the good and desirable changes God brings into our lives. It seems like a paradox, but even the very best blessing we receive from our Daddy in heaven can, if we're not careful, lead us to places we shouldn't go and into thinking thoughts that we should never entertain.

The "good" things that happen to us come with their own special set of challenges, don't they? If you want a biblical example, then take a look at the life of Saul, Israel's first monarch.

When the prophet Samuel informed Saul that God had chosen him to serve as Israel's king, Saul responded with what looked like the requisite humility: *But am I not a Benjamite, from the smallest tribe of Israel, and is not my clan the least of all the clans of the tribe of Benjamin? Why do you say such a thing to me?* (1 Samuel 9:21)

Saul started his reign spectacularly; but over time, human pride replaced dependence on God, and he placed his confidence in himself and not in his Daddy in heaven. He committed a series of terrible blunders, starting with overstepping his God-ordained bounds by doing Samuel's priestly job of offering a sacrifice to the Lord.

Together, those missteps led to one of the most tragic downfalls recorded in Scripture. Saul, once small in his own eyes (1 Samuel 15:17), allowed his regal position, authority, and wealth to cause him to see himself as something much bigger than God intended. And the bigger he became in his own eyes, the harder he fell.

And his fall was truly terrible.

Most of us find it easy to look down on an individual like Saul. We somehow assume that if our Daddy God were to appoint us to some high position or give us great success in our work, that we'd somehow naturally remain humble and give Him all the credit. But let's not fool ourselves! We're all fallen humans, prone to seeing ourselves in a flattering (but unrealistic) light when those "good" changes bless us. We become self-sufficient and overly self-confident, coming to believe we can handle everything by ourselves.

Our Daddy God has given us an antidote for this kind of poisonous thinking, a good medicine that my late pastor and good friend Ron Mehl often took: going straight to our knees before our Daddy God when He blesses us with success, thanking Him for His grace and mercy, and asking Him to remind us that it's all about Him, not us. It's about giving our Father in heaven all the credit and speaking and thinking in a way that demonstrates true humility and gratitude. And it's about filling our eyes not with ourselves, but with our Daddy God and with the people He's placed in our lives. It's always about *others: God and the people He has placed in our lives.*

Changes Caused by Difficulty

The challenges that success and other good life changes present us can look fairly subtle. We have to remain on the lookout so we can meet those challenges.

But what about changes that come to us through difficult, even awful, life events? Those aren't so subtle, are they? No one needs to tell you that the difficulty you're facing–the loss of a loved one, the loss of your physical health, a divorce or other broken relationship, the loss of a job or your investments—represents a massive, unwelcome change.

My life, no doubt like yours, can be defined in part as a series of changes, some of them good and welcome and some of them difficult and hard to take. And I can tell you with confidence that my Daddy God has been there for me through every change I've experienced. He's kept me humble (balanced and "low") when good times have me on a high, and He's kept me "up" when life has has thrown me the proverbial curve ball and has knocked me into the pit(s).

Let me return to the story of the failed television production company I started back in the 1990s. Remember that I had worked extremely hard for seven years before the funding suddenly dried up and the company shut down. And as if the death of that cherished dream weren't difficult enough, several months later, newly married and needing income, I found myself digging trenches on a construction site in 95-degree weather…for $12 an hour.

I didn't enjoy that change, not even remotely. It's one thing to be between ventures; it's quite another when necessity forces you to abandon your education and long-honed skills in order to do something very different. In my case "something very different" involved using a shovel and my two hands in order to get by. Here I was, a college-educated man, a few months from turning forty–and I had to use my education and training to cover myself with dirt and sweat, digging ditches? Not fair! Not right! Not a good use of my talents!

Then came that 95-degree day, when I stopped my digging for a moment, lifted my eyes toward heaven, and said, "God, what am I doing here?"

I will always remember His answer. As soon as the words left my lips, I heard His words in my heart. *David, you are exactly where I want you to be. Rest in that. And I'm proud of you.*

That was all I needed to hear from my Daddy in heaven. Suddenly, it was all okay. I was still standing in a trench in the beating sun with a shovel in my blistered hands, but that was all right. An incredible peace poured over me, because I knew that—in that moment—I was exactly where I was supposed to be.

God hadn't abandoned me or stopped caring, and all my training and education for "bigger things" hadn't been a waste of time and money. Life didn't make a lot of logical sense at that moment, but I knew beyond any doubt that my Daddy God still cared about me and about where my life was going.

And I knew He had a plan for me. What that plan might be, I had no clue. But I knew it existed and would be revealed at the right time.

In hindsight, I can see that God really did have me right where He wanted me in that difficult season of life. He had me in a place where I could show Him, and myself, that I was serious when I said I'd follow Him anywhere. He put me in the same place He put Abraham when He commanded him to sacrifice his long-awaited son of promise, Isaac (Genesis 22). He seemed to be asking me, *David, will you really follow Me anywhere I lead you and do whatever I ask you to do, even if it means changes you don't understand or enjoy?*

"Yes, God," I answered. "I'll follow You anywhere You lead me and do anything You ask me to do." I meant it. But it still wasn't easy.

Following our Daddy God's lead is often far from easy. It can be especially difficult when we go through unpleasant changes. These times can push us out of our comfort zones and force us to rely completely on Him, where before, just maybe, we still had a bit of self-dependency in us. These times can even cause us to question His love and devotion to us and make us wonder, if He loves us so much, how He has allowed life to become so hard.

A lot of Daddy God's kids seem to have missed this: He never promised us easy lives. He never guaranteed smooth, daisy-lined pathways through our years on earth. In fact, He promises quite the opposite.

When Jesus gave Peter a glimpse into his future, the snapshot didn't conjure up a lot of pleasant images (John 21:18-21). Peter wouldn't be retiring in some quiet Mediterranean villa to raise geraniums. On the contrary, it called for some changes far more difficult than I faced when my production company folded. Jesus told the apostle that when he grew old, others would take him where he would not want to go. They would control his earthly destiny, even down to the clothes he would have to wear.

Jesus said this, John added, to inform Peter of the kind of death he would suffer and how it would glorify God.

That's pretty sobering stuff! So how did Jesus follow up these solemn words? With softer words?

With a sonnet of praise?

Not really. He simply told His apostle, "Follow Me!"

Peter did follow Jesus, and everything His Lord had told him turned out to be true. But because Peter followed, he became one of the key, if not *the* key, human figures in establishing that first-generation church.

So long as you remain alive on this earth, you can expect changes of all kinds. But when you continue to follow your Daddy God, when you put yourself in that place of comfort and strength called His loving arms, He'll give you the strength and the wisdom, the faith and the courage, to endure any change that life throws your way.

Making Music…Even in Chains

Open Arms International, which I cofounded, hosts an annual Good Friday Breakfast for the city of Portland, Oregon. We see the breakfast as a gift to the city and as a way to show our appreciation for the support that so many of its people have given us since the ministry's 2003 inception.

Each year, we welcome a guest speaker to the breakfast. For me, one of the most memorable of those speakers was Captain Charlie

Plumb, who flew fighter jets in the Vietnam War. On his 75th and final mission, with only five days before he was to return home, Charlie got shot down and captured. He spent the next 2,103 days imprisoned in an eight-foot by eight-foot cell. He had to endure almost daily torture and abuse.

Understandably, Charlie suffered through a lot of despondency and turmoil during this horrific time in his life. Then one day, a fellow P.O.W. who recognized Charlie had landed in a bad place said to him, "Charlie, you want to know your biggest problem? Sounds like you're suffering from a fairly common disease. Around here we call it 'prison thinking.'"

Well, of course I have prison thinking! Charlie thought. *Look at me! I have four holes in my body where blood's running out. I have boils all over my front side, all over my back. I'm down to 115 pounds.*

My sole possession in life is a rag wrapped around my waist to hide my nudity. I am rotting away in a Communist prison camp–and now, to add insult to injury, they put me next to a positive thinker!

"Okay," Charlie said to his fellow prisoner, "tell me about this 'prison thinking.'"

"Don't you see?" the man asked. "When a fighter pilot is blown out of the sky...or a manager is rebuked one more time...or a salesperson is turned down one more time...or a mother is having challenges with that unruly child one more time...what's the first emotion for all of us? Three common voices shout at us:

"There's Voice 1: 'Oh God, why me? This is so terrible. What could be worse than this? This event will never have any value. The best I can do is to make it through this tough time and try to forget it.'

"Then there's Voice 2: 'It's not my fault, man. I didn't start this war. I didn't build that airplane.

I'm the victim. I have no control over my destiny.'

"And there's Voice 3: 'This has got to be somebody else's fault. Blame everybody you can think of. Blame the president, blame

Congress, blame the enemy.' The problem here, is when you start blaming other people for your problems, you give away control of your life."

"Okay," Charlie responded, "I guess I have a bad case of this prison thinking. What's the antidote for my disease?"

"First of all, you have to be a believer," the man answered. "Men come and go, some live and some die. If there's any one single common denominator of survival in this prison camp, it's that the guys who live *believe* they're going to live. They tap into sources of strength and power. They believe in their team; they believe in their products; they believe in their services; they believe in their Creator. They believe in the big plan...they're believers.

"You've got to have courage," he continued. "You're stepping up to the plate. It's the bottom of the ninth, we're twenty runs behind, and you've got to swing the bat like, 'We're going to win this game!'"

When I heard Charlie Plumb tell his story, I couldn't help but think of the prison experience of Paul and Silas. These two men of God got attacked by an angry crowd, beaten, and thrown in prison. But they never allowed their harsh treatment to discourage them or rob them of their faith and joy in God, or of their belief that all would ultimately turn out for God's glory. In the midst of their pain and suffering, instead of crying out, "Woe is me!" they did the most remarkable thing: they began praying and singing songs to God (Acts 16).

I have to admit that I don't always follow Paul's and Silas's example...or Charlie Plumb's, for that matter. When I'm in a difficult season, I sometimes (Okay, more often than I'd like to confess) give in to "prison thinking." When I'm going through challenges and changes, the last thing I want to do is make music and sing to the Lord. Too often, I still give into that common human response to feeling bound up and trapped by tough circumstances: I moan, I complain, and as they say in the UK, I 'whinge.'

But, thank God, I think I'm getting better. With the help of a good friend, I'm getting better. I once served on a church staff with a wonderful friend and fellow pastor named Jerry Shonk.

Jerry has one of the closest, most intimate relationships with God of anyone I know. I had been facing a very difficult and troubling situation, from which I didn't see a way of escape. Jerry knew about the situation, and one day he said something to me, something profound and deep...and incredibly *freeing*.

"Kiss the chains," he said, "and you'll be free."

Human nature doesn't particularly like change. We especially don't like those seasons of change that involve difficulties, heartaches, and anxiety. During those times, the changes make us feel as though we're imprisoned and clapped in irons. We know our heavenly Daddy has set us free, but we don't *feel* free. We know He has given us every reason to rejoice in Him, but we don't *feel* like rejoicing. And we know He has promised to use everything that happens to us for our good and for His glory, but we just can't see how anything good can come out of "this."

I would never be so presumptuous as to believe that I have all the answers every time someone is going through a difficult time of change. God has given me enough humility to admit that I don't know everything, including the "whys" for another person's difficulties.

But I believe with all my heart that our Daddy God loves us deeply and that He knows why these things happen. Not only that, nothing life brings our way has to be fruitless, for He has a plan for everything that He allows to happen to us. That is why we can find freedom, joy, and purpose for our difficulties. We can find liberty from the things that bind us when we choose to *Rejoice always, pray continually, give thanks in all circumstances; for this is God's will for you in Christ Jesus* (1 Thessalonians 5:16-18).

We can kiss the chains.

I'm still learning what that means. I'm still learning about the freedom that comes when I allow the music of praise for my Daddy

God to flow through me when I'm going through difficult life changes. And I'm still learning to trust His amazing promise: *And we know that in all things God works for the good of those who love him, who have been called according to his purpose* (Romans 8:28).

Your Daddy God has promised to be with you through even the most trying changes in your life. Not only that, but He has promised to guide you and teach you, as well as bless you and glorify Himself, as He helps you navigate through seasons of change.

So may I encourage you to listen to Charlie Plumb's prison teacher? Step up to the plate. It's the bottom of the ninth and you're twenty runs behind. Still, swing the bat like, "We're going to win this game!"

Because we are.

Chapter 13

DADDY, WILL YOU TEACH ME WHAT IS RIGHT?

Rachel and I had just gone to bed one night when we noticed a light from the hallway. We'd put the girls down for bed, so we knew one of two things had happened: either Diana and/or Belle had gotten up *or* we had forgotten to turn out the light. We knew we hadn't forgotten to douse the light, so we got up to investigate what our daughters might be up to.

We walked into the hallway and saw that indeed the light came from the girls' bedroom.

When we looked inside their bedroom, we couldn't believe our eyes.

Belle, just two years old at the time, was on her way back to the small sink in her bedroom for what appeared to be the umpteenth time. She had been filling a small child's teacup with water and pouring it repeatedly on her sister, who continued to sleep blissfully. Diana, although totally drenched, and lying in her own private lake, remained completely unaware of her sister's work.

"Belle!" we said, with one of those shouting whispers, "What are you doing?"

She turned, looked up at us and gave us a blank stare. Just a silly look on her face that communicated, as clear as day, that she had no idea how to respond. It was one of those "I don't know" looks.

I think I "get" that blank stare. I'm not sure Belle *knew* that she had done anything wrong. I'm not even sure she knew why she had soaked her sister. Who knows what goes through the head of a two-year-old? She may have had a perfectly logical two-year-old's reason to drench her sister with water, one teacup at a time. I have no doubt she was having fun.

I recognized immediately that a teaching moment had arrived. As a daddy, I've had more of those than I can count. I didn't find it an easy task at that moment, however—and not because Rachel and I felt especially angry or upset at Belle. In fact, we had to stifle our laughter.

If you're a parent, you know what I'm talking about. Your son or daughter needs some correction, but for some reason, the misdemeanor just tickles your funny bone. So when you have to get serious and administer some teaching and correction, you must first find a way to get "that look" off your face—the one where your eyes bulge out and your cheeks puff up as you hold your breath, trying hard not to laugh out loud.

Let's face it: kids, even when they do inappropriate things, can be really funny.

Rachel and I knew we needed to discipline Belle that night, and by discipline, I don't mean corporal punishment. Rather, we needed to teach her that pouring water on sleeping sisters is never a great idea.

In short order, we taught the lesson and got the girls back in bed. I say girls, plural, because we first had to get Diana out of her wading pool so we could change her sheets and towel her off. That night, Belle earned a new nickname: "Belle the Baptist."

After the festivities came to an end, Rachel and I did the best we could to cloak our smiles and laughter before we returned to our room and climbed back into bed.

Discipline as Teaching . . . and Loving

When Rachel and I verbally corrected Belle the Baptist, in fact, we were disciplining her. That's a tough one for many people to grasp, because they associate the word "discipline" with physical punishment. Very possibly, they grew up in homes in which the parents didn't always handle discipline in appropriate or constructive ways.

Although discipline sometimes involves fitting punishment, it has a lot more to do with sound teaching and careful instruction. In fact, the word "discipline" comes from the Latin word meaning "instruction" or "training." It means "to teach." Because parents love their children, they discipline and teach them in loving and appropriate ways.

Our heavenly Daddy wrote the book on that kind of thoughtful and caring discipline, and so it's a tragedy that sometimes the idea of His discipline frightens us. Without question, at times our Daddy God disciplines those He loves in strict or even painful ways. When we continuously behave in a manner that causes distance to grow between ourselves and our heavenly Daddy, He will do whatever He must do to get our attention and bring us back into relationship. Only when we remain in vital relationship with Him do we experience true life. Moving on through life apart from Him is more like a living death (John 15:6).

Although that kind of painful discipline is designed to produce a "harvest of righteousness," it never feels good. It's like a heavenly measles shot–momentarily painful but intended to produce a lifetime of good (Hebrews 12:11).

God had this kind of loving discipline in mind when He inspired David to write, *I will instruct you and teach you in the way you should go; I will counsel you with my loving eye on you* (Psalm 32:8).

As with any loving father, our Daddy God keeps His eyes on His kids and teaches them. His discipline brings instruction to us which shapes our character and enables us to live our lives in the way He intended. When we submit to His discipline and correction and allow Him to shape our character, we stay in close relationship with Him.

Yes, He loves us *that* much!

The same God who wants to be our loving heavenly Daddy also wants to be our Teacher. He wants to teach us the most important things about our relationship with Him, how we should relate to others, how we can best love our families and friends, and how to wisely conduct our personal and business affairs. Whatever we need to know, He wants to teach us.

A little later we'll look at *how* He teaches us. But for now, let's understand that our part in benefiting from our Daddy God's discipline—His teaching and instruction—is simply a willingness to listen so that we might learn.

Sporting a Teachable Spirit

Rachel and I spend time teaching our girls the basics of how to behave, both at home and in public. One of those basics is how to conduct themselves at the dinner table.

We teach our girls about the proper portion size to put in their mouths and instruct them to keep their mouths closed when they chew. We instruct them not to speak with their mouths full. (Have you ever met a child who just "knew" these things? I haven't. Children who haven't been taught good table manners make mealtimes…interesting.)

We also go a little beyond the basics of good table manners. We show our daughters where the silverware and water glasses go. We teach them that when they serve plates, they set them down in front of their guests on the left, and when they remove the plates, they do so from the right (I learned this in my days as a waiter). If they find multiple pieces of cutlery on each side of their plate, we teach them to begin with the piece of cutlery farthest out and to work their way in, corresponding to the meal courses.

As a father, I've learned that kids often learn like little sponges, absorbing everything their parents teach them. But I've also learned that they have moments when they seem more like stubborn little rocks, resisting every bit of teaching and instruction that comes their way while absorbing nothing.

In other words, kids are just fallen humans in miniature. They can get just as stubborn and resistant to good teaching as their parents. Belle and Diana do not differ at all in this respect from any other kids on the planet. Part of my job as Dad, therefore, is to teach them to be teachable—even as I receive exactly the same training from my heavenly Daddy.

I'm still a work in progress. I don't always get it right, but I still know that my Daddy God wants to teach me. Sometimes, however, I just don't want to be taught. And so I say a short prayer:

Daddy God, please help me to be more like a sponge than a stone!

We may not like hearing it, but at times, we all need to be taught through discipline. We don't always do things right. Sometimes our thoughts go in errant directions. Sometimes we wander away out of sheer ignorance and not out of any lack of desire to do the right thing, while at other times…

In so many ways, we're like two year olds, without a clue as to what we should be doing.

Hence, our need to let our Daddy God teach us.

Be honest, now. Do you ever chafe a little—or possibly roll your eyes—when someone wants to teach you something? I do. We want others to believe that we know what we're doing and that we're smart enough to figure things out on our own to make the right decision. In all honesty, we want to be seen as the brightest stars in our own little solar system. We don't want anyone or anything to diminish what we perceive to be the brightness of our own star.

I know I have some of that "chafeability" in me. Something inside me wants others to know how smart and gifted I am, how I already know whatever I might need to know. And I can't help but think that, at least sometimes, I give off that air even to the One who knows all. Although my Daddy God wants more than anything to teach me everything I need to know in order to live a full and satisfying life, I sometimes resist His instruction.

Do you know the word the Bible uses to describe a person who continually resists instruction, refusing to learn or be taught?

It calls that person a fool.

Solomon (the wisest guy who has ever lived) says in Proverbs 1:7, *The fear* (honor and respect) *of the Lord is the beginning of knowledge, but fools despise wisdom and discipline.*

He continues on in Proverbs 12:1, *Whoever loves discipline loves knowledge, but whoever hates correction is stupid.* These are tough words—"fool" and "stupid"—but the Bible doesn't shy away from them. It's just plain stupid to play the fool and set your jaw and continue to ignore or push away life-giving truth. It would be like a person swept away in a flash flood who refuses a rope lowered to him by a helicopter.

At the other end of the spectrum, Scripture gives us a great example of someone who has a teachable spirit:

Show me your ways, Lord, teach me your paths.
Guide me in your truth and teach me, for you are God my Savior,
and my hope is in you all day long
(Psalm 25:4-5).

Our Daddy God speaks to us and teaches us in several ways: through His written Word, the Bible; through the wisdom of others; through our personal experiences; even through His own "still, small voice."

The Bible makes it clear that when God wants to teach us something, we would do well to listen, to learn, and then to apply that knowledge to our lives. Scripture also tells us something about our heavenly Daddy's credentials as a Teacher: He knows everything. There is literally nothing He doesn't know.

Daddy God Knows What We Don't
Diana recently started learning multiplication at school. Her lessons have given me the opportunity to spend some fun learning time

with her, helping her to learn the multiplication table. I've been using multiplication flash cards to teach her the right answers to simple, mostly single-digit, multiplication problems. Our regimen goes something like the following:

Diana starts out by testing me, asking me what 6 x 7 equals. I rapidly spit out the answer: "42." Then comes 8 x 6. Just as quickly, I answer, "48." Then comes 9 x 9, and once I again, I blurt out, "81."

I'll admit that Diana does a great job of stroking my Daddy ego when we study together. I get a kick out of impressing my little girl with my vast knowledge of mathematics (at least, vast compared to hers). It always makes me smile as she looks at me, wide-eyed and in absolute awe, that I can throw the right answers out so quickly. In her little mind, there seems to be nothing that Daddy doesn't know.

But then comes the teaching time. I pose multiplication problems back to Diana, starting with the simplest equations. When I present her with a problem, she sits and thinks, and then she tries counting on her fingers. She often follows with more thinking and more counting on her fingers. Sometimes she gets the right answer, but much of the time she doesn't.

Diana is a bright little girl and one day soon she'll know the answers, not just to simple mathematical problems, but also to more complex ones. One day, when I ask her what 7 x 7 equals, she'll answer without hesitation, "49." But for now, she has a lot to learn. And I love taking the time to teach her.

We often use a simple two-word term to describe the process of committing to memory the multiplication tables, the alphabet, and other basics:

By heart.

The phrase indicates that we learn something so well that it becomes ingrained in us, so that we can easily recite it without even really thinking about it.

For now, Diana doesn't know her multiplication table by heart, but soon she will. And her Daddy? Well, I know a lot of things by heart, but I know I still need to work on some things. I also know my Daddy in heaven is working on me and teaching me the things I need to know.

For me, this is often a difficult part of my relationship with Him. I know He loves me and wants to administer His own kind of discipline and teaching, but I'm a lot like many other "grown-ups" in that I tend to think I already have all the answers. I don't want anyone to tell me anything or teach me something I think I know well enough on my own.

Okay, I'll just come right out and say it. *I'm stubborn.*

My Daddy God knows this unpleasant fact about me. He knows that part of my fallible human nature leads me to think I don't need a lot of instruction, that I already know what I need to do and where I need to go. He recognizes that I can be something of a know-it-all, since the same malady afflicts all of humanity. I believe that's why He inspired the writer of Proverbs to jot down a particular bit of wisdom not once, but twice: *There is a way that seems right to a man, but in the end it leads to death* (Proverbs 14:12, 16:25).

Since our Daddy God knows us so well, He knows we're prone to go our own way and do things as we see fit. But He also knows the biggest problem with His kids solving their own problems and charting their own way is that it leads to a lot of painful dead ends.

Dead ends are frustrating. Dead ends waste time.

Dead ends lead *nowhere.*

Our Daddy God wants His children to remember that they are children. Whether we've reached the ripe old age of forty or fifty or seventy, He wants us to remain in a place where we can hear His voice clearly. He wants us to look to Him and depend on His knowledge and wisdom with the same wide-eyed wonderment I see on my daughter's face when I rattle off the answers to math problems. He wants us to remain children in the sense that we continue to depend on Him and look to Him for instruction and guidance in every area of our lives.

On the other hand, God doesn't want us to respond to His teaching and instruction in an automated, robotic way. He doesn't want to fill our heads with a bunch of knowledge just so we can recite it back to Him or rattle it off to others.

No, our Daddy in heaven wants to lovingly teach us and instruct us. He wants us to receive what He has for us and have us learn it *by heart*. In other words, He wants us to make the things He teaches us, especially through His written Word, a part of who we are, at a soul level. He wants to instill His wisdom and knowledge into the very core of our being, that spiritual part of us that He created in His own image to hear and respond when He speaks to us.

A big part of having a teachable spirit is being able to humbly admit that while we don't have all the answers, God does. He wants to teach us everything we need to know in order to experience the abundant life Jesus promised us (John 10:10). And He accomplishes that objective primarily through the wisdom He's placed in the greatest book of all time, the Bible.

Do you *want* your Daddy God to teach you? Then make sure you spend time in the Bible, the source of teaching and wisdom He's given you. But as you do so, ask your heavenly Father to teach you. When you do this, He'll send His Holy Spirit to transfer the knowledge in your head to a lasting and productive place in your heart. You'll learn to live *by heart* and not *by head*.

Learning to Distinguish His Voice

For some reason, Belle likes standing up in chairs and in other places where standing isn't such a good idea.

I know. It's a kid thing. When I was her age I'm sure I did the same thing. However, she's paid a price for that odd practice–and it's been more than once.

One day when she stood up on her little chair, it toppled over, sending her on a swan dive to a face-plant on the floor. As a result, she got a bloodied lip and banged-up teeth.

One day, as Belle played in the seat of her stroller at home, she started standing up in it. When I saw her doing so, I looked at her and said in a firm voice, "Belle, do *not* stand up in your stroller." She instantly wheeled around, because she knows *that* tone of my "correcting voice," and she immediately sat down. But only a few minutes later, she repeated her stunt. This time, I mustered up my firmest daddy voice and said, "Belle?"

When she heard my voice, she turned toward me, saw my unhappy countenance, and sat down. I then added a little positive reinforcement, applauding her and telling her what a good girl she was for obeying her daddy. She lit up with a huge smile because she knew she had made her Daddy happy. A small thing, but I'll always remember that nice daddy-daughter moment.

Unfortunately, we have other moments too.

One afternoon, close to dinnertime, Belle came to me with a package of chewing gum and asked if she could have a piece. "No," I said, "I don't want you to have any right now, just before we eat." I thought I had taken care of the issue.

But Belle had other ideas.

About an hour later, as we got ready for dinner, I noticed that she had something in her mouth. She had decided that she didn't want to listen to her daddy's voice when he told her she couldn't have a piece of gum before dinner. Instead, she listened to the voice inside her own little head that said, *I want gum, and I want it now.*

Of course, Belle's decision didn't make me happy. Another teaching moment had arrived, this one about obeying her daddy even when she'd rather do something he has already asked her not to do. I led Belle into her bedroom, sat her down, and verbally reprimanded her for her disobedience. I took the moment to teach her (discipline her) with words of instruction.

Belle, like any small child, has moments when she chooses to go her own way rather than doing what her parents instruct her to do. But thankfully she is one of those tender souls whose heart aches when she knows she has disappointed her parents. As I spoke to Belle about her wrong decision, she burst into tears and told me how sorry she felt. Although it warmed my heart to see her remorse, that didn't save her from having to spend some time by herself in her room to think about how she had disobeyed and how she could make the right decision next time. For Belle staying in her room by herself is painful. She absolutely hates it. And that's the power of discipline: some form of pain (it doesn't have to be physical) to enforce corrective behavior.

Living life on this earth means making all sorts of decisions, some simple and easy and others more complicated and difficult. But it also means sorting through all the voices trying to "help" us with those decisions. If we're not careful, many of those voices can drown out the sound of our Daddy God's voice, leading us to make decisions and take actions that aren't always the best and that keep us from enjoying the close, intimate relationship He wants us to enjoy with Him.

What makes this all the more difficult and complicated is that we humans, fallen and imperfect as we are, too often like listening to our own voice rather than to God's. We like making decisions that please ourselves, whether or not they please Him. We like standing when we know He has instructed us to sit, and we like that pre-dinner piece of gum when He's already said, "No."

The Bible records many stories of people who listened to the sound of their own voices and desires rather than to the voice of God. They never had a good result.

God gave Eve and her husband free run in the Garden of Eden, but Eve chose to listen to the serpent's voice instead of to her Daddy God. And so mortality and death entered our world.

Many centuries later, the prophet Jonah listened to his own voice rather than to God's, fleeing to Tarshish rather than going to Ninevah where God had instructed him to go.

How about Moses, who in a fit of anger publicly disobeyed what the Lord had clearly instructed him to do?

And let's not forget King David, who listened to the wrong voice and so pursued an adulterous relationship with Bathsheba, leading to horrible long-term consequences for himself, his family, and his kingdom.

Men and women universally have a habit of listening to the wrong voice. It's a human problem that has dogged us since the beginning of time. It's as though a tug-of-war goes on inside our heads and hearts between our Daddy God's voice and all the other voices, including our own.

We live in a time when countless voices call to us to follow. Our ears get inundated 24/7 with voices calling to us through all sorts of media—magazines, newspapers, the Internet, radio, television programs and social media. Add to that the voices of our teachers and professors, entertainers and even famous athletes, very few of whom have what's best for us at heart, as does our Daddy God.

The biggest (and most dangerous) problem with these voices is that too often they represent worldviews in opposition to our Daddy God. Without His help, none of us has the ability to adequately filter out those discordant voices. And when we don't filter them out, they begin to seep into the edges of our thoughts—like floodwater seeps into a basement. As a result, we begin to listen a bit too attentively as they urge us to go *their* way. In time, those voices often become our own voice.

And then our heavenly Daddy steps in. He gives His children an opportunity, through His counsel (His written Word, the Bible), to benefit from His wisdom—and so avoid many of the mistakes and errors in judgment so common to us. He instructs us to step back from the costly mistakes and errors that can hurt us and others.

Your Daddy God never intended for you to go through life without His teaching and instruction. He didn't bring you into a relationship with Himself and then leave you on your own to walk blindly through life. He has promised that when you come alongside Him, He'll walk with you through this grand adventure of life, teaching you, instructing, and counseling you every step of the way.

To whose voice are you listening? What voice so influences you that it becomes your own? I hope it's the voice of your Daddy in heaven! You'll never, ever go wrong by listening to Him.

Hearing God . . . and Overcoming Sin

Our Open Arms Academy girls once played a soccer match against another school. At the same time, a ministry team from the U.K. was visiting us. A few of the U.K. team members knew a little something about soccer—or "football," as they call it—so they volunteered to referee the game.

About halfway through the contest, what seemed like a pretty serious argument broke out at midfield. As I got closer, I could see that one or two of the referees were quite upset and angry about something. I made my way to the edge of the chaos and quickly discovered that an accusation had surfaced against our rival team. The accusation turned out to be true. A grown woman had posed as a student on the other team in order to play in the game.

The chaos started getting wild enough that I stepped in and suggested that we suspend the game until we could sort everything out. We then talked to the adults supervising the opposing team and confirmed that the team had, in fact, cheated by allowing an adult woman to pose as a player. The opposing team offered, rightfully, to forfeit the game. (I felt proud of the girls from Open Arms Academy when they said they didn't want to accept the forfeit, but instead wanted to meet another day to find out which team was better.)

About two hours after the chaos had died down, the other team's manager and an official from the school made their way over to me to apologize. While I accepted the apology, I also recognized an open door for a father figure teaching moment (I was old enough to be both young men's father).

"Guys," I said, "in the future, do what is right."

I then challenged them to use the incident as a teaching moment for their girls: "I want you to promise me you'll do something. I want you to apologize to the girls on your team. I want you to admit your failure to them as leaders. You must set an example to them that it's not okay to cheat. It's your golden opportunity to set a right example for the next generation. Your girls will remember your example in a powerful and positive way when they get tempted to do wrong.

They'll also greatly respect your willingness to be honest and admit your failure. Just maybe, because of your example, they'll decide in the future to always do what is right."

The young men didn't know it, but a very personal element colored my conversation with them. As the daddy of two highly impressionable little girls, I know how important it is that I set the right example for them. I know they're watching me, and I know that what they see me doing when they're children will go a long way toward determining how they'll live as adults.

To me, that's a big part of what fatherhood is all about: using every teaching moment that God gives me to teach my children to consistently do what is right.

Our Daddy God sets the pattern for us. He teaches us, instructs us, and guides us in the right way, and then He gives us a chance to get out there and live according to what He's taught us. He knows we'll fail sometimes, but when we ask Him to, He always forgives us, cleans us up, and uses our failures as His own specially-designed teaching moments. Our Daddy God knows that we need Him to teach us and instruct us. He knows that if we don't receive His teaching and instruction, sin waits to master us, to control us, and to dominate us.

My mind goes to the sad story of Cain and Abel, recorded in Genesis 4. When Cain brought the Lord a less-than-desirable offering, God called him out for it. Cain felt demoralized and saw the rebuke as nothing more than an unfair comparison with his brother, Abel, who got accolades for giving God his best. Cain had a deadly solution: rather than doing what God had asked, he decided to get rid of the competition by committing the first murder in human history.

Just before Cain acted on his decision to kill his brother, the Lord had asked him, *"Why are you angry? Why is your face downcast? If you do what is right, will you not be accepted? But if you do not do what is right, sin is crouching at your door; it desires to have you, but you must rule over it"* (Genesis 4:6-7).

Two things stand out in this passage as I think about our Daddy God offering to freely teach and instruct us. First are these words, straight from the mouth of God: "sin...desires to have you." In other words, "sin is waiting to eat you for lunch." And that's what happened with Cain. When he yielded to the temptation to do wrong, sin ate him up.

Second, I see that God instructed Cain, *"you must master it [sin]."* I know my Daddy God well enough to say with absolute confidence that He never tells His kids to do something without giving them the resources they need to do it. What we cannot accomplish on our own, we can do through the power of the Holy Spirit.

For the kids of our heavenly Daddy God, it all comes down to Jesus. God knew from the very beginning that no matter how hard we humans try, we can never on our own hit the target called "righteousness" or "doing right." But He had a foolproof plan: He would offer His own Son so that we could have forgiveness for, and power over, sin.

Jesus came to give God's children freedom from the ultimate consequences of sin: eternal death. And when we allow Him to be our Master Teacher, He promises to instruct us and teach us how we should live. We become His willing students and He becomes our faithful Teacher–or as the Bible calls the followers of Christ during His earthly ministry, Jesus' "disciples."

The Lord gave Cain some vital teaching that he refused to hear. Will we hear that teaching today? God tells us that we don't have to allow sin to master us or rule over us. We can't overcome sin on our own, but *He* can. When you make your Daddy God your Teacher, He *will* give you the teaching, the wisdom, and the supernatural help you need to resist sin.

What sort of sin crouches at your door, desiring to eat you for lunch? Adultery? Murder? Jealousy? Greed? Sexual immorality? Pride? Lust? Remember, your Daddy God has promised to instruct you and teach you how to say "no" to all those things and "yes" to living in a way that keeps you in intimate contact with Him.

For the grace of God has appeared that offers salvation to all people. It teaches us to say "No" to ungodliness and worldly passions, and to live self-controlled, upright and godly lives in this present age (Titus 2:11-12).

Your Daddy doesn't want sin to eat you for lunch. That's why He provides a way of escape. His name is Jesus, and He wants to be your Savior, your Friend, your Counselor…and your faithful Teacher.

Chapter 14

DADDY, WILL YOU PROTECT ME?

Fresh out of high school and only eighteen years old, my brother Bill joined the United States Air Force. After finishing basic training and serving for several months, one day he got pulled from his specialized training when his background check revealed something that would prevent him from receiving the top secret clearance his target job required.

This made no sense to Bill. He couldn't think of one thing in his background that would have kept him from receiving the clearance. He soon received new orders to go to Las Vegas, where he would be trained as a "civil engineer"–military lingo for base garbage man. But before the paperwork for his transfer wrapped up, he checked into the hospital with a bad case of the flu.

Fortunately for Bill, he never made it to Las Vegas.

When news of Bill's failed background check reached our father's ears, Dad took it upon himself to call the Air Force Security Service headquarters in San Angelo, Texas, and speak with the head of command. He got through to a Colonel Phillips. When the colonel first heard Dad's name–William "Bill" Gallagher–he told Dad that he had served with a flight officer named Gallagher during World War II. It turned out that that old flight officer was our dad.

After Colonel Phillips and my father spent some time catching up with each other, talking about where their lives had taken them since the war, Dad asked the colonel to look into my brother's case.

After investigating the chain of events that had led to the reassignment, Colonel Phillips determined that my brother had run afoul of a simple case of mistaken identity. Another William Kevin Gallagher had begun training at the same time and on the same base as my brother, and this was the young man who had a few things in his past that raised the concerns.

Once my brother got discharged from the hospital, he received a transfer from Biloxi to San Angelo for training in the Security Service. That training afforded my brother much better working circumstances for the remainder of his military service. A very bad situation for my brother thus got turned around for good...all because our dad got involved in an effort to protect his son.

Something about being a dad brings out the protector and defender in a man. My own father had that in large measure. So do I. So do most earthly dads I know. Whether you look at it as pure paternal instinct or see it as something God instilled in us at the moment of creation, it seems that most earthly fathers have an innate desire to stand up and defend their offspring, regardless of the cost.

Daddy God: Our Protector and Defender

Every child needs and wants to know that Daddy is ready and willing to come to his or her defense and play the role of protector and defender during times of threat. Children, because they are smaller, weaker, and less mentally developed than adults, need to depend on someone bigger, stronger, and more experienced to stand with them in time of danger.

But...so do adults, I've learned.

Even after we grow up, we remain our Daddy God's children. He never intended that we rely solely on ourselves for protection from the dangers of life. We need someone Bigger, Stronger, and More Experienced to help us defeat the things in this life that want to take a toll on our souls.

As I live out my role as father to protect and defend my girls, a calling I believe comes straight from heaven, I know that I provide them with a picture of their Daddy God. When they watch me protect them and defend them, they see a small portion of God's nature and character and how He reacts when He sees His kids in any kind of danger.

I want Diana and Belle to understand two things. First, I want them to know there's nothing I won't do to protect and defend them from the many dangers they'll face growing up. Second, I want them to live in the absolute confidence that their ever-present Daddy God will never leave them to fend for themselves. Though the day will come when I'm gone and can no longer protect and defend them here on earth, their Father in heaven will always be here for them, forever.

A heartbreaking reality in the part of the world where I live and work is the huge number of children who have no protector and defender. Unfortunately, that reality is repeated all over the world in country after country. Here in Kenya, as well as in many other African nations, countless children have no daddy to step up and protect them from the many dangers that threaten them every day. As abandoned and forgotten kids, they're on their own, many of them almost from the moment of birth.

That's a huge part of what motivates me and the others serving at the Open Arms Village. We want to reach as many forsaken children as we possibly can. We want them to learn that even though their earthly daddies are nowhere to be found, their Daddy God is always there and always will be. We want them to know that He longs to be not only their loving, adoring Daddy in heaven, but also their Protector and Defender here on earth.

He's the loving, protective Daddy God of whom the psalmist wrote, *The Lord will keep you from all harm—he will watch over your life; the Lord will watch over your coming and going both now and forevermore* (Psalm 121:7-8).

He Protects His Children's Minds

My father was a member of the Lions Club. Every Christmas, the Lions Club in our area threw a party for the poor, disadvantaged kids of our community. One year, I got to accompany Dad to help out. I still remember how shocked and surprised I felt when one of my elementary school classmates and his siblings walked in for the party. They hadn't come to help, as I had; they were among the guests of honor. My classmate was one of the poor, disadvantaged kids whom I had come to serve.

Before that night, I had no idea that he was any different from me. If I thought about it at all, I guess I just assumed he lived in a home like mine, a home where his parents had the means to provide Christmas presents and a special dinner for their kids. But that night, I found out that he lived in a home very different from my own.

Since that night, I've spoken with that elementary school friend and learned that his home situation often embarrassed him deeply. He hated the thought that his classmates saw him as the kid from a poor family, and hated the fact that his hand-me-down clothes and tattered shoes set him apart as different.

My classmate's home situation made him feel, in a word, inferior. We might say, "Well, that shouldn't be," but it was that way. As a child, he felt the stares and sometimes the snickers and unkind remarks of his classmates, jabs that marked him out as an outsider. It hurt him–badly.

Truth be told, my classmate was far from the only kid I knew in school who suffered thoughtless but terrible mental abuse because he seemed "different." Kids often speak unkind words to their peers who live in homes where money is very tight. Such children frequently become the targets of ridicule. They pay in countless ways for having no choice but to wear old clothes and shoes, for having parents who just can't afford to buy them the latest school supplies. They become the kids on the outside looking in.

But it doesn't stop there. Kids who have a different physical appearance–maybe they aren't as pretty or handsome as their classmates, or they're heavier or skinnier than the others, or they have some kind of physical deformity–know the pain of being made fun of and ostracized. Kids who aren't as gifted athletically or blessed with other recognizable talents know how it feels to be "left out." Even kids with underdeveloped social skills often become targets for verbal abuse, left out of a circle of friends. Too often, they find themselves alone and alienated.

As I write, Belle and Diana are in elementary school, so I am readying myself to protect them from the myriad assaults I'm sure will come. I know that one day others will say hurtful things to them, flinging insults their way. These verbal arrows may prompt them to focus more on themselves and what they don't have, instead of on everything they do have because they belong to their Daddy God.

My daughters have already suffered some of these expected verbal assaults. At the tender age of five, one of my girls has come home on more than one occasion in tears because other children have said some very unkind things to her.

How many parents, when a child comes home hurt and upset about unkind words spoken by classmates, haven't thought about (if only for a moment) marching down to the school and setting things right? I think we all fantasize about a fiery confrontation, the kind of public altercation that would teach those mouthy little kids a lesson or two. Of course, we know that such a strategy is not always the highest and best way to handle such a situation. I know it too. So instead of trying to mete out some kind of retribution on my daughter's tormenters, I do everything I can to protect her mind from believing the nasty (and false) things other kids say to her. I try to prepare her to know how to handle the attacks that begin in primary school but which, in fact, will come at her in one form or another, her entire life.

As Diana and Belle's loving earthly daddy, I know that *the best way to protect their minds is to counter such cruel remarks with the truth.* I tell my girls that the kids who say unkind things about them don't know what they're talking about. But more importantly, I constantly remind them that their earthly daddy loves them…and that their Daddy in heaven loves them even more.

We all know that we live in a world that throws a torrent of mental and emotional bombs our way. While the world tosses its lies at us, however, our Daddy God remains our constant source of encouragement and truth. Good dads encourage their kids and build them up and let them know they are loved, which is exactly what my Father in heaven does for me…and for all of His children:

- When I feel powerless, my Daddy God reminds me, *I can do everything through him who gives me strength* (Philippians 4:13).
- When I feel unloved, He reminds me, *I have loved you with an everlasting love* (Jeremiah 31:3).
- When I feel like a hopeless sinner, He tells me, *as far as the east is from the west, so far has he removed our transgressions from us* (Psalm 103:12).
- When I wonder where this life is taking me, He promises me, *For I know the plans I have for you…plans to prosper you and not to harm you, plans to give you hope and a future* (Jeremiah 29:11).
- When I wonder what good can possibly come from some tough situation I'm in, He says, *in all things God works for the good of those who love him, who have been called according to his purpose* (Romans 8:28).

Attacks on our minds remain a constant threat in this world. The world throws a lot of darts at me, but I've learned that I don't have to let anything stick. I know my Daddy God, so I know what He thinks about me. Better yet, I know the promises He's made to me. And no better defense exists against the world's relentless mental assaults.

He Protects Us from Worry

I have a very active imagination that sometimes runs to places I wish it wouldn't go. I can create stories in my mind at the drop of a hat, and I often make myself the central character. My stories don't usually run toward simple drama, comedy, or fantasy. They tend more toward pure melodrama, or even horror, all combined with a heavy dose of suspense.

I'm quite good at mentally torturing myself, and I think I know why. If you imagine the worst possible scenario and stick yourself right in the middle of it, the actual reality probably won't be that bad. You end up experiencing the bad while you are braced for the worst.

Remember the story of Chicken Little? He got bonked on the head by a falling acorn, panicked, and then came to the catastrophically wrong conclusion that the sky was falling. I'm pretty sure I suffer from a bit of "Chicken Little Syndrome." I can turn a little acorn into a huge, overblown melodrama, and before I know it, my mind and emotions explode into a big, tangled mess.

I know I'm not alone in this. All of us can very easily fall into a similar trap (though some of us are far more susceptible to worry than others). We worry about our families, about our jobs and income, about the fragile state of our unstable world, about flu bugs and computer bugs and tree-eating bugs. The world overflows with oceans of serious issues far more troublesome than a little acorn falling out of a tree.

Yet our Daddy God's own Son has told us that we needn't and shouldn't let these things eat us up: *Therefore I tell you, do not worry about your life, what you will eat or drink; or about your body, what you will wear* (Matthew 6:25). Jesus understood and taught something that we all need to remember when we face issues that could nudge us toward worry. We must rely on our Daddy God, who sees the acorn for exactly what it is and who superintends every event in our lives. He is the One who protects our minds and emotions from spinning out of control. We don't need to obsess over life's worst-case scenarios, because our Daddy God continually watches over us.

Whether we face a genuinely serious problem or just smart a little after getting smacked on the head by a falling acorn, our Daddy God wants to protect our minds from worry. In place of anxiety, He wants to give us the perfect inner peace He's promised. Our Daddy God *will keep in perfect peace those whose minds are steadfast, because they trust in him* (Isaiah 26:3).

What a great promise! But what does it mean to have a "steadfast" mind? The apostle Paul enlarged on the idea when he wrote, *Do not be anxious about anything, but in every situation, by prayer and petition, with thanksgiving, present your requests to God. And the peace of God, which transcends all understanding, will guard your hearts and your minds in Christ Jesus* (Philippians 4:6-7). Really, it's a simple 1-2-3 proposition.
1. Talk to your Daddy God about whatever concerns you.
2. Thank Him for His protection and provision.
3. *Believe* Him on His word that He'll protect your heart and mind.

So whenever you find yourself sinking into worry, remember that the sky is *not* falling. Don't forget that Jesus is *upholding all things by the word of His power* (Hebrews 1:3 KJV), including the sky. Your Daddy God has all things under control!

He Protects His Children's Hearts

I'll never forget the first time I was "in love." Was I ever head over heels! I met my girlfriend at church when I was eighteen years old. We dated for about three years before I finally popped the question. Joy of joys! She said, "Yes."

But as excited as I felt, almost immediately after we became engaged, something quite unexpected and even shocking happened to me. A terrible, confusing, and consuming sense of fear swept over me. Such a dreadful feeling of terror enveloped me that within a day or two after proposing, I backed out. I felt like I had no choice. I just couldn't do anything else.

My girlfriend felt shaken and deeply hurt by my sudden reversal, and I felt utterly embarrassed and humiliated. I did love her, but the idea of a lifetime commitment simply terrified me.

Though I broke off our engagement–temporarily, I thought–I didn't end the relationship. I honestly hoped we could continue our courtship, and maybe one day I would no longer have such a paralyzing fear of getting married. But the damage had been done.

Not many weeks later, the love of my life met someone else (at church, no less), fell in love, and within eighteen months, she got married. My heart felt worse than broken; it had been crushed.

Why couldn't she just love me through my fear?

Most of us have suffered a broken heart. We've given our love to another person, whether to a close friend, a romantic interest, a spouse, or a son or daughter, only to have that person do or say something that hurt us badly. Even worse, that person might have severed the relationship completely, leaving us devastated at the loss of the close connection we once shared with that wonderful person.

Probably you've heard the old saying about getting over the pain of a broken relationship: "Time heals all wounds." Unfortunately, it's not always true. Many men and women respond to the pain of heartbreak by shutting themselves off from any chance of truly loving others again. In the end, they wind up alone, whether they allow anyone to get in close proximity to them or not. Loneliness can feel most intense in a crowd.

Our Daddy God never intended any of His children to live such an empty life, a bare existence of emotional and spiritual poverty.

God created the human heart to have not only the ability to give and receive love, but with the *need* to do just that.

Loving earthly daddies do whatever they must to protect their children's hearts. They don't, however, protect their kids from all suffering or hurt. How could they, even if they wanted to? Wise fathers understand that the risk of heartbreak is part of loving. It simply goes with the territory. So instead of protecting their kids from any chance of heartbreak, they show them how to avoid shutting off their hearts after someone has hurt them.

Our Daddy God knows that the worst pain and suffering His children can endure is *not* the pain of a broken heart, but the pain of a closed heart—a heart closed off to loving others. He doesn't protect us from a broken heart as much as a closed heart.

If you think about it, you will recognize that if anyone could understand the desire to escape the pain and hurt of a broken heart, it's our Daddy God. Remember, it was our Father in heaven who gave us everything He had in the person of His Son, Jesus Christ, only to watch His own people reject Him. And don't forget, it was Jesus Himself who suffered betrayal and abandonment from His very closest friends on earth, the twelve disciples.

The pain and suffering Jesus endured broke His heart, but never *closed* His heart. As Jesus heaved His dying breaths on the cross, He continued to love even His executioners. "Father, forgive them, for they do not know what they are doing." And after His resurrection, He reached out in love to one of His closest friends, Peter, who three times had denied even knowing Him. *Nothing* could keep Jesus from loving. Not rejection, not betrayal, not abandonment, not even an excruciating death. He didn't allow a broken heart to close His heart.

And God doesn't want anything to keep us from loving, either.

King David wrote of our Daddy God's compassion for those suffering from broken hearts: *The Lord is close to the brokenhearted and saves those who are crushed in spirit* (Psalm 34:18). Why is He "close to the brokenhearted"? He's so close because He truly understands the deep pain of heartbreak. And He's close because He wants to be right there with us, helping us to get through the pain.

He Protects Us from Ourselves

As loving and responsible parents, Rachel and I go to great lengths to protect our children from the threat of physical harm. One day when I thought through the many things we do to keep the girls safe and sound, I discovered I had a really long list.

We bundle them up with warm jackets when the temperature drops. We place covers on the electrical outlets so they don't accidentally electrocute themselves. We shutter the second-story bedroom windows so they can't fall through to the ground below. We place them in car seats and put seat belts on them to protect them in case of an accident. We keep an attentive eye on them in the bathtub so they don't drown.

I won't bore you with the whole list. I'm sure yours is (or was, or will be) just as long.

Rachel and I know we need to do these things to shield and watch over our daughters for one reason: they're kids who need protection, oftentimes from themselves. Diana and Belle aren't old enough or wise enough to keep themselves safe. Without the boundaries and protections we set up for them, sooner rather than later they would pay a heavy price as they inevitably put themselves in danger. Children need these boundaries and safeguards to protect them from themselves, to protect them from their own naivety and lack of common sense.

But really, doesn't that remain true for all of us, even long after we become adults? Don't we all need guidelines, boundaries, and safeguards to keep us from hurting ourselves and others?

Sometimes, we grown-ups are our own worst enemies. We're prone to making bad decisions that put us in harm's way, damage others around us, and injure our relationship with our Daddy God.

That's why we need Him to protect us and guide us. We never get too old to need Him as our Protector...oftentimes from ourselves.

Our Daddy in heaven knows we need His protection, so He has taken preventive measures to help protect us in all ways, whether physically, emotionally, socially, or spiritually. And He gives us much of that protection through the boundaries and guidelines (and, yes, *rules* for living) that He's recorded for us in the pages of Scripture. The Word provides us with many great protections, but it does its best work only so long as we pay attention to it and keep ourselves under it.

Adults don't always like the boundaries and protections our Daddy God has put in place. We often get that "Don't fence me in" attitude, and we imagine that He is just trying to limit our fun. But when we finally get it through our heads that He loves us and wants to protect us from physical, emotional, and spiritual harm, we learn to love those boundaries and protections.

This is partly why He has warned us in His written Word that we are to avoid sexual immorality. God created sex as an expression of love between a husband and wife, and when we step outside that divinely ordained boundary, we bring on ourselves all kinds of serious consequences, including broken hearts and confused minds, ruined relationships, physical sickness and disease, and unplanned pregnancies.

Likewise, our loving Daddy God has warned us against the abuse of alcohol. Just open your Bible, read Proverbs 23:29-35, and ask yourself if the consequences of drunkenness listed in that passage don't remind you of one or more people you know. God warns us of the trouble, physical pain, and other hurtful results of drinking too much. Does it seem fun or a little relaxing at first? Sure. But in time, if it isn't kept in moderation, it will bring us nothing but bondage and heartache.

These are just two common examples of the many kinds of threats that prompted our Daddy God to set up various boundaries or protections, all of them for our own good. And like it or not, all of us would do well to put ourselves under our Daddy God's protection by heeding the many instructions, warnings, and commandments He has communicated to us in the Bible.

Over time, as my daughters mature and learn how to look out for their own safety, Rachel and I will be able to pull back on some of the protections we set up for them during their childhood. One day, Diana and Belle will know to put on warm clothing when they venture outside the house on a cold day. They'll know not to put their fingers in electrical sockets, so we won't have to put covers on the outlets. They'll know not to goof around in front of an open second-story window, and they'll know how to buckle their own seat belts.

All these aspects of parenting will change over time for Rachel and me. But even when Diana and Belle become young adults, I hope I never stop teaching them the importance of obeying their Daddy God and honoring the protective boundaries He's put in place for all His kids.

No Better Place

Over time, I've gotten it through my thick head that my Daddy God always keeps a watchful, protective eye on me. That has been a process of learning for me, sometimes the hard way. But by this point in my life, I realize that I can find no better place to live than under His protective hand.

It's an amazing place. It's safe, it's secure...and best of all, it's the place where I can remain closely connected to my Creator, who also just happens to be my heavenly Daddy.

Chapter 15

DADDY, CAN YOU TEACH ME TO GIVE?

Belle was two-and-a-half years old when Diana first came to live with us, and for the first week or so, they both lived in paradise. They enjoyed playing together, talking together, and just enjoying one another's company.

But then, very suddenly, the novelty wore off.

Belle no longer wanted to share her home and family with this new trespasser. One Saturday morning, not long after Diana's arrival, I walked into the family room to hear and see Belle following her sister around, saying, "Go home! Go home! Go home!"

Little Belle had grown quite accustomed to being the one and only princess in the house and decided she had no intention of sharing her royal seat of honor with anyone else. She thought it better to have Diana gone entirely than to risk having to share anything with her.

Children reveal their selfish natures more readily than adults. Because they are more self-centered than the rest of us? No, I actually think it's because most of them lack any kind of guile. When they think something, they just say it. And when someone encroaches on their territory, like Diana did with Belle, or gets too close to their treasured possessions, children have no problem at all in letting the interlopers know they're not welcome.

Go home! Go home! Go home! Mine! Mine! Mine! Give it back!

From our youngest days, all of us–from parents to plumbers, from hairstylists to real estate agents, from landscapers to company bosses, from kings and queens to presidents to prime ministers–every human being on the planet shares a common disease. We all suffer from selfishness.

Our Daddy God never intended for it to be that way. From the moment of creation, He wanted all His people to live in perfect harmony, to share what they had. That all changed, of course, when sin shattered the human experience. That's the bad news.

The good news is that our Daddy God not only tells His kids to share and to give of themselves, He actually teaches us, through His own words and His own example, how we can live generously today. How we can share what we've been given right now. And even better, how we can give and share without a struggle and without the tears and tantrums that can come when we feel like we're losing something that we desperately want to hang on to.

Generosity, a Learned Behavior
The goal for Open Arms Village has always been to bring in married couples, a husband and a wife, to serve as houseparents. The ideal for a child, we believe, is to have both a mother and a father in the home. And though the majority of children's homes have single women doing an excellent job as housemothers, we believe that children are most blessed and receive the most benefits by having a fatherly role model in the home as well.

When Rachel and I began sharing our vision of having married couples serve as houseparents, our idea sparked a surprising amount of skepticism. "Well, good luck with that," we would hear. "It's very difficult to find healthy and happy married couples who will take on the challenge of being a mom and dad to up to twenty children."

But that ideal remains our goal. In spite of the challenges, we haven't wavered. In fact, all of our homes have married couples serving as parents, and the results have been nothing short of amazing.

God has brought us some incredibly generous couples–generous with their time, their financial resources, and with their love and commitments to truly needy children–to help us fulfill our vision of giving parentless children a mom and a dad.

But I'd also like to give a shout-out, as the saying goes, to an even more amazing group of people who help make Open Arms Village such a wonderful place to live. They make it possible for otherwise destitute Kenyan children to find family, love, and refuge. I'm referring to the biological children of the adults we call our houseparents.

In some ways, they are the hidden heroes.

Every one of our houseparent couples has at least two or three of their own biological children. And when these couples move into our Village and into the homes in which they will serve, their children go from having one or two siblings to having up to twenty. Literally overnight, these children must transition from having their parents to themselves to having to share them with more than a dozen other very needy children.

The biological children of these couples don't have a lot of choice in the matter, and they have to make incredible sacrifices as they learn to share their parents with so many other children. As you'd expect, they have to undergo a period of great adjustment. This period can feel extremely difficult and challenging for these kids and understandably so.

Nevertheless, I have heard some really inspiring stories of children not merely adapting to their new family situations, but stepping up to genuinely love their new "siblings." One housefather said to me, "You know, Kevin originally had a really hard time coming to the Village and having our formerly small and otherwise intimate family grow so large. But he has come to me a few times and told me how much he loves his new brothers and sisters. He says he's glad we came here to serve–and he wouldn't have it any other way."

Children, although selfish by nature (like their parents), have a remarkable ability to adapt. More quickly than we sometimes expect, they can learn to share what was once only theirs, or something they shared with only a few. And because of our specific circumstances in the Village, the kids here must learn to share with *many* others.

A heart attitude of generosity and giving doesn't come naturally to most of us. I wish it developed more easily after we became adults, but we all know it often doesn't work out that way. As we become adults, we become less and less dependent on others to make our decisions for us. We become the "deciders" and "determiners" and we must make decisions as to what we (and those in our charge) are going to do. When we lose sight of the wonderful fact that we are still children of our Daddy God, even though we are adults, it becomes easy to default to the attitude, "I'm going to make decisions that most directly benefit me and my family and that cause us the least amount of personal discomfort."

Our Daddy God, however, insists that we develop a sharing, giving spirit. In fact, He can (and does) instill this quality in us. In a very real way, this spirit of generosity gets back to our seeing ourselves as children of our Daddy God, the most generous Person in the universe. And our Daddy God seeks to give us a heart attitude like His, that looks out for others who live outside our own walls.

He knows how to work with selfish human hearts. He's had a great deal of experience at that.

This includes, of course, the work He's had to do in me. Some time ago, He provided me with an unforgettable lesson on the value of giving, even when it involves inconvenience and sacrifice.

Learning to Let Go and Give

At times I've struggled with the idea of letting go of things. Like just about everyone I know, something inside me tells me that I need to cling tightly to the items I've worked so hard to earn. Knowing this about me, my Daddy God gives me opportunities to practice "letting go" and giving.

A couple of my American friends visited me in Kenya a few years ago, and as part of their "Africa Adventure," I took them to the Great Rift Valley (Kenya's version of the Grand Canyon). There is a beautiful waterfall there that I had passed while driving on many other occasions. When I told them I'd like to hike to it, they quickly agreed to accompany me on this one-day adventure.

After we arrived at a spot along the main highway closest to the waterfall, we went "off-road" and drove as far as we could before the dirt road ended. There, we parked our truck and began walking. The waterfall still lay quite a distance away.

We hadn't walked very far when we met a farmer and his wife, hard at work harvesting soybeans. We stopped walking and engaged this farmer, Paul, in casual conversation. He asked us where we were headed. No doubt, he didn't often see *mzungus* (*mzungu* is a Swahili word for people of European descent, or "white people") walking around his community, and our presence intrigued him. When we told Paul that we wanted to hike to the waterfall, he eagerly offered to lead us there. We gladly accepted his offer; Paul's wife returned home, and he began leading us to our destination.

As I walked directly behind Paul, I took notice of his shoes: old, tattered Adidas footwear that reminded me of my first pair of Adidas sneakers, the white leather ones with the three red stripes, dating back to the 1970s. Only Paul's shoes were in far worse shape than mine ever were. The uppers of both shoes had separated from the soles, and I wondered how he even kept them on his feet. In America, we would have thrown them away years before; but not in Kenya. Paul had no other shoes. I found out later that in his younger days, he had been a runner, and those battered old Adidas had served as his running shoes long before.

Before I had walked many more steps, I heard "the voice" speaking to me.

David, I want you to give Paul your shoes.

Far too often, when I hear that voice, I immediately chalk it up to "my imagination," or maybe "something I've eaten." I started playing that mental game on this day. But the voice came again, even more clearly this time.

David, I want you to give Paul your shoes.

I told myself that I hadn't heard the voice correctly. This couldn't possibly be what He wanted. (I've heard His voice countless times in my life. But if He's speaking to me of personal sacrifice, I tend to want to close my ears a bit.) I had on an almost brand-new pair of Columbia Sportswear hiking shoes, and giving them away didn't make sense to me. I really *liked* my shoes and didn't want to part with them. Besides (and this is where the voice of practicality tried to outtalk the voice of my Daddy God), a good pair of hiking shoes aren't just a luxury in that part of the world. They're a necessity.

"But I need these shoes!" I silently protested. "If I give them to Paul, I won't have a good pair for myself."

But the voice wouldn't leave me alone. By now, I've learned that I never win an argument with *that* voice, so I quickly went into negotiating mode, something I'm pretty good at. I silently replied, "Okay, okay. I'll give up my shoes. But I'll do it at the end of the day, after our long hike to the waterfall."

No, the voice replied, I don't want you to wait. *I want you to give them to him right now.*

"Right now? Are you *sure?*"

Yes, I'm sure. Right now.

I asked Paul to stop, and our little caravan came to an abrupt halt. I explained to Paul that I was a follower of God and His Son, Jesus, and that as we were walking, God had given me some very clear instructions.

"Paul," I said, "God has told me to give you my shoes. I need to know if you want them. I would just ask one thing: Would you give me your shoes in exchange for mine? Can I have your shoes to wear?"

With a look of complete astonishment on his face, Paul answered, "Yes." (Who in his right mind would turn down a new pair of Columbia Sportswear hiking shoes?)

We exchanged shoes right then and there, and I could see Paul getting quite emotional. He began crying a little, just enough that he had to wipe away the tears. He then said, "I want to know more about your God. Can you tell me more? If you don't mind, would you be willing to come back to my house so my wife can hear about your God too?"

My friends and I had looked forward to seeing the waterfall, but this was such an obvious "God moment" that we knew we could not continue our hike. God had called us to something else, something far bigger than a recreational hike to a waterfall, something eternal. As it turned out, I didn't need those shoes for a long hike that day.

We immediately reversed course and walked back down the hill to Paul's house, where we met his wife, as well as about a dozen others. There, we shared God's love through Jesus for Paul and his wife and their friends. That afternoon, Paul and his wife, as well as a half-dozen or so of their friends, invited Jesus to be part of their lives.

At that moment, my beautiful new pair of Columbia Sportswear shoes became a distant memory. In fact, I don't recall thinking about them at all.

When the time came for us to leave, one of the women there, Alice, asked if we could give her a lift back down the hill to the highway. She lived in a neighboring village farther down the hill, and we readily agreed to her request.

Once we all hopped in the car and began our ride down the hill, Alice said, "I think I should tell you what just happened back there. What just happened changed Paul's life and that of his family and friends. But you should know that it wasn't the gift of your shoes that changed his life."

"Really?" we said. "What was it?"

"It was when he saw you put on his shoes and walk in them that his life was changed," Alice replied. "I am a Christian, and people from my church down in the valley have carried the good news of Jesus to Paul's community for several years. Today was the first day that anyone in that community has opened their hearts to Jesus."

I spent the rest of that day walking in Paul's shoes, quite literally. Although we didn't complete our hike to the waterfall, we still had some walking to do. I have slightly bigger feet than Paul does, so I felt grateful that the uppers of his shoes had separated from the lowers. I walked around with my feet overhanging the soles. No, it didn't feel comfortable. But it felt more rewarding than I will ever be able to put into words.

I'm so grateful that my Daddy God allowed me to play a part in Paul's new, eternal destiny, and in that of his family and some of his friends. When I followed His clear instructions to give up something of so little consequence to me–an $80 pair of shoes– He allowed me to make an investment in something eternal. My friends and I got to witness, and even play a part in, something truly miraculous.

I know a lot of people who struggle with this idea of "hearing God's voice." My guess is that they hear it, but don't always want to pay attention to it. They don't want to listen to His voice because they're afraid of what it might require of them–which is so often true in my own life.

For those who truly want to hear God's voice, here's a sure-fire recipe for knowing and discerning it. If what you're hearing:

➢ Is going to be a blessing or a benefit to another person, it is God's voice
➢ Is going to cost you something (like a new pair of shoes), it is God's voice
➢ Involves personal sacrifice (including some level of suffering or discomfort), it is God's voice

Paul wasn't the only one transformed that day. So was I. I learned that even the smallest act of obedient giving can make a huge difference in someone's life and in my Daddy God's kingdom. Though I truly believed I had a practical, even noble, reason to hang on to those shoes, in the end, I let go and let God do what He does best. I gave this man the shoes off my feet, but my Daddy God gave him eternal life.

As the cliché goes, it was a small price to pay. These days, I look forward to such opportunities to pay again whenever my heavenly Daddy God speaks to me and says, David, give.

What I Have Isn't "Mine" Alone
Mine! Mine! Mine!

What parent hasn't heard the shrill protest, "Mine!" coming from the mouth of a toy-obsessed child? When that child suddenly notices another child challenging his ownership—or even the mere possession—of something valued, the words just erupt. It's an unavoidable part of being a parent.

One night, as I sat down to dinner with Rachel and the girls, Diana told me how that afternoon Mommy had made a pineapple upside-down cake for us to enjoy for dessert. With a look of great delight on her sweet little face, she told me how Mommy had let her lick the pan, after it had cooled, so she could enjoy all the crusty, sugary bits of goodness left behind after the cake's removal.

I felt a little cheeky, so I decided to tease Diana a bit. With a very serious face I inquired, "Why didn't you call *me* so I could have some?" I asked. My daughter gave me a sheepish look that said what she wouldn't say with words: "I didn't want you to have any. I wanted it all for myself." Rest assured, I broke into a small grin and winked at her when her silence betrayed her.

Hey, if I had been her I wouldn't have called me either. I knew what Diana was thinking, and not only because I've learned how the mind of a child works. I also know my own mind.

And it occurred to me that my Daddy God knows my mind far better than I know my daughter's.

I'm well into my fifties. I've followed Jesus for decades. At times I hear myself silently shouting 'Mine! Mine! Mine!'–even after all these years. Shouldn't that unlovely part of human nature have started to improve by now? I'm happy to say that I am better about giving and sharing now than I was when I was younger. But the desire to hang on to things is still very much present in my life, and still tries to exert its power over me. I know that, left to my own devices, I want to hoard things for myself. I sometimes catch myself thinking about what I need to do, what I need to earn, and what I need to stockpile so that I can make a better life for myself and my family.

I know, of course, that there's nothing wrong with earning a good wage so that you can adequately provide for your spouse and children. God explicitly tells us in Scripture that we fathers are to work in order to provide for our families. He even says, *If anyone does not provide for his relatives, and especially for his immediate family, he has denied the faith and is worse than an unbeliever* (1 Timothy 5:8).

But at the same time, a far bigger question looms. What does our Daddy God want us to do with our worldly resources? How are we to use them? How much do we keep for ourselves and how much do we give away?

That's a tough one for many of us. We're conditioned to believe that we should keep what we have so that we can take better care of ourselves, our spouse, and children. We also believe we should keep what we've earned because it can give us greater levels of comfort, greater levels of respect from others, and greater levels of power and control over our lives. And before we leave this life, we often buy into the old tradition that everything we have accumulated should be left to our immediate family. We believe that before we die we are to exercise our "will" to keep it all in the family, and by doing so, that we have somehow still held onto our wealth because it has stayed in our bloodline. Are you brave enough to ask this simple question: "Daddy God, what do you want me to do with my earthly wealth? What is your will for how I exercise my will?" Is it possible that our Daddy God who tells us to give things away doesn't share the same idea of wealth transition that culture and tradition has taught us?

Indeed, Daddy God's paradigm looks very different. His own Son, Jesus, taught His followers to share with others the material blessings they had received. He also taught them that an attitude of generosity is the key to further heavenly blessings: *Give, and it will be given to you. A good measure, pressed down, shaken together and running over, will be poured into your lap. For with the measure you use, it will be measured to you* (Luke 6:38).

Our Daddy God loves blessing His kids, both with material blessings and with all other types of blessings. But He also warns us against seeing ourselves as "owners" of what He gives us. *Everything* really belongs to Him. He just makes us stewards, for a time, of what has always been His anyway.

It's Not Always about the Money

God has made it abundantly clear in His written Word that He desires His kids to become a giving and generous people. Most often, we associate this notion of generosity with the financial or material blessings God gives us. But I don't think that's all He has in mind.

What about those of us who lack the resources to write a big check to a worthy charity? For reasons He alone knows, our heavenly Daddy doesn't bless every one of His kids with great financial resources. To some, he gives much; to others, He gives less.

"David," someone says, "I know God wants me to share from what I have. But I don't have much to give. So many times, it's a stretch just to pay all our monthly bills, put food on the table for the kids, and cover all the other expenses of living."

God never asks us to give what we don't have. But lest we make the mistake that "what I have" is confined to material wealth, let me offer another perspective.

In college, as I studied business, I also spent time obtaining my real estate license. I planned to finish my degree and then enter the world of real estate development. Land and buildings had always intrigued me, and I knew I could probably make a handsome living in that field.

But then one day, I heard my Daddy God's voice telling me to head in a different direction. I'll admit that I felt a sense of disappointment when He made it clear to me that He wanted me to go to Bible school instead of into the big-dollar world of real estate. Although I felt like my dream was dying, today, many years later, I feel nothing but gratitude that I didn't allow my disappointment to steer me in another direction.

It turned out my Daddy God wanted to use the gifts and talents He had given me–gifts and talents I didn't really recognize in college–to give to many others, and often in ways that had little to do with money.

Fast forward more than two decades. When we began to search for land in east Africa on which to build the Open Arms Village, I was forty-six years old. Since then, I've spent the better part of a decade building the Village, which serves not only orphaned and abandoned children but also the community around us.

As I look back, I think I would have succeeded in the world of real estate. I'd also like to think that I would have given generously out of the financial success my career would have made possible. But by doing what I'm doing now, God has allowed me to give in ways I never could have otherwise, had I pursued a lucrative career in real estate. I'm not getting financially rich doing what I'm doing now, but God has blessed me with other riches, the kind that comes from making a difference in the lives and eternal destinations of His most precious creation. I can honestly say that I wouldn't trade what I have now for all the real estate success in the world.

Whatever your gifts, talents, passions, and dreams may be, they're not "all about you." In fact, if Daddy God is involved in your life, I can assure you that those things have far less to do with you than you might imagine. The question we all must answer is, "How do my passions and giftings bless others?" God has given each of us abilities and resources we can use to give to others, as they have need. Our part in the deal is to simply listen to Him when He tells us how He wants us to put those resources to work. And if we're not hearing Him giving us such direction, then it's time to *ask*.

Richly Diverse

Let's take a quick look at a group of men and women who, collectively, had an amazing set of gifts and talents. The early church in a Grecian city called Corinth had a wonderfully diverse mixture of individuals with an equally diverse set of God-given abilities.

The apostle Paul wrote to the members of this church, *There are different kinds of gifts, but the same Spirit distributes them. There are different kinds of service, but the same Lord. There are different kinds of working, but in all of them and in everyone it is the same God at work* (1 Corinthians 12:4-6). Paul further explained that God wanted the gifts He had given each of these believers to benefit everyone in the congregation, for the larger good of the kingdom of God.

The same principle holds true for our Daddy God's kids today. The question we must all seek to answer is, "How can I use my gifts and my passions to serve and bless others?" And when our Daddy in heaven gives us that answer, we must begin to take on the nature of a servant, a servant God has equipped for a life of sacrificial giving.

"Sacrificial" may not be your favorite word. It isn't mine, either.

We tend to associate it with hardship, pain, and setting our jaw to do something unpleasant. We don't often connect it with joy—yet, we probably should. The apostle Paul certainly did. He once wrote to some Christian friends in Philippi, *Even if I am being poured* out like a drink offering on the sacrifice and service coming from your faith, I am glad and rejoice with all of you. So you too should be glad and rejoice with me (Philippians 2:17-18).

God loves our heartfelt sacrifices, but many of those sacrifices (even most?) have nothing to do with money: *The sacrifices of God are a broken spirit; a broken and contrite heart, O God, you will not despise* (Psalm 51:17).

I wonder: Can we learn to be generous and share with others whatever blessings our Daddy God sends our way?

"Paying it Forward" When God Blesses

Rachel and I have been blessed with some amazing friendships. Two such friends are our Open Arms cofounders, John and Rosemary Lancaster, an amazing couple from the United Kingdom. For as long as we have known John and Rosemary, they are two people who have set their sights on heaven and have made earthly decisions with eternity clearly in mind.

In the latter half of their lives, God blessed the Lancasters with incredible financial wealth. After John's company went public, he and Rosemary became very prosperous, literally overnight. Neither of them had grown up with much in the way of material wealth, and early in their marriage, they didn't exactly roll in cash, either.

But whether they had little or plenty, they always thought of others and always sought to bless them. So by the time they became financially wealthy, they were ready to put their money to good use. They wanted to help others who had no one else to help them, to reach out to the poorest of the poor.

Now, many years later, they continue to build their legacy of giving. The Lancasters live as if their personal motto is, *we brought nothing into the world, and we can take nothing out of it* (1 Timothy 6:7). They seem to understand the truth of the old saying, "You can't take it with you," so they keep themselves occupied giving away the things they can't keep anyway, in order to bless and benefit others.

John and Rosemary inspire those of us who know them because their acquisition of wealth didn't change them. They remain grounded, humble, sincere people who desire to do their Daddy God's work. They know where their real treasure lies. They hold material things loosely and know that God has blessed them, not only to provide for themselves and for their family, but for many others as well. As a result, they continually invest their time, energy, giftings, and resources in people and things that have eternal significance. They want their lives to *count*.

Our Daddy God calls each of His kids to live generously, to share with others the gifts He's already showered on them. He asks that we learn to put others first and to avoid focusing only on ourselves and on our closest loved ones. And He promises that when we give—whether of our finances, our worldly possessions, or ourselves—that in return, He'll bless us again.

That's how it works with our Daddy God. When we give out of the blessings He's given us, He turns it around and blesses us even more. Then, when we give of those additional blessings, He blesses even more. And after that…

Just set your heart and mind on giving generously of whatever your heavenly Daddy has given you, and then sit back and watch the variety of amazing things He'll choose to do with your "sacrifice."

If you want joy, that's where to find it.

Chapter 16

DADDY, CAN I COUNT ON YOU?

Many years before I met the love of my life, Rachel, I courted a young woman who lived in North Carolina, more than 2,200 miles from my home in Portland, Oregon. Because of the geographical distance between us, we picked "Somewhere Out There" as "our song," the Grammy Award-winning ballad by Linda Ronstadt and James Ingram featured in the 1986 animated movie *An American Tail*.

In my zeal for my special friend, I bought a beautiful and expensive (to me, anyway) crystal music box that played our song. On my first trip to her home in North Carolina, I gave it to her. What a special moment!

A month or two after my trip, I spoke with her on the phone one night. I asked about the music box.

"Are you enjoying it?" I inquired. I noted an ever-so-slight pause before she answered, and I knew I needed to dig deeper.

"What's wrong?" I asked. "Did it break?"

"Well...yes, it did. It fell off my dresser. The crystal top broke."

"Oh, that's too bad," I said. "The good news is that I can get a replacement piece of glass for the top. Can you send it to me?"

"Um, well, no, I can't." "You can't? Why not?"

"Because I don't have it."

"What do you mean, you don't have it?"

"Well, I threw it out because it was broken."

In a strange way, that fractured music box symbolized the beginning of the fractures in our relationship. I had presented that box as a gift to someone who meant a great deal to me, and it became obvious that it meant a lot more to me than it did to her. I considered the damaged music box well worth saving and repairing. To her, however, it wasn't worth the effort. So she discarded my gift with little thought.

We kept our relationship going for a short while after the incident, but eventually it became more and more difficult to keep things together. The day finally came when I put my cards on the table. I wanted to tell her some of the wrong things I had done in my life. With a good and well-meaning heart that yearned for intimacy with this woman, I tried to be as open and transparent as possible. Looking back, I think what I really wanted to know was whether or not she would still love me despite some of my poor choices.

It turned out to be "or not." She didn't, and she couldn't.

My friend couldn't cope with the knowledge of my failures. Our relationship quickly eroded and ended.

When I think of my friend, the broken music box, and all that I had hoped it represented, I'm reminded that virtually everything in this world–including human relationships–is susceptible to change and irreparable damage.

Things break. People change. Hopes evaporate.

And we find ourselves wondering what or whom we can depend on to go the distance with us. We wonder who will believe in us in spite of our failures and shortcomings.

The greatest news of all is that our Daddy God's kids, each and every one of us, can always count on Him to fix what is broken, to preserve what seems hopelessly decayed, and to restore what has been destroyed. We can count on Him to stick with us. Even in our brokenness He never, ever entertains the thought of setting us aside or throwing us away. Never.

Even though precious things on earth sometimes break or die, including our earthly relationships, we can always count on our

Daddy God. In the midst of our unsettled feelings, anxiety, or heartbreak, we can rely on Him to comfort us in His loving arms. When we feel shaken to the core by something valuable slipping from our grasp, we can rest secure in knowing that He stays the same, yesterday, today, and forever.

Grateful That Daddy God Will Never Change
Like many people, memories of my dad come in two categories. Some memories are great while others are not-so-great. I know my siblings would say exactly the same thing.

One memory that still makes me smile is the time Dad worked with me to build my Pinewood Derby car for Boy Scouts. He had come up with a strategy to drill holes into the soft wood on the underside of my car and fill them with lead. His idea was that the extra weight (adding weight is allowed up to a certain amount) would make the car go faster, but it didn't work out that way. When the starting gate opened, my car just sat there. It was too heavy to move. Others had almost crossed the finished line by the time mine finally started moving. Do I need to tell you I came in dead last? Following that race (the car's one and only) I nicknamed my car "the slug." While I appreciated his efforts, it did occur to me that my dad, a dentist, should have stuck with filling cavities, and not Pinewood Derby cars.

If I really thought about it, I know there are other good memories sprinkled along the way through my childhood. But for intensity, they don't hold a candle to the bad ones. The bad ones left indelible, painful impressions on me and my siblings.

While there's no need go into detail about my father's shortcomings, suffice it to say that Dad could be very distant emotionally. He sometimes said hurtful, mean things to his children, and eventually he walked out of our house, never to return.

To this day, if it were possible, my siblings and I would go back in time to see if our father could become a different man. We'd want to keep the good things but change many others. We'd want a dad who didn't saddle us with unhealthy and unreasonable expectations, who spoke to us with kindness and care, and who came home from work every day, eager to spend quality time with his wife and kids.

I doubt we're alone in this kind of wishful thinking. If you were to ask many adults if they wished their earthly fathers had been different in some way, I'm guessing that a thoughtful, pained look would crease the faces of far too many of them. And then they'd slowly agree that, yes, they wish their dads had done some things differently. Recently a friend of mine wrote to me saying, "I had a strong Christian dad who was a wonderful provider and faithful man, but who didn't take much personal interest in his boys. I am grateful to God for him in so many ways, but I had very little sense that he was proud of me or wanted my company." That refrain is repeated over and over again by so many people. Many of us, if we had the power to change anyone, would want our fathers to become more loving, affectionate, and communicative—and less suspicious, prone to angry outbursts, or moody. We'd want the good things to stay and the hurtful stuff to leave.

And yet, most of us who didn't have the greatest earthly dads would probably acknowledge that, despite their many warts, they had moments worth remembering and cherishing. And even individuals who grew up in homes where Dad sported a close resemblance to Ward Cleaver have to acknowledge that even their loving, giving daddies had out-of-character moments when they came up a bit short on the love and generosity their families needed.

I'm not picking on dads; I am one myself. I know my own tendency to sometimes get angry and moody. But I know that earthly daddies are just like all other human beings: imperfect, fallible and prone to mistakes, with their own wounds and scars that keep them from being the kind of fathers God intended them to be. And all too often those scars and wounds were inflicted on them by *their* dads. Those mistakes, both the intentional and unintentional kind, can permanently hurt us. And so sometimes we wish we could change the things about Dad that still cause us pain.

How blessed we are to have a heavenly Daddy who is perfect, who never makes mistakes, and who specializes in healing His kids' hurts! Best of all, He has never changed and never will.

Our Daddy God is the same in the twenty-first century as He was at the time of creation. He's the same perfectly holy, just, and loving God He always has been. And because He is that kind of Daddy God, we can always count on Him.

A Consistent Heavenly Daddy

I attended Elizabeth Hayhurst Grade School in southwest Portland, and there had the pleasure and privilege of getting to know the school principal, Francis V. "Mac" Magaurn.

Everyone adored Mr. Magaurn. He always seemed happy, upbeat, smiled a lot, and made everyone around him feel good. Sure, he ran a tight ship and refused to put up with foolishness, but he had the respect of parents, faculty, and students alike. He could be tough when he needed to be, but he was always fair. Everyone knew him as a man who loved his job and loved the kids placed in his charge.

Mr. Magaurn's personal trademark, something he became well-known for both far and wide, was an apparently inexhaustible supply of Tootsie Rolls. He never seemed to run out of his stash of the little treats–in his office, in his pockets, in his car. Tootsie Rolls followed him like day follows night. And he didn't hoard them just to satisfy his own sweet tooth. He doled out his Tootsie Rolls with generous abandon. He seemed to have a sense for those having a bad day and almost always had a Tootsie Roll at the ready.

Maybe it was because we both had Irish last names, but Mr. Magaurn seemed to take to me. In fact his nickname for me was "Irish." The best birthday card I ever got– and I still have it–came from Mr. Magaurn. I'm sure the huge card cost him a fortune, by greeting card standards, anyway. When he gave it to me, I thought, *This birthday card is almost as big as I am!* It had a bell inside that rang when I opened it.

Over the years, I've thought a lot about Mr. Magaurn. And it's occurred to me more than once that the best thing he had going for him as an educator was that he genuinely loved children. He had committed himself to educating them and molding them. He didn't represent only a source of fear for children (back when school principals nearly always had the "educational tools" known as wooden paddles, hidden away in their offices), but provided a picture of genuine love and concern for "his" kids.

Mr. Magaurn modeled for me many of the qualities of what an earthly daddy should be: tough and firm when he needed to be, but always tender, loving, caring and kind. You always knew where you stood with Mr. Magaurn. His absolute consistency meant you knew what he expected of you and you knew what discipline he'd mete out, if necessary. Most of all, though, you knew Mr. Magaurn was genuinely and deeply committed to the children he so obviously loved.

Today, I think of Mr. Magaurn as an amazing, though imperfect, representation not only of a loving earthly father, but also of our Daddy God. We kids saw him as the "ruler" of this kingdom called Elizabeth Hayhurst Grade School–the older, wiser supreme authority who had the final answer for everything and everyone. When we got out of line, we knew the consequences and repercussions that would follow; but we also knew that doing something good would bring rewards, kind words, and yes, Tootsie Rolls...sometimes, for no apparent reason at all.

Doesn't that sound a lot like God? I've seen Him act in just this way in my life and in the lives of others, including those whose stories found a permanent place in the pages of Scripture.

When we remain in a close Father/child relationship with our

Daddy God, He helps us to feel secure, at ease, and at peace in the world He created. Our sense of peace arises from our deep-rooted sense of security in Him. We feel secure because we know who is in charge and because we know that the One in charge also loves us, keeping His watchful eye upon us at all times.

Something deep within our hearts cries out for security and stability. We want to know we have a reliable place to which we can return or retreat to when our world gets turned upside-down and sideways. As children, we need daddies and mommies who consistently give us both their love and their discipline. We still need that mix of love and discipline as adults, though we may not fully realize it or understand why.

Insecurity in our lives takes a terrible toll, and sometimes the hurt lasts a lifetime. But your Daddy God never intended you to live that way! Early in the book of Exodus He declared His name to Moses as: *"I AM WHO I AM."* He is who He is, and He will be who He is. He is the same all-powerful, all-knowing, all-holy God who created the universe. Over 2,000 years ago, in the little book of 1 John, the apostle declared *God is love*. And He still is! He loved you before you came to be, He loves you now, and He will always love you.

How Will They Remember Me?

Imperfect and changeable as we earthly fathers may be, it's vitally important that we show consistent love, kindness, and affection toward our sons and daughters. I must never forget that my behaviors and attitudes have a huge effect on my girls. How they view me, even after I'm long gone, will go a long way toward how they view their Daddy in heaven. So I often ask myself several questions:

- Will they remember being afraid of me when I got in a bad, impatient mood?
- Will they remember me as being kind?
- Will they remember me as being forgiving?

- Will they remember me as being generous?
- Will they remember me as someone who put others first?
- Will they remember me as someone who followed through and did what I told them I would do?
- Will they remember witnessing my love and devotion to my Daddy God by seeing me in prayer and reading His Word?

I want my daughters to know that they can put their faith and trust in a Daddy God who is faithful and trustworthy. And more than almost anything, I want them to catch a glimpse of their perfect Father in heaven—even when they observe their imperfect earthly daddy. I want them to learn that they can lean on Him, not only because I have taught them about His character and nature, but because I've done my best to reflect those things in how I live and love.

We earthly dads will never perfectly reflect our Daddy in heaven. I know I don't. We're human, and we make mistakes—and sometimes some real doozies. Even the best of us daddies trip, stumble, and sometimes fall flat on our faces.

But we do have an absolutely perfect daddy. In a world full of inconsistencies, our Daddy in heaven is 100 percent consistent in every way, hour by hour, day by day, and year by year. He never, *ever* fails to live up to His perfect nature. He is perfect in His holiness, perfect in His love, perfect in His mercy…perfect in every way. He never fails us.

In this life full of uncertainties, changes, hurt, accidents, and dangers, we can still bank on one constant, and that's our Daddy God. We can count on Him as our place of refuge, no matter what.

Daddy God Does What He Says He'll Do

Frankly, I sometimes fail to keep my word. As hard as I try to do what I promise, I sometimes fail. And I *hate* failing in that area, because I know that my failures negatively affect those around me, including my wife and my two little girls.

I never, ever want my daughters to think that they can't count on me to keep my promises. I never want to be like the father depicted in the old Harry Chapin song, *Cat's In The Cradle*. The song is about a boy who just wants to spend time with his dad – even just playing with him – but his dad is so busy that he keeps putting his son off saying, "Another time." And in the end the boy says to his dad, "It's okay."

But we all know that it really isn't okay.

As kids, we may try to put on a brave face and convince ourselves that "it's all right," but deep down we know that it isn't all right at all. It isn't okay when a daddy doesn't spend time with his kids, and when he makes promises to them that he doesn't keep.

I suppose that if I had the power to change one thing about all earthly fathers, it would concern this promise-keeping thing. I'd simply snap my fingers and every daddy in the world would keep every promise he makes to his kids.

The ugly truth is that too many daddies make promises they can't keep–and maybe have no intention of keeping. But one Daddy has an amazing track record of never breaking even the smallest promise He ever made. The Bible declares, *God is not a man, that he should lie, nor a son of man, that he should change his mind. Does he speak and then not act? Does he promise and not fulfill?* (Numbers 23:19). The answer, of course, is "no."

Our heavenly Daddy isn't like me, who tries hard to keep his promises but sometimes fails, or like Daddy Matthew or Daddy Tom or Daddy _____(fill in your own name). He *always* does what He says He'll do. He has a 100 percent track record of keeping every one of His promises, even though He sometimes fulfills them in ways no one could ever expect. Let's take a brief look back into one crucial period in the history of God's people and remind ourselves how He always keeps His promises.

About 3,400 years ago, way back during the time of the Exodus when God brought His people out of Egypt, He made it abundantly clear that nothing would thwart Him from keeping His promise to give the Israelites a new land to live in–not even His kids' own stubbornness and sin. He promised the nation through Moses,

I am the Lord, and I will bring you out from under the yoke of the Egyptians. I will free you from being slaves to them, and I will redeem you with an outstretched arm and with mighty acts of judgment. I will take you as my own people, and I will be your God. Then you will know that I am the Lord your God, who brought you out from under the yoke of the Egyptians. And I will bring you to the land I swore with uplifted hand to give to Abraham, to Isaac and to Jacob. I will give it to you as a possession. I am the Lord (Exodus 6:6-8).

After the Lord fulfilled His promise, despite the Israelites' complaining and repeated acts of rebellion and sin, Moses' successor, Joshua, said this to his people: *You know with all your heart and soul that not one of all the good promises the Lord your God gave you has failed. Every promise has been fulfilled; not one has failed* (Joshua 23:14).

At the very same time, this passage both convicts and comforts me. It convicts me because it reminds me that I can always do a better job of being the kind of daddy my daughters can count on. It comforts me because it reminds me that my own Daddy God has *never once* made a promise that He's failed to keep.

This is why you, as one of your Daddy God's kids, can feel secure in His love. It's why you can live in complete peace. It's why you can rest in Him and…

- ➢ …stop worrying and just give your cares to your Daddy in heaven, knowing that He promises to give you peace (Philippians 4:6-7);
- ➢ …persevere through anything, knowing that your Daddy God will hold you steady when you keep your heart and mind focused on Him (Isaiah 26:3);
- ➢ …depend on God for strength and comfort during difficult times (Psalm 46:1);
- ➢ …trust God to give you direction (Proverbs 3:5-6);

> ...depend on God for everything you need, including peace for your soul and direction in His ways, even when walking through the worst of life's valleys (Psalm 23:1-4). You and I can always–*always*–count on our Daddy God, simply because He never, ever, ever fails to keep His promises.

Our Daddy God Always Believes in His Kids

I well remember an ugly argument between my dad and my older sister, Kerry, and the physical confrontation that resulted.

Kerry was only twelve at the time, but Dad sometimes had her clean his dental office. The argument came after Kerry and her friend, Becky, had cleaned his office. As the two girls went about their work one day, they came across a box of disposable syringes. As pre-teen girls, they both decided to have some fun with their discovery. They each took a syringe, filled it with water, and started a water fight.

When Dad found the two "used" syringes in the office wastebasket, he jumped to the conclusion that Kerry and her friend had been doing drugs in his office. The accusations flew and naturally, she denied them. But when Dad didn't believe that Kerry and her friend had merely engaged in some innocent fun, he decided to beat "the truth" out of her. In his rage, he slapped her across the face with a smack loud enough to be heard in China.

Kerry still carries the memory of that moment of our father's rage. So do I, because I was there. I've never forgotten it. She also carries with her the knowledge of how it drastically changed the course of her life. *If he really believes that's who I am,* she thought, *then I might as well become that person.* Our dad's lack of faith and trust in his daughter caused her to begin living down to his low expectations.

And it cost Kerry dearly, for a number of years.

How different is our Daddy God! He loves us and tells us that we have a staggering future ahead of us. And so He says to us things like this:

Our Daddy Who Art in Heaven

You are a chosen people...God's very own possession. As a result, you can show others the goodness of God, for he called you out of the darkness into his wonderful light (1 Peter 2:9 NLT).

I take great comfort and deep encouragement in knowing that my heavenly Daddy believes in me. Yes, this same Daddy God who knows how selfish and prideful I can be, who knows that my thoughts can go where He doesn't want them to go, who knows how prone I am to acting like an independent know-it-all...*that* God believes in me.

And He believes in you too.

In His love for you He believes the *best* about you and not the worst.

Our Daddy God knows, of course, that on our own, we're helpless. He knows that no matter how hard we may try, we will mess up, sometimes badly. And He knows that if He doesn't step in Himself, we have no power to act like His chosen people, or as God's own possession. Jesus, our Daddy God in the flesh, said it best when He told His followers, *Apart from me you can do nothing* (John 15:5).

Think about those words, "apart from me." Jesus knew that humans, left to their own devices, have no lasting power to do anything good and no lasting power to stop doing whatever they know to be wrong. The situation gets completely turned around, however, when we factor in the Lord's promise that He will send His own Spirit to live inside every one of His kids. His Spirit brings His power into our lives. His power is much different than our power. His power is supernatural, it's eternal, and the effects of His power are lasting.

Our Daddy God believes in us, not because we have earned His trust, but because He knows what we can do when He gives us His very own Spirit. When we allow the Holy Spirit to guide us, teach us, correct us, and empower us, then we come alive to Him and to all His possibilities for us. We don't need to live down to low expectations, but we get to live on a very high plane indeed, through our Daddy God's own power working inside us and through us.

He Finishes What He Starts
Our Daddy God never says something and then doesn't follow through. Nor does He ever make a promise and then fail to keep it. He never fails to finish anything He starts—and that includes supporting, believing in, and empowering His kids to be and to do everything He created them to be and to do.

That very thought moved the apostle Paul to confidently write, *he who began a good work in you will carry it on to completion until the day of Christ Jesus* (Philippians 1:6).

Our Daddy God knows our full potential. And He'll never stop working with us and empowering us so that we reach that potential. He's always treated His kids that way, and He'll never stop.

Kerry has it right. Even though she spent some years living down to our dad's low expectations, she now answers every one of the Accuser's words with this wonderful promise from her Daddy God: *Love bears all things, believes all things, hopes all things, endures all things. Love never fails* (1 Corinthians 13:7-8 NKJV).

I can't think of many things that more powerfully encourage, comfort, and excite me than to know that my Daddy God believes in me. He believes in me because He loves me. His love for me will never fail!

It never has and it never will.

EPILOGUE

You might have noticed that none of the chapters in this book are titled something like "Daddy, Will You Love Me?" or "Daddy, Can You Love Me?" This is because I have tried to fill each and every chapter with varying aspects of His character and His nature, all of which together loudly proclaim God's love for you. I am hopeful you felt His love for you as you read page by page.

I also hope that your "takeaways" from this book are truly life-changing. I know better than anyone that I could never write anything that would be life-changing. However, I do know whose Spirit and words can change lives, and I am hopeful that I have written enough of His words in this book that His Holy Spirit can indeed bring life and healing to you through them.

The things that you glean from this book will be unique and specific to you. Here are at least a few things that I am hopeful will be part of your takeaway:

- Believe that you are your Daddy God's son or daughter no matter what your age.
- Believe that your Daddy God wants the absolute best for you as His child and works hard to make sure you have everything you need.
- Believe that your Daddy God doesn't ever want you to become too "grown-up" and lose your dependency on Him.

- Believe that you sit at His dining table and He provides for you because you belong there as His child and as part of His family.
- Believe that nothing–especially nothing you've done and nothing that has been done to you–can destroy your Daddy God's love for you.
- Believe that your Daddy God not only loves you but is interested in you.
- Believe that He's always with you and sees you–even in your darkest night when you can't see Him.

Believe. That can be a big problem for a lot of people. That's not a surprise to God and He knows that. The most significant first step is a simple request of God that echoes the heart-cry of a man who asked Jesus to heal his boy (Mark 9:23-24). In a very obvious sign of his own inner struggle to believe, he cried out to Jesus, *"I do believe; help me overcome my unbelief!"*

Jesus' own words to this man are just as much for us now as they were for that man then, *"Everything is possible for him who believes."*

Believe in the One who created you and called you into existence–your Daddy God–and in His Son Jesus. Not only believe in Him but invite Him "in" because He wants to be a part of your life. Your heavenly Daddy is right outside the door of your heart waiting for your invitation to come in. Just be prepared though. Once you let Him in you won't be able to get rid of Him. But that's a good thing.

> *"But to all who believed him and accepted him, he gave the right to become children of God. They are reborn–not with a physical birth resulting from human passion or plan, but a birth that comes from God."*
> – John 1:12-13 NLT[1]

Epilogue

God is closer than you think. Believe it.

For I am convinced that neither death nor life, neither angels nor demons, neither the present nor the future, nor any powers, neither height nor depth, nor anything else in all creation, will be able to separate us from the love of God that is in Christ Jesus our Lord.
– Romans 8:38-39

For God so loved the world that he gave his one and only Son, that whoever believes in him shall not perish but have eternal life.
– John 3:16

ABOUT THE AUTHOR

David Grant Gallagher is a native of Portland, Oregon, in the United States, but now lives much of the year in Eldoret, Kenya, with his wife Rachel and their two daughters, Diana and Belle.

David is a graduate of Portland State University with a degree in business administration and is also a graduate of L.I.F.E. Bible College in San Dimas, California with a degree in biblical theology. He furthered his theological studies by taking graduate courses at Multnomah University in Portland, Oregon.

David is the CEO and co-founder, along with his wife Rachel and with John and Rosemary Lancaster in the UK, of Open Arms International. Open Arms International's mission is to provide relief from physical, emotional, and spiritual suffering through medical expertise, education and Christian ministry. David and Rachel, along with their team of staff, volunteers, and donors, have founded and built Open Arms Village which is located outside of Eldoret, Kenya in Africa.

Open Arms Village welcomes visitors and has built beautiful Guest Lodges for that purpose.

To learn more about Open Arms Village, the various outreaches that Open Arms has in Eldoret, and for a tour or visit to the Village, please go to **openarmsinternational.org**

David is a dynamic leader with a global vision for compassionate ministry and evangelism. He is available for speaking engagements at businesses, schools, civic group meetings and churches. Inquiries can be made by visiting **davidgrantgallagher.com** or by writing him at:

davidgrantgallagher@gmail.com

David Grant Gallagher
PO Box 25795
Portland, Oregon 97298-0795